POSTCOLONIAL AUTOMOBILITY

Postcolonial Automobility

. . . .

Car Culture in West Africa

Lindsey B. Green-Simms

MINNESOTA

University of Minnesota Press
Minneapolis
London

The University of Minnesota Press gratefully acknowledges financial support for the publication of this book from the Helen Tartar First Book Subvention Fund of the American Comparative Literature Association.

An earlier version of chapter 2 appeared as "No Danger No Delay: Wole Soyinka and the Perils of the Road," *Journal of Postcolonial Writing* 46, no. 1 (March 2010): 53–64, available online at www.tandfonline.com. Portions of chapters 3 and 4 appeared in "The Return of the Mercedes: From Ousmane Sembène to Kenneth Nnebue," in *Viewing African Cinema in the Twenty-First Century: FESPACO Art Films and the Nollywood Video Revolution,* ed. Mahir Saul and Ralph Austen, 209–24 (Athens: Ohio University Press, 2010); copyright 2010 Ohio University Press; this material is reprinted by permission of Ohio University Press, www.ohioswallow.com.

Published by the University of Minnesota Press
111 Third Avenue South, Suite 290
Minneapolis, MN 55401-2520
http://www.upress.umn.edu

A Cataloging-in-Publication record for this book is available from the Library of Congress.
ISBN 978-1-5179-0113-4 (hc)
ISBN 978-1-5179-0114-1 (pb)

For Oliver and Leo,
who love cars and trucks

Contents

Acknowledgments

THE IDEA FOR *Postcolonial Automobility* began amid conversations about globalization, mobility, and postcoloniality at the University of Minnesota in the early 2000s when I was a graduate student in the Department of Cultural Studies and Comparative Literature. Discussions in seminars with Timothy Brennan, Charles Sugnet, John Mowitt, and Cesare Casarino shaped the initial questions in this project, and these faculty members, along with Shaden Tageldin, provided invaluable intellectual guidance and support. I am also grateful for feedback from fellow Minnesota graduate students Stephen Groening, Alicia Gibson, and Andrew Opitz. At Duke University Ranjana Khanna, Negar Mottahedeh, and Charles Piot and faculty and graduate students in the women's studies department provided thoughtful comments that helped to guide my revisions. At American University, I am deeply grateful to my colleagues Richard Sha, David Pike, Despina Kakoudaki, and Erik Dussere for their insightful and constructive notes on more recent iterations. This book also owes a huge debt to Africanist colleagues who provided vital feedback on chapters at various stages throughout my writing process: Ralph Austen, Mahir Saul, Sarah Lincoln, Carmela Garritano, Noah Tsika, Ato Quayson, Tsitsi Jaji, Jennifer Hart, Joshua Grace, Kenneth Harrow, Lindiwe Dovey, and Nicole Rizutto. At the University of Minnesota Press, Richard Morrison was an early supporter of this project, and Danielle Kasprzak, along with her amazing team, saw it through to the end. A special thanks goes to Jesse Weaver Shipley, Marian Aguiar, and an earlier anonymous reviewer at the University of Minnesota Press for pushing me to refine key questions.

Throughout the life of this book a number of friends and colleagues have been treasured interlocutors and supporters whether they knew it or not. Frieda Ekotto has been a dedicated mentor since my days as an undergraduate at the University of Michigan. Fellow travelers and road trippers Carole Patrikakos, Rosalind Fredericks, Cori Princell, Annie Lenth, and

Ella Martin helped me to think through the practicalities of automobility in Senegal, Mauritania, Cameroon, Mali, and Burkina Faso. In Senegal the M'Bengue family were wonderful hosts, while Rudy Gomes taught me as much about Wolof as he did about politics, music, and 4x4s. Conversations in Lagos with Rudolf Gaudio, Matthew Brown, Onookome Okome, Bond Emeruwa, Kabat Esosa Egbon, Tunde Kelani, Alexandra Koruba-Fi, and Unoma Azuah provided me with a better understanding of Nigerian urban life as well as the ever-changing Nollywood industry, while Socrate Safo taught me much about the Ghanaian video industry in Accra. During the course of writing I have had the privilege of thinking through many of the ideas that shape this book with Carmen McCain, John Nimis, Moradewun Adejunmobi, Brian Larkin, John McCall, Birgit Meyer, Serena Dankwa, Teju Olaniyan, Susan Andrade, Simon Lewis, Lily Saint, Paul Ugor, Matthew Omelsky, Wendy Belcher, Jonathan Haynes, Caren Kaplan, Francis Nyamnjoh, Samantha Pinto, Elisabeth R. Anker, Carl LeVan, Susan Shepler, Shalini Ayyagari, and many, many others who have influenced my thinking in both big and small ways. A special thanks goes to Connor Ryan, Peter Bloom, and Jean-Pierre Bekolo, who helped me source some of the images and screen grabs for this book. I would like to express my gratitude to my American University literature department colleagues Amanda Berry, Fiona Brideoke, Kyle Dargan, Danielle Evans, Dustin Friedman, Stephanie Grant, John Hyman, David Keplinger, Keith Leonard, Jonathan Loesberg, Richard McCann, Jeffrey Middents, Madhavi Menon, Marianne Noble, Deborah Payne, Tom Ratekin, Roberta Rubenstein, Anita Sherman, Kathleen Smith, Rachel Louise Snyder, Linda Voris, and Lily Wong, who, along with those American University colleagues mentioned above, have provided much-appreciated support and camaraderie and a warm intellectual home here in Washington, D.C.

Parts of this project were presented at the University of Pennsylvania, the University of Wisconsin, Wesleyan University, and Brown University. I am grateful to those who invited me and to the audiences who asked curious and formative questions about my work in progress. I received research funding from the Doctoral Dissertation Fellowship and the Harold Leonard Memorial Fellowship in Film Studies at the University of Minnesota, a Postdoctoral Fellowship in Women's Studies at Duke, and a junior-year research leave at American University. I am also grateful to be a recipient of the Helen Tartar First Book Subvention Fund awarded by the American Comparative Literature Association.

Finally, a huge thank you to my family, whose love, support, and encouragement has helped make me who I am. My parents, Stuart and Debra, my sisters, Kimberly, Carly, and Alexandra, and my in-laws, Barbara and Edward Greenberg, deserve my deepest gratitude. And nothing would be possible without Amy, who, for the past twenty years, has copyedited everything I have written, talked through countless drafts and ideas, shared my happiest moments, and been an endless source of love and inspiration. This book is dedicated to our two little boys and all that they may set out to accomplish.

INTRODUCTION

Cars, Cultural Production, and Global Modernity

The motor-car is the epitome of "objects," the Leading-Object, and this fact should be kept in mind.

—Henri Lefebvre, *Everyday Life in the Modern World*

Anyone who thinks evil of you, may this car run them over in their sleep. This car will hunt out your enemies, pursue their bad spirits, grind them into the road. Your car will drive over fire and be safe. It will drive into the ocean and be safe. It has friends in the spirit world. Its friend there, a car just like this one, will hunt down your enemies. They will not be safe from you. A bomb will fall on this car and it will be safe. I have opened the road for this car. It will travel all roads. It will arrive safely at all destinations.

—Ben Okri, *The Famished Road*

TOWARD THE END of Chimamanda Adichie's best-selling novel *Americanah* (2013), Ifemelu, a Nigerian woman who has just returned to Lagos after over a decade of living in America, sits beside her ex-boyfriend as they drive to his private club in upscale Victoria Island. Adichie writes that Ifemelu "would remember this moment, sitting beside Obinze in his Range Rover, stalled in traffic, listening to [Nigerian music] . . . beside them a shiny Honda, the latest model, and in front of them an ancient Datsun that looked a hundred years old" (544). The moment is memorable for Ifemelu because she has finally rekindled her romance with Obinze. But it is also memorable for all that it says about the new Lagos that Ifemelu returns to in 2009. The now-wealthy Obinze has acquired his Range Rover, along with a beautiful house, bank accounts, and a BMW, at a time when the Nigerian middle class is expanding under increased democracy and an array of business opportunities. Obinze himself has been rewarded for the part he plays in undervaluing real estate that is then bought up cheaply and resold at a high profit margin. And though he now feels uncomfortable with all the material objects he has acquired, this does not stop him from driving to his club in luxury. The driver of the new Honda has also presumably done well for him- or herself, but the Range Rover and the Honda share the road with the driver of the old Datsun who, like the majority of Nigerians, moves through the city with less ease and comfort. And all three of the cars are stuck together in the notoriously crippling Lagos traffic. Here, then, so many of the contradictions of modern Lagos play out on the road, in cars, and around cars.

Though it is a novel about so many things—race, gender, migration, romance—*Americanah* affords readers a specific insight into what Nigerian automobility and car culture look like in two distinct postcolonial moments. In the 1990s, when Nigeria was under the military rule of Sani Abacha and before Ifemelu left for America, "The country was starved of hope, cars stuck for days in long, sweaty petrol lines, pensioners raising wilting placards demanding their pay (55). Ifemelu's mother attends a church where she has the only shabby car in the parking lot because she hopes that she will be blessed with a nice car like the other worshippers. University students burn cars in front of the vice chancellor's house in protest of constant faculty strikes. And, at the same time, wealthy criminals "who donated cars with the ease of people giving away chewing gum" (62) are able to cruise the city with impunity. Years later when Ifemelu returns to Nigeria, the petrol lines have disappeared and hope, at least for select members of the educated middle class, has been restored. Ifemelu's previously unemployed father has a job at a bank and one of the first things he does is to purchase new tires for her mother's car and buy a mobile phone, ensuring the family's mobility.

But, at the same time, the roads and street life of Lagos in 2009 are as frenetic as they have always been. No longer accustomed to the chaos and energy, Ifemelu is inundated with scenes she had forgotten about: "At first Lagos assaulted her; the sun-dazed haste, the yellow buses full of squashed limbs, the sweating hawkers racing after cars, the advertisements on hulking billboards" (475). Despite the obvious presence of new wealth, Ifemelu observes the roadside rubbish, the accident victim lying on the side of the street, and the patina of the decaying buildings. And even in this new Lagos infrastructural impediments become a prime topic of conversation. When her friend Ranyinudo picks her up from the airport the immediate talk is about traffic, power outages, parking woes, and how Ranyinudo wants her married boyfriend to buy her a jeep before she breaks up with him because the roads are so terrible.

Americanah reveals how automobility and daily experiences on the road are a vital part of social life in Lagos: they are intertwined with identity, longing, and status in a way that seems particularly pressing and unrelenting. This is not to say that cars are radically different in America—in fact, many of Ifemelu's initial observations upon arriving in the United States reveal that car culture is more similar than she assumed. Ifemelu, surprised that the cars in America are not new and shiny, finds them "disappointingly matte" (127). And when she observes her aunt's wheezing American car that stands in contrast to the "green, glossy, intimidatingly streamlined" (54) Mazda she drove in Nigeria, it becomes clear that class rather than geographical location often determines what one drives. But after a very short period of time, cars in the American scenes of the novel are simply part of the landscape. They may be covered in snow, or parked in a parking lot of the organic grocery store, or playing loud music as they pass by, but people do not seem to fixate on them or integrate them into daily conversation with the same intensity as they do in Lagos. Unlike the Nigerian characters, the American characters are never introduced along with the type of car they drive, they do not seem to be particularly consumed with the need to acquire new cars, they do not carry on long conversations in stalled city traffic, and they almost never talk about infrastructural failures. Of course, cars in the United States are still objects that are crucial for mobility, they are still important signifiers of wealth and status, and they still break down, but what *Americanah* illustrates is that they are not discussed with either the same urgency or the same ambivalence.

The goal of *Postcolonial Automobility* is to examine the ways that aesthetic forms like *Americanah* set in motion the various and contradictory forms that automobility takes in postcolonial West Africa. The car, with its promise of autonomous, unfettered mobility—implicated in the term "automobility"—has often been called the commodity par excellence of postwar modernity and has perhaps been one of the most globally experienced technologies of the twentieth- and twenty-first centuries.[1] But as Adichie's novel indicates, despite its presence across the world and its iconicity in globally consumed media, the automobile is often experienced and valued in particular ways outside of a "First World" context. What the literary and visual texts that anchor this study do, then, is make palpable the complex ways that automobility in West Africa is, at once, an everyday practice, an ethos, a fantasy of autonomy and mobility, and an affective experience intimately tied to modern social life. As such, a study of automobility is also necessarily an exploration of the complicated ways that consumption, mobility, stasis, scarcity, and excess all intersect along West Africa's bumpy and multidirectional roads. The aim of *Postcolonial Automobility* is therefore to track the complex relationship African subjects have to cars and to automobility at a time when global modernity is simultaneously alienating and enticing, as it has been since the globalizing colonial encounter and as it continues to be today.

The Literary and Cinematic Life of Cars

In their introduction to *The Speed of Change: Motor Vehicles and People in Africa, 1890–2000*, Jan-Bart Gewald, Sabine Luning, and Klaas van Walraven argue that though "the arrival of the motor vehicle was the single most important factor for change in Africa in the twentieth century" there has been surprisingly little systematic research done on motorcars (2009a, 1). Furthermore, they suggest, works that focus on motorcars in Africa, with a handful of notable exceptions, tend to sideline the multiple ways that motorcars affect the everyday lives of Africans in rural and urban environments. And yet motorcars have profoundly impacted social life and day-to-day mobility and have become important practical and symbolic technologies. Historically, as the editors of *The Speed of Change* suggest, "the colonial state relied heavily on motor vehicles for the extension and enforcement of its control at a symbolic and functional level" (4). Roads were built, often with conscripted or coerced labor, in order to export goods to the metropole, sell products back to colonial subjects, patrol towns, and maintain order. During both colonial and postcolonial times, motor vehicles were used to collect taxes, police borders, spread missionary values, and promote health care and other developmentalist projects, often at costs to the environment and to local communities. Both cars and roads, then, have been key to "disciplining a subject population" (5).

But, at the same time, as I'll be discussing in chapter 1, African entrepreneurs were quick to appropriate the technology of the motorcar, and as soon as cars began to be imported into Africa in the early 1900s, African businessmen began to repurpose them in order to transport both goods and people. These businessmen formed a system of informal collective transportation, not dependent on government, public bus routes, or the railway, that still today provides many people employment opportunities and affordable transport options. Moreover, as Gewald et al. argue, it is important to note that while cars might have been used to discipline colonial populations, they were also often very important technologies for anticolonial political movements. In Ghana, for instance, propaganda vans toured the countryside to campaign for Kwame Nkrumah, and in Niger in the 1950s motor vehicles were instrumental in political rallies and in enhancing political competition (5). What this all suggests is that cars in Africa have ambivalent pasts and presents, that they can be technologies of oppression and alienation as well as sources of agency.

Though the impact of the motorcar on African social life might be underrepresented in the social sciences, African films and literature have often registered and recorded the ways that cars mediate African subjects' relation to both modernity and mobility. In countless texts, African writers and filmmakers deploy cars as emblems of social and material change, the processes of urbanization, or the shifting gender dynamics that shape Africa in different historical moments. In one of the most notable literary representations of African car ownership during the colonial era, the trickster Wangrin in Amadou Hampaté Bâ's *The Fortunes of Wangrin* (2000) buys a sports car that "[speeds] along at 60 miles an hour—at a time when a Delahaye lorry couldn't be pushed faster than 20 miles an hour[—]" (172) and uses it to sell provisions to a railway company that was laying down tracks. Here, the car is a symbol of Wangrin's ingenuity and success as a resistant colonial subject. In novels taking place shortly after independence was achieved in the late 1950s and early 1960s, cars, especially luxury ones, tend to be associated with the corrupt and neocolonial elite. This is the case in novels like Chinua Achebe's *No Longer at Ease* (1969), Nkem Nwankwo's *My Mercedes Is Bigger Than Yours* (1975), Ousmane Sembene's[2] *Xala* (1973), and Ayi Kwei Armah's *The Beautyful Ones Are Not Yet Born* (1968). In the 1980s and 1990s a few feminist novels like Mariama Bâ's *So Long a Letter* (1981) and Ama Ata Aidoo's *Changes: A Love Story* (1991) began to feature women drivers and often associated the car with women's freedom, albeit in complicated ways. There are also those texts—Wole Soyinka's play *The Road* (1965) and Ben Okri's novel *The Famished Road* (1991) are the most famous examples, while Nnedi Okorafor's *Lagoon* (2014) is perhaps the most recent—that write about road spirits and, as can be seen in the case of Okri's incantation in the above epigraph, the spirituality of vehicles themselves. Furthermore, scenes of traffic and gridlock appear with regularity in a wide range of West African urban novels. The sociologist Wendy Griswold, who systematically surveyed 467 Nigerian novels written between 1952 and 1992 (every Nigerian novel that she could identify and locate), found that the single most common scene in Nigerian literature was that of a traffic jam, or "go-slow." And indeed traffic jams and road accidents continue to be staples of Nigerian literature in texts like *Americanah, Lagoon,* Chris Abani's *GraceLand* (2004), Adaobi Tricia Nwaubani's *I Do Not Come to You by Chance* (2009), and A. Igoni Barrett's *Blackass* (2015).

In African screen media, motorcars have become powerful visual tropes and are often crucial to painting scenes of both development and underdevelopment. Cars have figured prominently in both the plot and mise-en-scène of a significant number of West African art films, like Flora Gomes's *Blue Eyes of Yonta* (1992), Abderrahmane Sissako's *Heremakono* (2002), Sembene's *Xala* (1975) and *Faat Kiné* (2000), Jean-Pierre Bekolo's *Quartier Mozart* (1992) and *Les Saignantes* (2005), Jean-Marie Teno's *Clando* (1996), Jean Odoutan's *Barbecue Pejo* (2000), Moussa Touré's *TGV* (1998), Olivier Delahaye and Dani Kouyaté's *Soleils* (2013), and Philippe Lacôte's *Run* (2014). In these films cars are not just part of the background scenery but are often used to comment on the dialectics of mobility and immobility in West African social life. And while cars in many of these art films are prone to breakdown, the Nigerian and Ghanaian video films that have become incredibly popular across the continent are filled with perfectly working Mercedes-Benzes and SUVs that, though not always purchased with clean money, are key to the video films' aesthetics of wealth and glamour. Furthermore, as is the case with West African literature, both celluloid and video films sometimes link the car to witchcraft and occult practices. Thus, even while many African countries have some of the lowest motorization rates in the world and private cars are only driven by a relatively small portion of the population, African cinematic and literary texts seem to have a fascination with the moving vehicle.[3] The contradictory and socially symbolic ways that cars are deployed in West African films and literature indicate that motor vehicles in Africa "appear to have taken on values over and above their mere utilitarian function" (Gewald et al. 2009a, 4).

Of course motor vehicles everywhere, not just in Africa, have symbolic and social significance. But what is often overlooked in studies of automobility is that while the utilitarian functions of automobiles do not vary significantly—they are almost always used to get someone or something from point A to point B—the way in which they are valued, exchanged, and integrated into social life often depends on their particular cultural and historical context. In "The Cultural Biography of Things: Commoditization as Process," Igor Kopytoff advocates a way of studying an object by providing it with its own cultural biography to understand what makes it significant in a given culture. The example he provides is, conveniently, the automobile in Africa: "The biography of the car in Africa would reveal a wealth of cultural data: the way it was acquired, how and from whom the money was assembled to pay for it, the relationship of the seller to the buyer, the uses to which the car is regularly put, the identity of its most frequent passengers and of those who borrow it" (1986, 67). Since the essay was published several anthropologists have taken up Kopytoff's challenge by writing brief cultural biographies of the car in Africa. For instance, Jojada Verrips and Birgit Meyer's "Kwaku's Car: The Struggles and Stories of a Ghanaian Long-Distance Taxi-Driver" and Brenda Chalfin's "Cars, the Customs Service, and Sumptuary Rule in Neoliberal Ghana" both examine the cultural biography of the car in Ghana. Both essays look at the business of importing used cars often purchased at auctions in Europe, the bureaucracy of taxing and licensing these cars, the built-in system of bribery, the relationship between cars and spirituality, and, in the case of "Kwaku's Car," the endless cycle of breakdown, repair, and making do without proper spare parts. Even a cursory look at the list of issues these essays cover reveals how the car in West Africa requires a biography quite different from the car in America or other "First World" countries. As Kopytoff suggests, such culturally informed studies reveal much about the way objects lead different lives in different places.

Given the diverse cultural biographies of cars and the particular sociohistorical and economic conditions of West Africa, my intent in this book is to explore the specific experiences of automobility and the feelings that it generates in the region. To do so, I examine films, novels, popular videos, plays, and poems, all meaning-making devices that are techniques or tools through which human beings constitute their relationship to the material world, each with its own unique form that focuses on the different shapes automobility takes in particular times and places. What I want to emphasize, though, is that the cultural texts I examine do not simply represent cars or reflect automobility in West Africa. More importantly, they provide a canvas on which the complexities of what Daniel Miller calls the "intimate relationship between cars and people" play out (2001b, 16). As Caroline Levine argues, fictional narratives can be understood as "productive thought experiments that allow us to imagine the subtle unfolding activity of multiple social forms" (19). In other words, the aesthetic objects discussed here are productive heuristic forms that explore the conflicting, contradictory, and overlapping lived experiences and forms of automobility, experiences and forms that are thoroughly intertwined with everyday social life in West Africa and shaped by the region's particular historical, cultural, economic, and political conditions. Throughout the book, then, the aesthetic objects I read put into relief the "multiple social forms" entangled with automobility.[4] By looking at how West African writers and media practitioners position the automobile in their stories, I am able to consider how cars in the region become both coveted and maligned, how automobiles are a part of West Africans' lived practices as consumers in an unevenly globalized world, and how people sense and internalize technology in areas where it often does not function at its optimal capacity.

Toward a Regional Automobility

I focus on West Africa in particular because creating a regional cultural study has certain intellectual advantages over a national project or one that attempts to take into account the entire continent. As I discuss in my first chapter, the history of motorization across Anglophone and Francophone West Africa, despite local differences, followed many of the same overall patterns. Colonialists were at first reluctant to motorize West Africa, but as cars became lighter and cheaper and African entrepreneurs began importing and driving automobiles, motorcars became an indispensable part of the colonial administration. And today, again despite some local differences, motorcars throughout West Africa follow similar patterns of distribution, consumption, and exchange. While a handful of cities like Ouagadougou, Lagos, and N'Goundéré have strong motorbike cultures, for the most part roads throughout the region are dominated by different types of informal shared taxis. These taxis (sometimes called "bush taxis") are either cars, often referred to by the number of places they have, with a seven-seater or five-seater being the most common, or minivans and small buses that go by different names in different countries: the *tro-tro* in Ghana, the *car rapide* or *Ndiaga Ndiaye* in Senegal, and the *danfo* or *bolekaja* (no longer in use) in Nigeria.

As Joost Beuving notes, most motorcars in West Africa today are second-hand vehicles imported from Western Europe that often arrive first in Cotonou, Benin, and then find their way to markets in Dakar, Abidjan, Tema, Lomé, Lagos, and Douala. This particular trade route developed, according to Beuving, in the 1990s in response to deregulation and the removal of trade barriers. It was made possible in part by the expanding number of West Africans living abroad with access to European cars and in part by concessions that the Beninese government made to an association of wealthy second-hand car dealers who had migrated to Cotonou (Beuving 2009, 128, 134). Moreover, changes to the Cotonou car market reflect car consumption throughout the region so that when traders in Benin began importing German and Japanese cars in the mid-1990s instead of French cars, this indicated a shift in the types of cars being driven across the entire region. And, likewise, the age of the cars being imported into Cotonou tells us much about the quality of cars being driven: the estimated age of a car imported into Cotonou in the late 1990s and early years of the twenty-first century was between fourteen and sixteen years, with only 1 to 5 percent being new or nearly new and some being as old as twenty-five years (134). Though the quality and quantity of cars driven in each West African country differs, vehicles are, for the most part, decidedly much older than those driven in Europe or the United States, where the average age of a car on the road is eight and eleven years, respectively (Curtain 2013). And this disparity between the age of automobiles in West Africa and the age of automobiles in Europe and the United States remains today even as demands for newer vehicles in Africa increase with improved economic conditions and laws in countries like Nigeria, Senegal, Ghana, and Ivory Coast now technically prohibit the importation of older vehicles.

As the example of Cotonou shows, car markets in West Africa have a specifically regional character that is influenced not just by decisions made by the nation-state but also by changes like neoliberalism, structural adjustment, urbanization, and migration seen across West Africa after the Cold War.[5] Thus, the car markets in West Africa are much like the local markets that Manthia Diawara discusses in his widely cited essay "Toward a Regional Imaginary in Africa." Focusing on West African marketplaces as sites of regional and transnational flows of capital, commodities, technologies, and imaginaries, Diawara argues that underscoring the way that goods and culture circulate in a regional context can challenge both the homogenizing forces of globalization and the nation's complicity with multinational capitalism. Given the long history of cultural exchange, migration, and border crossing between West African countries, Diawara writes that "what is urgent in West Africa today is less a contrived unity based on an innate cultural identity and heritage, but a regional identity in motion that is based on linguistic affinities, economic reality, geographic proximity, as defined by the similarities in political and cultural dispositions grounded in history and patterns of consumption" (1998, 124). Certainly, this is not meant to erase local differences or to forget that West Africa is an incredibly diverse region with hundreds of different ethnic groups and religions, different histories of European colonization, and different postcolonial political realities. Nor does it mean that the distinct legal and educational systems, languages, and cultures that respective colonial powers left behind are no longer relevant. But what it does mean is that there is a need to make space for studies that focus on the "patterns of consumption" and experiences of modernity that are shared across the region and that recognizing these connections helps to create narratives that neither subsume Africa into the homogenous global nor posit African nation-states as isolated units.

Across West Africa driving culture and street life have many similarities and follow many of the same general trends. To begin with, West African driving has a certain gendered dynamic. Historically, though market women were some of the earliest riders of informal, collective transport and though vans in both colonial Ghana and Nigeria were so filled with market women that they were referred to as "mammy wagons," driving itself has been considered a male activity.[6] Even today it is rare to find a woman driving a taxi or commercial vehicle. But women do indeed own and drive private cars, and as I discuss in chapter 5, self-made market women and financially independent women throughout the region are often characterized by the luxury cars they drive. In several Francophone countries, for instance, wealthy cloth traders are called Mama Benzes or Nana Benzes because they drive Mercedes-Benzes. This means that cars in West Africa are both associated with patriarchal power structures and, at the same time, seen as a sign of women's empowerment and liberation.

Furthermore, because roads are often inadequately maintained and are statistically some of the most dangerous in the world (see chapter 2) and because automobiles are often quite old, car travel in West Africa has a distinct, precarious quality.[7] And yet due to the lack of formal regulation, West African streets are, as Ato Quayson argues, characterized by a level of dynamism, spontaneity, and flexibility. Roads are lively spaces filled with street hawkers who mingle with traffic, vehicles are painted with slogans and mottoes, and sidewalks, storefronts, and merchants spill out into the street allowing inhabitants to create new uses and meanings for road space.[8] Anxieties about the dangers of driving are therefore often mixed with the excitement and pleasures of street life and consumer culture.

Focusing on the regional particularities of West African car culture allows me to focus on how West African cultural texts theorize the specific contradictions of West African automobility. But at the same time, I should emphasize that West Africa is not isolated from the rest of the continent or somehow singular, especially considering that much of the African continent is saturated by the same global and economic forces. Although different flows of trade and consumption as well as strong cultural and historical differences across the African continent would reveal that the car has a different cultural life outside of West Africa, there would nevertheless be many overlaps, many ways in which the part would be able to stand in for the whole. Therefore *Postcolonial Automobility* is as much a study of the regional as it is an attempt to contribute to the many important discussions of what James Ferguson refers to as Africa's "place-in-the-world" (2006, 6), a shorthand for discussing the multiple ways that Africa is both connected to and disconnected from modern, global planetary networks. What I discuss throughout the book, then, is how automobility can be a way to examine these inclusions and exclusions and how automobility as a narrative about freedom, modernity, and mobility must be reconfigured when the car is examined within an African context rather than a Western context, when the specific obstacles, patterns of consumption, and gendered dynamics of postcolonial car culture are taken as the point of departure.

Automobility "Misplaced"

Though the term "automobility" has been used colloquially since the beginning of the twentieth century to describe the type of movement associated with the motorcar,[9] it is also a concept that is deeply entangled with the automobile's promise of autonomous, unfettered mobility. Cotten Seiler, for instance, argues that automobility is a term that signifies the myths, ideologies, and supposed freedoms of American-ness and that the "sensations of agency, self-determination, entitlement, privacy, sovereignty, transgression and speed"(2008, 41) of automobility became key to defining what it meant to be American.[10] Though automobility has clearly become a global phenomenon, what Seiler, like other cultural scholars, emphasizes is that the term "automobility" has come to mean more than just the type of mobility enabled by the use of the automobile.

Originally, the "auto" in "automobile" referred to the idea of a self-propelled motor vehicle free from dependence on an animal, and it marked the automobile as a self-directed vehicle liberated from the restrictions of a rail track and able to move in any direction whatsoever (Featherstone 2005, 1). Thus, the implication is that this self-moving vehicle enables a freedom of movement for its drivers: it conjoins the modern subject's dual desires for increased mobility and a larger degree of individualization. James Flink refers in particular to the way the car engendered an age of "mass personal automobility" in America, stressing the very individualized and privatized nature of this collective phenomenon. For Sudhir Chella Rajan the automobile is "the (literally) concrete articulation of liberal society's promise to its citizens" (2006, 112–13), the leading object of a post-Enlightenment order that has not yet given up on the idea of the free and autonomous individual. John Urry takes the notion of automobility one step further by elaborating an entire system that incorporates not only cars and drivers but roads, traffic signals, parking, and fuel into a self-organizing, *auto*-poetic system. Urry argues that the notion of automobility captures both the humanist notion of autobiography, or self-making, as well as the machine's capacity for automation (2005, 26). Automobility, for Urry, indicates the idea of an autonomous human linked to an automatic machine through a network of roads, technologies, and policies. In all of these accounts of automobility, the car is valued as an agent of autonomous mobility for the modern consumer-citizen.

Automobility therefore hinges on two mutually dependent ideals: mobility and autonomy. As several scholars have noted, mobility is often seen as a fundamental aspect, a right even, of modern culture. Tim Cresswell argues that while "the idea of mobility as liberty and freedom" would not have made much sense in feudal societies that valued fixity, mobility gained prestige as cities grew in the early modern period (2006, 15). Creswell notes that it was thinkers like Thomas Hobbes and later William Blackstone who argued that unimpeded mobility was essential for liberty and was "an absolute right of man," and he goes on to suggest that these ideas have become so self-evident that "the word *modern* seems to evoke images of technological mobility—the car, the plane, the spaceship" (15). Likewise, Marian Aguiar, writing about the ideological importance of trains in colonial India, argues that "mobility came to act as a material register for who was modern, a phenomenon that continues to this day" (2011, xv). And Seiler notes that mobility is both a "disciplinary technology and a form of capital . . . an arena of contest and performative display" (2008, 11) in the modern era. Automobility couples this experience of mobility with the ideal of autonomy, an ideal that has in moral and political philosophy been equated with liberty, sovereignty, self-rule, dignity, integrity, independence, and self-knowledge (Dworkin 1988, 6). Like mobility, autonomy is typically considered to be an attractive quality and one that is enabled by the automobile. But unlike mobility, autonomy is often an unattainable ideal.

Although some people have more access to mobility than others and some mobility is forced rather than voluntary, it is clear that people and things throughout the world do indeed move.[11] But the concept of the sui generis and completely sovereign, autonomous individual has been debunked by intellectual traditions as wide-ranging as Marxism, psychoanalysis, feminism, structural anthropology, and Foucauldian poststructuralism, all theories of thought that understand the human subject as socially determined, bound by class, labor, family, gender, kinship, or historical epistemes. Nancy Yousef, in her study of the notion of autonomy in Enlightenment philosophy and Romantic literature, argues that even in Enlightenment thought itself, the idea of the self-made autonomous man was never taken as a given fact: it was never assumed that man had actually created himself out of nothing. Where the idea held sway, she suggests, was in its "theoretical and imaginative implications" (2004, 19), in its ability to assuage anxieties and fears that derived from feeling weak, helpless, and dependent. The idea of autonomy enabled people to view themselves as self-determining individuals, free from the oppressive institutions of authority, instead of as helpless individuals at the mercy of others. Automobility as an expression of autonomy works in a similar way. Like the socially determined human subject, the automobile and its driver exist within a system of dependent relations. These dependencies include, but are by no means limited to, manufacturers, laborers, laws, police officers, roads, signs, advertisements, geographers, oil companies, gas stations, and gas-station clerks. Automobility as an expression of pure autonomy is therefore essentially nonsensical. And yet, as an ideal and as a modern ethos, automobility, just like autonomy, persists.[12]

But what happens when the car is taken out of its American and Western context and placed into an environment where modernity is just as often a status one hopes to achieve as it is a given state (Ferguson 2008, 189), where autonomous mobility is often thwarted by crumbling infrastructure and worn out vehicles, and where cars are more often used for collective rather than private, individualized transport? How do narratives of automobility travel and resonate? How is autonomy recalibrated in a West African context? What I suggest is that automobility in West Africa is what the Brazilian literary critic Roberto Schwarz calls a "misplaced idea." For Schwarz, a misplaced idea is a concept that emerges from specific developments in one country but when it is transplanted into a new cultural context, it begins to fissure and expose many of its original inconsistencies and forms of dissonance. Discussing the various European "ideas" that were transformed by Brazilians, Schwarz writes, "We didn't invent Romanticism, Naturalism, Modernism, *or the car industry,* none of which prevented us from adopting them. But adopting them did not imply that we reproduced the social system of their countries of origin" (1992, 34, emphasis added). For Schwarz, both the automobile and the narrative text emerge from and are determined by the specific socioeconomic and historical contradictions of their birthplaces. But when cars or artistic movements are transplanted into an entirely new context, their original inconsistencies become apparent in different and more pronounced ways and in ways that can be read through narrative art forms. He calls these ideas "misplaced" not because they do not belong in their new settings but because by incorporating the social contradictions of their new milieu, they seem "off-center" or off-kilter in revealing and often generative ways.

Understanding automobility as "misplaced" helps to underscore the way that many of the ideals of automobility are indeed still present throughout West Africa—the car, as is the case in the West, is seen as something that will provide status, independence, and personal freedom—even though the historical conditions that created the system of mass individualized automobility are largely absent. African automobility, like African modernity, is therefore neither "alternative," as some theorists would have it, nor fundamentally different or easily categorized as "non-Western." Rather, automobility in West Africa is conditioned by distinct experiences that bring out the already latent contradictions in the term and, as many of the chapters here will show, often lead to unique or creative adaptations.

Though this book is primarily concerned with the specific affective experiences and ambiguities of car culture and automobility in West Africa, it is also my hope that thinking through the ways that West African automobility is conditioned as much by freedom, liberty, and mobility as it is by inertia, congestion, precarity, and (sometimes unfulfilled) consumer desires will shed light on what Schwarz refers to as the original inconsistencies of the idea. Since it is technically impossible to be both a fully autonomous human subject and one who is dependent on a machine as well as the entire sociotechnical institution that supports it, automobility is characterized, from the outset, by core antagonisms. It is for this reason that Steffen Böhm, Campbell Jones, Chris Land, and Matthew Peterson, the editors of the collection *Against Automobility* (2006), have proposed viewing automobility as a disciplinary regime rather than a self-organizing system. Their focus is almost exclusively on the West, but pointing to the proliferation of traffic jams, dependency on nonrenewable resources, ecological devastation, and the prevalence of accidents, they assert that within the regime of automobility "the pursuit of individual mobility becomes collective immobility" (9). For these scholars, automobility is fundamentally an "impossible" system not simply because it is unsustainable but because it is inherently contradictory: it produces as much inertia and destruction as it does mobility.

Moreover, when one takes into consideration race, class, gender, and the historical and economic reasons that certain social groups in the West (which is no more monolithic than "Africa") have had unequal access to private property, it becomes clear that automobility is not simply a privileged experience in the West and a frustrated one in Africa. Seiler, for instance, discusses the way that the car in midcentury America was part of a culture of consumerism and national citizenry that was coded as white and male (2008, 7). As Jeremy Packer argues, automobility was often regulated in part because certain demographic groups in the United States, notably women, youth, and African Americans, were historically considered unsafe drivers. Packer writes, "The unsafe form of automobility [these groups] employ (overstressed commuting, motorcycling, pimping, hitchhiking) have largely been used to legitimate the monitoring, regulating, and minimizing of access to and use of the automobility system" (2008, 9). Automobility may therefore be just as misplaced in certain communities in the United States as it is in West Africa.

Nevertheless, though the instabilities and inconsistencies of automobility are certainly not exclusive to any particular geographical region, what I argue here is that in West Africa they do have a prominence that makes them particularly influential to subject formation. As Brian Larkin argues, technologies and infrastructures in colonial and postcolonial Africa "have proved to be unruly and difficult to control" but "their failure to carry out their technical and symbolic function" is just as important in shaping social life as their success (2008, 250). Simply put, understanding the ways that West African subjects navigate their world means giving full attention to the ways that they manage their ideals and expectations about technological objects that sometimes function well and sometimes manifest the structural and economic uncertainties that characterize postcolonial daily life.

By posing the question of what automobility and car culture look like when they are "misplaced" or when African texts, rather than literary and cinematic works from the United States or Europe, are the focus, I analyze some of the messy ways that African subjects navigate their role as global consumers in a rapidly and still unevenly globalizing world where cars, like most technologies, are very much present but not always experienced in a globally uniform way. What this means is that the encounter between the African subject and global technology cannot fit neatly into developmentalist or modernization narratives, nor can it be a story of lack and absence. More specifically, thinking through automobility as a misplaced idea means complicating its relationship to the global Fordist and post-Fordist narratives to which it is usually tied. As Julie Graham writes, "From a critical feminist perspective, existing theories of Fordism and Post-Fordism offer a 'totalizing' rendition of capitalist development which fails to acknowledge multiplicity and difference in social life" (1991, 53). Building on the work of these feminist critiques of modernism and Africanist critiques of globalization, I want, therefore, to emphasize how the Fordist and post-Fordist discourses that have uniformly excluded Africa and African experiences of automobility participate in a discourse in which African mobility, as Joshua Grace argues, "is so often presented as unnatural, disconcerting, or as an indication of social crisis and decline" (2013, 405). Moreover, understanding the links between the modernist, Fordist discussions and the post-Fordist theories of globalization underscores the fact that debates about African development and modernization are far from being settled.

From Fordism to Post-Fordism

During the 1950s and 1960s, the Golden Age of Fordism, Fordist models of development, following the hopes and aspiration of Ford himself, insisted that all societies would eventually achieve the level of production and consumerism as the West. Though Fordism began in America, to Henry Ford, who claimed that the practices that he put into place in his factories would establish a "natural, universal" code of freedom, this system of production was a global one. For Ford, the eight-hour, five-dollar workday, the streamlining of the automobile, and the building of a car "for the great multitude" (2008, 52) were part of a democratic world vision that would eliminate poverty and allow each individual to maximize his or her personal freedom.[13] Fordism was therefore both a way of organizing factory labor according to a Taylorist model and a rigid model of labor that would lead to higher salaries and higher levels of consumerism. This is perhaps why the car is so central to Walt W. Rostow's *The Stages of Economic Growth: A Non-Communist Manifesto* (1960), one of the foundational texts of modernization theory, which purports that underdeveloped countries would eventually "catch up" to the West. For Rostow the mass diffusion of the automobile was the most decisive signal that a society had reached the last of several stages of development. Widespread automobile ownership would therefore epitomize the achievement of development in the stage that he called the "age of high mass-consumption" (4) and measure the advancement of the lifestyle patterns of societies. Rostow, like other proponents of modernization, believed that Fordist-style capitalism was the only road available to modernization.

However, beyond Rostow's developmentalist claims, Fordism is not a narrative that is typically paired with colonial or postcolonial history, as Kristin Ross notes in *Fast Cars, Clean Bodies: Decolonization and the Reordering of French Culture* (1995). Rather, Ross argues that there has been a tendency to keep the two stories separate, to see modernization in the West as completely unconnected to and uninfluenced by events occurring in the colonies or ex-colonies. Ross, however, makes an important intervention by linking narratives of Fordism and modernization to the story of decolonization. She traces how the arrival of new consumer goods in France during the period of decolonization helped France to situate colonialism as a thing of the past—France could define itself as a modern nation by separating itself from its former colonies that were figured as "dirty and backward" (78). Moreover, turning toward French cinema of the time, Ross shows how the car in decolonizing France was central in shaping this new modern identity by creating new forms of factory production, a newly mobile work force, a new *jeune cadre* (managerial class), new forms of masculinity, and a new "sublime" experience of everyday life that, significantly, relied on the labor of ex-colonial immigrants. But while Ross examines the ways that the car defined forward-looking France against its former colonies, no monograph has yet examined the social and symbolic function of the car in the ex-colonies.[14]

Understanding how existing theories of Fordism play out in West Africa means, first of all, acknowledging that the postwar period of decolonization and independence was a "modernizing" one for West Africa, just as it was for both of its two main former European rulers. In the same decade that Ross examines—the mid-1950s to the mid-1960s—the number of automobiles in West Africa more than doubled, while roads and modern infrastructure in and between cities multiplied at a quicker rate than ever before ("L'évolution des marchés ouest-africains de l'automobile" 1966). And, as I will discuss further in chapter 1, this is partially the result of the importation of Ford cars that had become popular before World War II because they were cheaper and lighter than other brands and much easier on African roads. Thus, African ex-colonies were indeed going through their own period of urbanization and development, creating new spatial arrangements and expanding a middle class that was not too unlike the *jeune cadre* Ross describes. In the immediate decolonization period, modernity was often expressed as a hope for the future, a period where a "new man" could be reborn through technological development. Young cosmopolitan men in Accra at the time even referred to themselves as Jaguars and cultivated a sense of style worthy of the modern, high-class car of their dreams.[15] Commercial drivers were seen as "cultural heroes" (Van der Geest 2009, 261) and were representative of a cosmopolitan class that could come and go as they pleased (Hart 2016, 208). Furthermore, the car became particularly important in newly independent Africa because it embodied both independence and its hoped for financial rewards.

However, Fordism in West Africa at the time was experienced in distinct and often uneven ways. While collective transport often flourished, the private automobile quickly became a sign of the divide between the postcolonial elite and the masses whose lives remained essentially the same after independence. Rather than becoming part of the sublimity of everyday life, private cars, as can be seen in texts like Armah's *The Beautyful Ones Are Not Yet Born* and Sembene's *Xala,* were some of the most visible signs of the excesses of the national bourgeoisie. And though in Europe and the United States cars in the mid-1960s were either becoming or already "integrated into the banality of the everyday" (Ross 1995, 29), car ownership in West Africa remained relatively low. Whereas by 1966 around 25 percent of the population owned a car in most industrialized countries, in West Africa the rate hovered around 1 percent and only in the more well-off countries ("L'évolution des marchés ouest-africains de l'automobile"). While riding in motor vehicles might have been a part of everyday life for many West Africans, owning them was certainly not. Moreover, while cars in France, Britain, or the United States were often shiny and new objects, fresh off the assembly line, the vehicles arriving in West African ports were more likely to be second hand, in some cases overhauled war vehicles. Although Ivory Coast, Senegal, and Nigeria each had a few small assembly plants for European carmakers at the time, no West African country was producing its own vehicles. The Fordist regime that was penetrating Western Europe, and that had already swept up America, was therefore experienced in West Africa as something dissonant and nonsynchronous—neither fully present, nor fully absent.

And though post-Fordism describes shifts in forms of consumption and production, it too is a global narrative that often elides global differences. While Fordism was premised on industrial conditions, post-Fordism describes the change, following the global recession of the 1970s, to economies based on flexibility and rapid turnover in labor practices, production, and consumption (Harvey 1990, 159). According to David Harvey, the changes that characterize post-Fordism include the weakening of unions, the opening up of labor markets across the globe, outsourcing, the growth of the service industry, quickly changing fashions, and new, innovative technologies. In narratives of post-Fordism, the automobile itself becomes less of a central character but one that is, nevertheless, key to understanding the story. For instance, Michael Hardt and Antonio Negri cite the shift from Fordism to Toyotism as one example of what they call Empire, the new political logic of a universal globalization. They argue that Toyotism is based on an inversion of the Fordist relation between production and consumption. Whereas Fordism produced standardized vehicles and had little need to listen to its consumers, Toyotism involves a "rapid feedback loop" (2000, 290) where, in theory, the decision to produce a vehicle comes after consumers have already decided it should be produced. In this argument the post-Fordist shift in the way cars are produced signifies the postmodernization of the global economy in a smooth, decentralized world.

But while theories of post-Fordism track a supposedly global shift from Taylorist modes of production to flexible accumulation, West African countries, still with no automobile industries of their own, have experienced a different shift, one where "post-Fordist" precarity and flexibility of labor are not in fact new and where Fordism often becomes repositioned as an unfulfilled dream. A post in the Facebook group The Nigeria Nostalgia Project 1960–1980 illustrates this perfectly. On May 27, 2013, one of the group's members posted a picture of an old Volkswagen assembly line in Lagos circa 1975/1976. Other group members responded by writing comments that lamented failed leadership and the lack of industrialization in contemporary Nigeria, comparing Nigeria unfavorably to countries like Brazil that moved from assembly to the manufacturing of cars rather than from assembly to simply importing them. One commenter notes distastefully that the assembly line in the photo is now a storage facility for imported rice.[16] Here, then, post-Fordism is experienced not as a move to the future but as what Charles Piot calls a "nostalgia for the future," a "longing for a future that replaces untoward pasts" (2010, 30), or a longing for a past when the future seemed possible. But at the same time, West Africans have indeed been affected by the rapid spread of consumer goods and technologies produced in a post-Fordist world, as can be seen in my brief reading of *Americanah* above. What characterizes post-Fordism in West Africa, then, is the same paradox that characterized Fordism—it is neither fully present, nor fully absent.

Global Modernity

Understanding global modernity in a West African context therefore means recognizing the unevenness of capitalist modes of production and consumption and, at the same time, acknowledging the fact that African subjects are constantly interacting with and creating meaning through global technologies, consumer objects, and media. Accordingly, it is important to underscore that, despite the fact that Fordist and post-Fordist conditions might not be neatly mapped onto a West African context, African subjects are indeed global subjects. And, as Jean-François Bayart cogently argues, global subjects are the product of a globalization that should be thought of as a mode of belonging rather than as a practice of dispossession. Positioning globalization as a process that begins in the colonial era, Bayart uses Michel Foucault's concept of governmentality to argue for an understanding of globalization as a historical encounter between "techniques of domination" and "techniques of the self." In other words, Bayart sees the global subject as one who must submit to global forces of inequality but who, at the same time, invents daily life "in a personal way" through encounters with the material world (2007, 209–10). Echoing Daniel Miller, Bayart suggests that this is why "things matter," why consumption, even as it objectifies and alienates, is also part of self-realization, of being, acting, and existing in a global world. Like Bayart, I understand the global to be a paradoxical rather than universal or homogenizing signifier that has its roots in encounters and economies that predate the shift to post-Fordism by over a century.

What does it mean, then, to talk about a global modernity? Typically, modernity, one of the most debated terms in social theory (Cresswell 2006, 16), has been considered to be a temporal category. Whether it is being used to describe a time period, a technological advancement, or a "cast of mind," it usually "involves the idea of the 'new,' the break, the departure" from a past moment (Brennan 2008, 43). However, what Ferguson convincingly argues is that for African subjects "modernity has always been a matter not simply of past and present, but up and down. The aspiration to modernity has been an aspiration to rise in the world in economic and political terms; to improve one's way of life, one's standing, one's place-in-the-world" (2006, 32). Rejecting the idea that we should see global inequalities in terms of temporality (i.e., some nations are just behind others), Ferguson writes that modernity "has come to be simply a status—a standard of living to which some have rights by birth and from which others are simply, but unequivocally, excluded" (189). This formulation is useful for two reasons. First, it deflects the chronocentric emphasis of modernity—an emphasis repeated in the now-prevalent African Rising stories (which seem to eerily replicate the predictions of Rostow) and in the modernization rhetoric used to justify projects that do little more than make access to African cities and their high-end commercial centers easier for the wealthy (Malaquais 2011, 9). And second, refiguring modernity as a standard or status provides a way of understanding how modernity can be both elusive and "at large" in the same exact space.

"Global modernity," as I use the term, is therefore a paradoxical, sometimes aspirational, and often uneven experience that has much more to do with "relations of membership" (Ferguson 2006, 187) than with teleological projects of modernization or with a deterritorialized, new (capitalist) world order. And it is my contention in this book that automobility is a paradigmatic experience of a global modernity, that it affords particular insights into West African economies of desire and modes of belonging. Examining automobility critically therefore forces one to go beyond the equally totalizing narratives of bleak underdevelopment or inevitable progress that still persist today. I see automobility, like global modernity itself, as an experience infused with both "violence and pleasure" (Bayart 2007, 251), precariousness and prestige, and exclusion and inclusion. And though Fordist and post-Fordist narratives are certainly "misplaced" in West Africa, automobility, as a claim of autonomous, unfettered mobility, remains a powerful discourse to the construction of the modern self, just as the automobile continues to give meaning to the ways that African citizens inhabit their global world.

Infrastructures of Feeling

Throughout this book, I engage close readings of literary and cinematic texts in order to highlight the many ambivalences and overdeterminations of postcolonial automobility in an increasingly global West Africa. At the same time, I want to attend to the way that these texts pay attention to the materiality of the automobile itself and how it is intertwined with the specific historical and social formations in West Africa, issues of class and gender, and the realities of infrastructural failures and longings. Such an approach, which combines disciplinary methodologies, allows me to discuss the ways that fictional works manifest the sensations, anxieties, and affects evinced by the automobile. It also helps me to analyze how men and women, rich and poor, rural and urban, might have very different experiences of automobility. Methodologically, then, I make use of a form of postcolonial criticism that, following Achille Mbembe in *On The Postcolony* (2001), foregrounds social practices and embodied relations that involve "doing, seeing, hearing, tasting, and touching" (6). Focusing, as Mbembe does, on "*time as lived*" (8, emphasis in original) and "what it means to be a subject in contexts of instability and crisis" (17) is key, I believe, to understanding the complexity of everyday life for different subjects in West Africa and avoiding some of the abstract language of "hybridity," "nomadism" or "in-betweenness" that dominates much of postcolonial and globalization theory.[17] My goal is to examine how writers and filmmakers use the car to account for the ways that postcolonial, West African subjects inhabit and create meaning through their material and infrastructural world, a world made up not of Deleuzian "lines of flight" or virtual superhighways that globalization theorists are so keen on praising but of actual roads that need to be traversed on a daily basis.

In her introductory article to the January 2007 special issue of *PMLA,* Patricia Yaeger makes a call for precisely this kind of work on literature from the Global South. She writes, "My premise is that our [current] intellectual apparatus, like the wage puzzle, is inadequate for describing the pleasures and pounding of most urban lives, or the fact that many city dwellers survive despite all odds. How can our ethical and imaginative engagements with others around the world be worked into our scholarly infrastructures? . . . What is it like to be stuck, night and day, dreaming of infrastructure?" (5). Since the *PMLA* special issue, books like Larkin's *Signal and Noise: Media, Infrastructure, and Urban Culture in Nigeria* (2008), Michael Rubenstein's *Public Works: Infrastructure, Irish Modernism, and the Postcolonial* (2010), and Aguiar's *Tracking Modernity: India's Railway Culture and the Culture of Mobility* (2011) have quite brilliantly begun to provide such an intellectual apparatus. These works, which go beyond Yaeger's emphasis on the city, examine the structures of feeling generated by media and infrastructure (Larkin), public utilities (Rubenstein), and modes of transport like the train (Aguiar). It is my intention that *Postcolonial Automobility* will be a part of the larger discussions, which the *PMLA* issue and works by these scholars have begun, that focus on what literature and media can tell us about infrastructure and mobility and the feelings of pleasure, longing, desire, fear, and frustration that they produce. As Mimi Sheller argues, automobility "is implicated in a deep context of affective and embodied relations between people, machines and spaces of mobility and dwelling, in which emotions and the senses play a key part" (2005, 221). And as Bruce Robbins reminds us in his aptly titled article "The Smell of Infrastructure," infrastructure and access to it has often been the object of political struggle even when it "smells," when no one, it seems, is paying any attention to it. The car, then, is not simply a convenient metaphor or symptom of atomistic capitalist relations. It is also a social object that engenders ways of being, feeling, and acting in the modern world: it is an object that reflects and refracts various surfaces, from its own body, to the road on which it drives, to the social image of its driver.

A large part of what I explore in this book are the particular "infrastructures of feeling" that writers and filmmakers capture. What I mean by an infrastructure of feeling is quite similar to what Raymond Williams means when he describes a structure of feeling as a social experience, or set of "meanings and values as they are actively lived and felt" (1978, 132) in a particular historical moment. But by using the term "infrastructure" rather than "structure," I want to emphasize the feelings and "affective elements" (132) associated with the materiality of built structures and objects. Infrastructures of feeling are therefore sets of social and affective experiences that are conditioned by everyday interactions with infrastructural elements, and, as Williams suggests, these sets of feelings are often most visible in art and literature. As Yaeger reminds us, "*Infra* means beneath, below, or inferior to, while *infrastructure* represents the equipment, facilities, services, and supporting structures needed for a city's or region's functioning" (2007, 15). Infrastructure therefore always entails a "play of surface and depth (subways, water mains), of hypervisibility (bridges) and invisibility (the electrical grid)" (16). Yaeger's point here is to emphasize the fact that "infrastructure's role in literature is unpredictable and varied" (16), that there is no easy parallel between the "deep structures of cities" and the "deep structures" of the texts about them. What this means to me is that cultural texts do not simply transcode buried ideological formations, as Fredric Jameson famously argues. Though they do indeed reveal quite a bit about the hidden contradictions of capitalist society, they also, at the same time, invite readers or viewers to pay attention to the complex and surface ways that people interact with and are shaped by everyday material life and to the specific forms of technology and infrastructure that allow bodies to inhabit the world the way that they do. Infrastructures of feeling therefore are those meanings and affects that entail a constant entanglement of "surface and depth." Accordingly, this study aims to bring the deep contradictions of automobility to the surface in part by reading surfaces: by calling attention to the shiny, sleek, dinged, or damaged surfaces of automobiles and the surfaces of the roads that they occupy.[18]

This consideration of both the surface and ideological depth of the automobile is indebted, methodologically, to Roland Barthes's famous essay on the Citroën D.S. (which is pronounced the same as *déesse* [goddess] in French). Barthes calls the new Citroën a magical object, comparing it to Gothic cathedrals "created by unknown artists" and "consumed in image if not in usage" by a whole population (1957, 88). He describes how the surfaces of the car show no signs of factory assemblage, how the dashboard and levers make the car into a sleek and seamless object: "The lines of union are touched, the upholstery palpated, the seats tried, the doors caressed, the cushions fondled" (90). Reading the surface of the automobile, Barthes makes a potent argument about its ideological underpinnings. The Citroën is a reminder of the way human labor is erased and objects like the *déesse* become worshiped: it is "the very essence of petit-bourgeois advancement" (90). Barthes's reading relies on the outer shell of the car, the touch and feel of its interior surfaces, and, at the same time, the deeper meaning it reveals about labor and consumption.

But perhaps even more germane is the methodological approach taken by Luise White in *Speaking with the Vampires: Rumor and History in Colonial Africa* (2000), a book that discusses popular rumors in colonial East Africa about bloodsucking vampires who would capture victims in fire trucks, vans, and ambulances. White argues that, in part, these rumors can be explained by the fact that fire trucks painted the color of blood were occasionally used in blood drives, and ambulances emblazoned with suggestive red crosses were used to take sick people to hospitals from which they did not always return.[19] But White also claims that these stories, which "are about vehicles in unexpected places, used for unintended purposes" (130), must be understood in the larger context of the reservations and fears that many Africans had about a new sector of skilled laborers who worked for a colonial administration whose motives and policies were not always clear. Because many of the early vehicles had no windows, there was much fear and anxiety about the type of equipment they might contain, and many people found it hard to understand precisely what these new laborers did to receive a wage that was often significantly more substantial than what one would receive for casual labor (133). While I'll be discussing the contemporary link between occult practices and cars in Nigerian video films in chapter 4, my point here is to show how White toggles back and forth between surface and depth in order to explain the affective register of cars. What the vehicles looked like (painted red, windowless, etc.) mattered but so did various "hidden" aspects of the labor practices associated with them. Like White, I try to keep these various levels in mind when analyzing the stories that African authors and filmmakers tell about cars.

Roadmap

The chapters in this book all discuss the ways automobility and its attending infrastructures of feeling make themselves known and felt through different aesthetic objects. As Urry writes, "The car's significance is that it reconfigures civil society involving distinct ways of dwelling, travelling and socializing in, and through, an automobilised time-space" (2000, 15). Each chapter therefore takes up the various ways that the contradictions and tensions of these ways of "dwelling, travelling and socializing" in the car are refracted through and theorized in different West African literary and cinematic art forms. While the first chapter focuses on the history of motorization from the colonial moment to the decolonizing decades following World War II, the remaining chapters trace the way the historical contradictions and tensions surrounding African automobility are both repeated and transformed in aesthetic forms from the post-independence period of the 1960s and 1970s to the neoliberal era of the 1990s and early 2000s. The goal of the first chapter is therefore to show that whereas historicist versions of African economic development position the motorcar as part of Africa's road to modernization, in reality it was, and still is, part of a process that has been continually thwarted and overdetermined. Examining various events or episodes, like the first failed attempt in 1900 by French businessman Félix Dubois to bring a fleet of automobiles into modern-day Mali, alongside key literary and cinematic texts of the first half of the twentieth century, allows me to underscore how African subjects have been historically both included in and excluded from car culture and ownership. In order to reveal the ambivalences and conflicts present in the process of motorization, I concentrate on illustrative examples that have largely been absent from mainstream historical accounts of economic development and discuss how Europeans were often ambivalent or even hostile to the idea of motorizing Africa, while African entrepreneurs took the lead in importing automobiles and establishing the system of informal transportation that exists today.

Chapter 2 focuses on the tragedy of motorcar accidents through a close reading of Wole Soyinka's 1965 post-independence play *The Road* about Nigerian lorry drivers living on the urban periphery. Here, I read the road as a Bakhtinian chronotope—a space-time matrix—that includes various lived times of postcoloniality. Soyinka draws on Yoruba mythology and Ogun, the god of the road, to elaborate his philosophical views of a road that unleashes destruction and impedes progress while also creating the psychic strength needed for progress and survival. Soyinka's road also serves as a paradigmatic postcolonial space-time that comprises the swings, inertias, and "meaningful acts" (Mbembe 2001, 6) that determine how subjectivity is formed. In the work of Soyinka, who played a crucial role in founding the Nigerian Federal Road Safety Corps, automobility becomes legible not only in the movement of the drivers but also in the wreckage of their accidents, in the fallen bodies and spare parts, as well as in the psychological debris that accumulates in the consciousness of the characters. This chapter discusses how *The Road* uses the theatrical form to emphasize both the traumatizing effects of the road and the everyday heroism of the post-independence drivers and touts who have learned to survive it.

While my first two chapters discuss West African collective forms of transport, the last three focus more on private vehicles, which, because they are objects that are simultaneously coveted and viewed with deep ambivalence, are disproportionately represented in African film and literature. Chapters 3 and 4 both focus on the car in West African screen media. In chapter 3, I turn to Francophone cinema, discussing in detail Ousmane Sembene's *Xala* and Jean-Pierre Bekolo's *Quartier Mozart*. While media scholars like Kristin Ross have often focused on the shared qualities of film and cars—such as movement, image, standardization, mechanization, and displacement—this chapter discusses how African Francophone films reconfigure the link between the moving image and the moving vehicle by disallowing the automobile to represent a continuous, rational forward movement. Both *Xala* and *Quartier Mozart* engage with stasis just as much as with alternative forms of movement, and the tropes of mobility and immobility become important to understanding the filmmakers' critiques of patriarchal power structures. But whereas *Xala* focuses more on the failure of the postcolonial elite in the post-independence period, *Quartier Mozart* is a playful exploration of what movement might look like in the midst of structural adjustment and the crisis of the 1990s.

In Francophone films, private cars, because of their association with the neocolonial and patriarchal elite, are often parodied and mocked, shown to be stuck, undriveable, or otherwise immobilized. But in Nollywood, the low-budget video films that started to become incredibly popular in Nigeria and Anglophone Africa in the 1990s, the private luxury car is a highly coveted object, typically seen driving down paved roads in posh neighborhoods. My fourth chapter discusses how Nollywood videos, rather than highlighting the conditions of uneven development as the Francophone films do, center on stories of upwardly mobile neoliberal subjects and their shiny, new things. However, while video films may gleefully depict modern capitalist subjects, they also morally condemn those who become part of that commodity culture by trouncing on social codes integral to the welfare of the community at large. My readings of several popular Nollywood films, including Kenneth Nnebue's *Living in Bondage* (1992), Ojiofor Ezeanyaeche's *Blood Money* (1996), and Afam Okereke's *Boys Cot* (2007), underscore the ongoing tension between fantasies of material success depicted in the video films and the anxiety produced when wealth is acquired through criminality, witchcraft, magic, or fraud.

In my final chapter, "Women in Traffic," I look at the way that feminist texts rewrite and work in dialogue with the male-centered films and novels where the car stands in for patriarchal power and capitalist achievement. I argue that in films and novels where women are the drivers the car figures much less as a sign of upward mobility and elite status and instead highlights the ambivalence with which financially independent women move through West African urban centers. In the works I discuss—Ama Ata Aidoo's novel *Changes* and Sembene's film *Faat Kiné*—both female protagonists must negotiate their status as consumers and commodities in modern, neoliberal urban Africa. On the one hand, driving and car ownership seem to allow women certain social and economic advantages, but, on the other hand, the car can also register disillusionment with feminist fantasies of autonomy. What both texts explore are the "possibilities feminism might have within the neoliberalism in which it is taking shape" (Grewal 2005, 3).

Postcolonial Automobility sets forth an understanding of global modernity as a paradoxical social experience, formed not only by the speed of the new or the global but also, at the same time, by experiences of what I call "suspended animation," moments of pause, interruption, and disruption. In scientific discourse, suspended animation refers to the stopping or slowing of vital organs or to a body that has been frozen and may later be brought back to life. Accordingly, the idea of suspended animation implies a temporary interruption, a deferral of movement rather than a complete cessation. An automobile in suspended animation might be one that is waiting for a new spare part, one that has misfired, one that has crashed, one whose driver is no longer willing or allowed to drive, one that is stuck in the sand or mud, or one whose carcass has been put to other uses. In the 1980s and 1990s, the World Bank's push toward the free market in West Africa resulted in a liberalization of the importation of used vehicles and an influx of very old and poorly functioning cars and trucks. In the 1990s in Cameroon, where more than 84 percent of all cars had been in circulation between thirteen and twenty-two years *after* being imported as used vehicles (Tamo Tatiésté and Bidja 2002, 488), these substandard cars came to be called *congelés* (frozens). The name, however, according to Xavier Godard and Pierre Teurnier, was not only given to the cars because they were often immobilized on the roads. It was also intended to link the cars to the frozen imported chickens—also imposed on Cameroonians as part of structural adjustment programs—that were regarded to be far inferior to those raised locally. Thus, Cameroonians linked the substandard cars, their lack of national autonomy, and the stalling of their economic progress in one word: *congelé.* My use of the phrase "suspended animation" is intended to evoke both these multiple freezings and their potential for reanimation, a potential captured in both the form and content of many of the texts I examine.

What is central to my discussion of West African automobility is how this interplay of mobility and immobility is entangled with everyday experiences of postcolonial capitalism. Although the authors and filmmakers I discuss all demonstrate some level of ambivalence toward capitalist consumption, they also acknowledge how integral it is to becoming a modern, global subject. Indeed, the fact that scarcity and abundance comingle in such close proximity in the African postcolony creates a situation where it is not always easy to either fully embrace or denounce the pleasures that automobility has to offer. Therefore, throughout *Postcolonial Automobility* I analyze the car as the sign through which to read the overdetermined flows of global capital and as an object through which to assess the dangers, vulnerabilities, and pleasures global commodity culture produces for African subjects.

· CHAPTER 1 ·

The Hum of Progress: Motorcars and the Modernization of West Africa

The hum of our motors must always mingle with the splendour of the scenery and with the memories evoked by it. That hum has a beauty of its own. It is the song of progress, the rhythm of human effort chanting its victory over the elements.

—André Citroën (quoting Georges-Marie Haardt and Louis Audouin-Dubreuil)

For the speed of change brought about by the motor-car is visible in all fields of human endeavor on the Continent.... Arguably, the arrival of the motor vehicle was the single most important factor for change in Africa in the twentieth century. Its impact extended across the totality of human existence; from ecological devastation to economic advancement, from cultural transformation to political change, and from social perceptions through to a myriad of other dimensions.

—Jan-Bart Gewald, Sabine Luning, and Klaas van Walraven, *The Speed of Change*

IN JOYCE CARY'S NOVEL *Mister Johnson* (1939), set in colonial northern Nigeria, Officer Rudbeck is obsessed with building roads in his district: "He spends his afternoons riding or driving about the country inspecting bridges; and he loves to make maps and draw on them in dotted lines or red ink" (39). Like Rudbeck, Cary himself served as a district officer during the interwar years and he too took an "unusually keen pleasure" in road building (Moody 1967, 145). For both Rudbeck and Cary, constructing roads was an enthusiasm they learned from superior officers; it was a concrete, tangible, and measurable way to bring progress and "civilization" to the colonies (146) and one of the ways an ambitious officer could "leave his mark" and connect his region to the outside world (Hay 1971, 95). As a junior officer, Rudbeck had "caught the belief that to build a road, any road anywhere, is the noblest work a man can do" (Cary, 49).

However, Rudbeck's eagerness is not shared by other officers, and he has difficulty securing the funding he needs to build his dream road. Most notably, he is opposed by his predecessor Blore, "who considers motor roads to be the ruin of Africa, bringing swindlers, thieves and whores, disease, vice and corruption, and the vulgarities of trade, among decent, unspoiled tribesmen" (48). The Nigerians in *Mister Johnson* are no more unified on the matter than the British. The Emir and Waziri, the local leaders, agree with Blore and are fearful of the way that roads will erode traditional order. But for the clerk Mister Johnson, roads are a way to advance his career and please Rudbeck. When the money for the road runs out, he devises a comical plan to turn road building into a game and brings in beer and drummers to encourage the workers. The road building gang, like Johnson himself, becomes excited about the possibility of the road to expand their world, to bring trade and prosperity.

Though the labor of building a road by hand was hardly as fun and lighthearted as *Mister Johnson* makes it seem, the novel does exhibit the differing feelings that colonialists and Africans had about roads and motorization. Throughout much of the colonial period, the building of infrastructures like roads and bridges and the introduction of cars were met with a mixture of enthusiasm and trepidation, pleasure and anxiety. These often contradictory (infra)structures of feeling reflected the fact that roads and cars were often the sites of intense conflict and ambivalence.[1] The goal of this chapter is to highlight, through different episodes and events, the multiple ways that automobility has been an ambivalent experience from the moment the first car was introduced into West Africa. The car was a slippery technology that was at one moment triumphed and another maligned and that was always many things at once. My intention here is not to provide an encyclopedic history of motorization in West Africa, a task that would be difficult given both the limited available research on road transport (Gewald et al. 2009a, 2) and all the local variations and vicissitudes throughout the region. Rather, what this chapter focuses on are flashpoints and illustrative instances when the conflicting feelings about motorization and automobility in the colonial era become apparent. Here, then, I lay the groundwork for how I read the postcolonial aesthetic forms in the rest of this book.

In the first half of this chapter I discuss how some of the early initiatives to motorize Africa were met with resistance by colonial officers for various political and philosophical reasons. While some officers feared that the car would disrupt fragile social structures, others felt that it would compete with the railways, and many were put off by harsh climate conditions, lack of available spare parts, and the poor quality of the roads that led to chronic breakdown. The automobile that was continually in a state of suspended animation was a rather inconvenient symbol of progress. Colonial officers also expressed concern about whether Africans could handle this new, democratizing technology. However, after World War I, the motorcar, at least in the French colonies, became a symbol of European industrialization that could spread the benefits of technology to the less "civilized" colonies. Colonial documentaries, most notably those depicting the famous trans-Saharan and trans-African Citroën crossings, recast the motorcar as a conquering hero with distinct economic and military advantages.

In the second part of this chapter I argue that it was often Africans, not Europeans, who were at the vanguard of encouraging both motorization and the construction of surfaced roads. During the interwar years, African entrepreneurs were some of the most innovative pioneers in importing automobiles and establishing motorized mass transit. In many cases, drivers enjoyed a particularly high status in society and were often seen as emissaries of cosmopolitan fashion and modernity. Likewise, during the period of decolonization, African intellectuals and political leaders advocated the building of infrastructural projects, which, they argued, were being neglected by Europeans. They claimed that only sovereign African nations could bring about true social and economic development, in essence turning the tables on the Europeans whose pretensions of universalism could no longer be sustained.

According to the historian John Iliffe, the motorcar was the most influential innovation of the midcolonial period in Africa. Iliffe, like most historians of the period, agrees that the expansion of road transport stimulated internal trade, reduced the cost of transporting materials, opened up new circuits of commerce, and provided opportunities for indigenous as well as European transporters. The automobile and lorry are therefore often figured into a grand narrative of African modernization and development. This chapter, however, focuses on stories of the motorcar that have been marginalized in larger historical accounts of African development, stories that complicate and often contradict the narrative of continual modernization and show that Africans were often modernizing in ways that Europeans did not intend. The episodes examined in this chapter show that the motorization of West Africa was a process that was overdetermined by ambiguous intentions, politics of domination, technological hurdles, and various forms of African reinvention and creativity.

The Colonial Encounter

As Michael Adas, Daniel Headrick, Brian Larkin, Luise White, and Jan-Bart Gewald have variously argued, technological objects in Africa became central in colonial projects not simply because they were tools of colonial domination but also because they came to embody the technological mastery and supposed superiority of their bearers. But at the same time, technologies, just like churches and colonial schools, also participated in a project that incorporated colonial subjects into a culture of global modernity.[2] Therefore, technological objects like the motorcar were at certain moments symbols of Europe's dominance,[3] of its unique and distinctive scientific advancement, and, at other moments, part of a universal and democratizing technological culture in which both Europeans and non-Europeans could participate. This contradiction—this constant tension between what Frederick Cooper and Ann Laura Stoler aptly describe as "the dialectics of inclusion and exclusion" (1997, 3)—lays at the heart of the colonial project of modernization and also, I argue, accounts for the conflicting and shifting experiences of automobility in colonial West Africa.

Following Jean-François Bayart, I argue that colonization can be understood as a "founding moment" in globalization (2007, 148). As Bayart suggests, colonization was "less a duet than a polyphony, a series of improvisations on the modes of action available to the historical societies when they were forced to 'encounter' one another and overlap with each other by the fact of empire" (148). This improvisational character meant that although colonization was "a regime of domination [that was] literally conducted at gun point and with the lash of the whip," it was also, at the same time, "an experience of subjectivation . . . a painful process of self-reconstruction" (148). In other words, colonialism was an encounter that was shaped by the juxtaposition of modes of domination and practices of self-realization, by colonialists' attempts to "pacify" and rule over their supposedly less modern subjects and by Africans' insistence on appropriating and refashioning modernity. The history of West African motorization and the forms of automobility that begin to take shape during the colonial period are therefore part of a longer, ongoing experience of modernization and globalization, one that is ambivalent, multidimensional, and often complicated by the actions and words of Africans who forge their own relationships with Western technology.

Though my focus here is on West Africa as a region, there were, of course, key differences between British and French colonization. In general, French colonization aimed to integrate and assimilate the colonies into the metropole, a practice termed "association." The French typically viewed colonization as a "civilizing mission," tended to rule through a centralized administration based in Paris, and allowed a select number of Africans who received a French education, called *évolués,* to become French citizens. The British colonial practice of indirect rule relied more on keeping local institutions in place and ruling through established local chiefs who, though subordinate to the British, participated in governing in ways that traditional rulers in French colonies did not. And whereas the French infamously relied on forced labor, the British abolished the practice in the early stages of colonialism. However, it is important to note that within each empire, and oftentimes within the same country, different policies and philosophies about colonization often coexisted and came into conflict with each other. And, as Mahmood Mamdani argues, British indirect rule and French direct rule were often "complementary ways of native control" (1996, 18). In other words, both British and French colonialism shared certain fundamental features that involved ruling over and subduing indigenous populations.[4]

Moreover, while the differences between French and British rule have clearly shaped postcolonial institutions and cultures, they do not appear to have had a major impact on the overall process of motorization. As Jennifer Hart argues, when it came to road construction even the distinction between forced and paid labor might be exaggerated. British indirect rule created a system where traditional chiefs were paid to supervise the construction of rural roads. In theory, they were supposed to pay the laborers, but in practice the chiefs often pocketed the money and used forced labor anyway (2016, 54). Furthermore, in both British and French colonies cars were initially met with ambivalence by the colonial rulers. But when lightweight Fords and better technology were introduced after World War I much of the anxiety dissipated, though neither colonial power would fully commit to a project of modernization until after World War II (Cooper 2005, 145). And though the French created more professional and financial obstacles for indigenous transporters, in both Francophone and Anglophone colonies "indigenous transport" (the catch-all phrase used to indicate the vans and trucks owned and operated by Africans) flourished in similar ways and for similar reasons. Europeans were often dismayed and shocked at the way overloaded and cheap indigenous transport vulgarized the prestige value of the motorcar.[5] However, indigenous transport was a key part of the motorization of West Africa and was proof that the colonies did not always modernize in the way that Europeans expected. The practices of motorization in colonial West Africa therefore followed a regional pattern, albeit one with many local variations and one dependent on levels of economic development and urbanization, that was continually shaped by the dialectics of inclusion and exclusion, mobility and suspended animation, and progress and stasis.

Ambiguous Beginnings

In February of 1900, newspapers across the world reported enthusiastically on the first automobile journey in French West Africa. The drive, the result of efforts by the journalist and businessman Félix Dubois, was completed by the governor of French West Africa, Jean-Baptiste Chaudié, who traveled fifteen kilometers per hour from Toukoto to Kati in present-day Mali, reducing the length of a fourteen-day journey by eleven days. However, despite the initial excitement of the international press, this first effort to bring automobiles into West Africa has been largely ignored in historical accounts of the motorization of Africa. The omission is not entirely surprising given that Félix Dubois's attempt to establish regular motor transport in the French Sudan was ultimately a failure, one that ended with the colonial government seizing his automobiles and supplies and discharging his staff. But the reasons for the oversight of Dubois's venture may also have to do with the story's internal incongruities that do not fit neatly into any preestablished narratives of colonialism and modernization. In an ambitiously researched article published on the occasion of the 1973 conference of the Société française d'histoire d'outre-mer, Yves J. Saint-Martin revives the story of Dubois's "audacious enterprise" in order to pay homage to the forgotten pioneer. Saint-Martin's essay is largely a hagiographic project that attempts to praise the motives of Dubois and to malign those who stood in his way, and Saint-Martin's not-so-subtle goal is to re-narrate Dubois's failures into a story that ends, ultimately, with a success. Dubois, he concludes, was simply ahead of his time. However, what emerges in the many details that Saint-Martin provides is a story of competing agendas and conflicting beliefs as to whether it was advisable to bring motorcars into West Africa.

According to Saint-Martin, Dubois was motivated by a spirit of colonial humanism. Dubois believed cars to be the solution for eliminating the horrors of human porterage that he had seen firsthand in 1897 when he had accompanied Captain Cazemajou on a mission to Chad. There, Dubois had witnessed Cazemajou forcefully recruit and mistreat African porters, who were, at the time, the backbone of transportation in the region. Dubois publicly criticized the captain and argued that Cazemajou's behavior was "counter-propaganda," for it went against the ideals of a civilizing colonization as pronounced by the French Third Republic. But Dubois's objections were routinely dismissed, and the captain demoted him. When Cazemajou summarily executed ten of the porters for attempting to desert, Dubois abandoned the mission and returned to France. The following year, at the 1898 Automobile Exposition in Paris, Dubois came up with a potential solution to the inefficient and inhumane system of human porterage in the French Sudan, and he began to court investors to help him bring the De Dietrich gasoline truck he saw at the exposition to West Africa.

While Dubois's initial motives might have been humanitarian, they were also motivated by capitalist impulses. He believed and was able to convince his investors that the motorization of Africa could be a very profitable endeavor. Dubois estimated that to transport a ton of merchandise from Kayes to Bamako (where there was not yet a railroad) one needed forty porters and fifteen days, which would cost approximately one thousand francs. Dubois established a transport company that promised to do the job for much less, and he told his shareholders that they could expect their stock to yield generous dividends. Consequently, Dubois received wide support in the business community and also found an ally in Lieutenant Governor Louis Edgar de Trentinian, a key figure in the colonial administration. But others were less enthusiastic. The military, for instance, was strongly against the idea. They were already overburdened with providing security and recruiting a workforce to build the railroad. Dubois's automobiles would need additional roads, bridges, and military support—an entire infrastructure for automobility—that would divert resources from more immediate and reliable projects. Military officials published satiric articles making fun of Dubois's proposal, calling it "*l'auto*maboul*isme,*" *maboul* being the French word for "nut" or "loony." (The slur, I suggest, was also a likely reference to Georges Méliès's 1899 film *L'automaboulisme et autorité,* in which two clowns turn driving into an absurd and dangerous sport.) Furthermore, officials in Konakry—the only other area in French West Africa where there were somewhat suitable roads—turned down Dubois's proposal to begin automobile services, presumably for similar reasons. Governor Chaudié also remained very skeptical about the likelihood of Dubois's success.

Saint-Martin attributes Chaudié's hesitation to his weak character and lack of vision, disparagingly describing him as "timid" and a "porpoise." But Saint-Martin also hints at another possible explanation for Chaudié's uncertainty about motorcar transport. Saint-Martin describes how the governor's initial but hesitant optimism was dampened by the continual breakdowns that he experienced on his test drive to Kati. On several occasions, the car had to be pushed by hand, and the chassis and mechanisms proved to be too fragile to handle the heat and the poor roads. Furthermore, what seemed to bother Chaudié was that photographers and journalists were present to record the journey. Thus, it is reasonable to assume that Chaudié might have feared that the story of his "successful" test drive would be overshadowed by all of its setbacks and mishaps, by its constant state of suspended animation. Rather than seeing the journey as one of triumph of the machine over nature, Chaudié may have feared that the technological failures of the colonizers would take center stage, exposing their weaknesses and the limits of their technological prowess at a time when the French were still trying to consolidate their power in the region. Although it is of course impossible to know Chaudié's thoughts, Saint-Martin notes that the colonial government was very quick to annul its contract with Dubois once it became clear that the fifty-five motorcars he imported would need more maintenance than originally anticipated. When Dubois fell into debt, the government immediately seized his materials and repatriated the fifty Chinese mechanics that had been brought in to work with Dubois. Dubois had trouble regaining support, and as progress on the construction of a railway in the French Sudan continued, cars were increasingly seen to be an unnecessary nuisance.

However, roughly a decade after Dubois's premature attempt to motorize West Africa, automobiles began to trickle into the region. Dahomey (present-day Benin) imported its first car in 1910, Togo had about three automobiles four years after that, and, by 1913, there was a regular transport service operating in northern Nigeria.[6] Likewise, the first motorcar was introduced in the Gold Coast (present-day Ghana) in 1902 but was eventually dumped into the sea because it was unusable. But by 1908 eleven cars and sixteen lorries were registered in the country (Hart 2016, 45). In theory, motor roads were cheaper to build than railways, and they made more economic sense because they could be easily abandoned if they became unproductive. They were also less likely to be shut down in the face of minor setbacks like a washed-out embankment, common during the heavy tropical rains (Hawkins 1958, 91). However, since colonial governments had already heavily invested in the railways, motor roads were originally intended only to be feeders to the railways or, as in the case of Dubois's proposed itinerary, to connect railways with river transport. In the Gold Coast, the general manager of the railway argued that while the railway could pay for itself through users' fees and taxes, roads placed an unfair burden on inhabitants and colonial coffers because everyone had to pay for the infrastructure that only a few used (Hart 2016, 48). In both British and French colonies, roads were therefore seen as unwanted competition to the railway, and in certain cases legislation taxed and even forbade motor transport on routes that were served by the rail (Austen 1987, 127). Furthermore, many colonists before World War I opposed road building for purely practical reasons—cars at the time were so heavy that they tore up roads, making repairs an expensive and unending task (Hopkins 1973, 196).

In some cases Europeans also expressed ambivalence about the extent to which Africans should be owning cars, especially for personal use. Erdmute Alber analyzes instances in northern Dahomey during World War I in which automobiles became the center of political tensions between local chiefs and colonial officers. In two separate instances, local chiefs, using compensation money they had received for recruiting soldiers for the colonial army, bought automobiles only to be duped out of them by colonial officers. The chiefs had asked the colonial officers to help facilitate the purchase of the automobiles, but the officers saw an opportunity to take advantage of the situation, and knowing that the chiefs would be unable to afford maintenance, spare parts, or gasoline, the officers intended to use the cars for their own personal benefit. The matter was complicated by the fact that the local chiefs were acting on the encouragement of the governor of Dahomey, who introduced them to the sport of driving on his tour to bolster the efforts of the recruitment campaigns. Since cars were not yet standard issue for colonial officers (the governor was the only official to have one at the time), the officers believed they were justified in taking advantage of the chiefs' enthusiasm and newfound compensation money. To them, it was unthinkable that African leaders should have access to automobiles before European officers. During the legal investigation that ensued, the officers consistently accused the chiefs of not being developed enough to be part of the car-driving elite and questioned the ability of Africans, including their chiefs, to maintain and possess automobiles (Alber 2002, 82). The irony, which Alber fails to acknowledge, is that Africans were already doing so with a considerable amount of skill and innovation. But throughout the early twentieth century, motorization, from colonists' debates about road building to their discussions about car ownership, was inconsistent, and it belied an underlying ambivalence about the goals and profitability of modernization and development.

Of Caterpillars and Colonization

Though colonial governments were ambivalent or torn about the level of technological advancement they wanted in the colonies, there were certainly private citizens who saw merit in promulgating the benefits of Western technomodernity. During the interwar years, as colonial film vans toured through rural Anglophone Africa showing films that promoted Western values (see chapter 3), French documentary filmmakers participated in the media's effort to support colonial expansion.[7] One of the most famous documentary films of the time was Léon Poirier's *La croisière noire* (*The Black Cruise,* 1926), a film that chronicled a twenty-month trans-African road trip from Algeria through western, central, and southern Africa to Madagascar by Citroën half-tracks. By using editing techniques and voice-over narration, the film was able to map a coherent project of a Western modernity traversing and transforming an exotic and decidedly premodern African landscape. Such grand narratives of the civilizing mission could then be projected back to the French public who often knew nothing of either the conflicting agendas in the colonial territories or of their destructive nature as they altered both landscapes and cultural formations.

André Citroën, the French carmaker who brought Taylorist assembly techniques to Europe, originally intended his half-track vehicles for travel in the Sahara. The Citroën caterpillars, as they were affectionately called, were motorcars equipped with two front wheels and a back rubber band tread that would unroll under the vehicle—they could travel over sand or mud without sinking in, and they could travel over rugged territory without deteriorating.[8] Citroën called them "the invention that Jules Verne couldn't dream of: the steel dromedary that drinks gasoline and oil" (Audouin-Dubreuil 2005, 73). The caterpillar cars were first used in a trek from Touggourt, Algeria, to Timbuktu in present-day Mali, and resulted in a popular documentary by Paul Castelnau called *La traversée du Sahara* (*Traversing the Sahara,* 1923). Both the Saharan and trans-African trips were led by Georges-Marie Haardt and Louis Audouin-Dubreuil, who subsequently published their journals of the trips under the titles *La première traversée du Sahara en automobile: De Touggourt à Tombouctou par l'Atlantide* (*Across the Sahara by Motor Car: From Touggourt to Timbuctoo,* 1924) and *La croisière noire* (*The Black Journey,* 1927).[9] The books were intended to complement the films and provide curious readers with even more details about the missions that were marketed as acts of heroism. They were also part of a larger promotional package that demonstrated to the world the new era of an industrial France with the Citroën brand at its center.[10] *La croisière noire,* which was accompanied by various museum exhibitions, several shorter documentaries about the trek, and its own musical score with live orchestra, opened at a grand gala event at the Paris Opera with French president Gaston Doumergue in attendance.[11] Brett Berliner, who links the "*black* cruise" to jazz-age France's "negrophilism," reads the film as a "cultural expression of postwar French imagination and pacific conquest" that combined "exotic," "primitive," and sexualized Africans with French nationalistic pride (2002, 190).[12]

According to Citroën, bringing automobiles to the African continent was part of a spirit of colonial humanism that could spread the benefits of industrialism and progress to the "uncivilized" corners of the globe. Much like Félix Dubois, Citroën believed that this humanitarian project could simultaneously benefit native Africans, help establish communications between France's African territories, and yield generous profits. The Citroën crossings therefore form part of a historical legacy in which motor vehicles were offered up as roaming symbols of a superior civilization.[13] To the viewers in Europe, the sight of automobiles on a continent deemed to be untouched by modernity, with areas previously impenetrable by anyone other than the most intrepid of explorers, was ultimate proof that nothing was beyond the reach of technological progress.

The trans-Saharan journey had a number of objectives. The half-tracks were armed and militarized reconnaissance vehicles exploring the potential for military air bases; they were intended to pave the way for motorcar tourism; and they followed the itinerary of a proposed trans-Saharan railway that would connect North and West Africa.[14] However, what seemed to take priority for Citroën and the expedition leaders was exploring quickly. Citroën charged Haardt and Audouin-Dubreuil with the task of reaching Timbuktu in twenty-one days in order to prove that the half-tracks could not only traverse rough terrain but do so with unprecedented velocity. In their journal, Haardt and Audouin-Dubreuil exhibit an obsession with time and speed as they dutifully record their mileage and average speed per day as well as the precise times of their arrivals and departures. They include the time that a particular mountain comes into view or a repair is made; sometimes the reader is informed what time they go to sleep or wake up. As the expedition leaders state, "It is just as well that the inhabitants of the Sahara should know that the power of France, represented in this effective manner, can now move at the rate of several hundred miles a day over any sort of ground" (Haardt and Audouin-Dubreuil 1924, 50). If in the nineteenth century, "the comings and goings [of] trains (and steamships) proclaimed the Europeans' mastery of time and space and demonstrated their capacity for precision and discipline" (Adas 1990, 224), the Citroën films sought to demonstrate how the motorcar (and, more specifically, the half-track) came to represent the crowning achievement of this mastery in the twentieth century.

In the film of the Saharan journey the sense of speed is captured in the opening sequence when long shots of camel caravans are juxtaposed with shots of the modern caterpillar cars traversing the desert to supplant them. The sequence is a manifestation of Citroën's declaration that "le chameau est mort—la Citroën le remplace" (the camel is dead—the Citroën is replacing it) (qtd. in Reynolds 1996, 98). While Haardt and Audouin-Dubreuil's journal expresses anxiety about whether or not the trip to Timbuktu will be accomplished in twenty-one days, Castelnau's film represents a fait accompli, a travelogue in which exotic desert tribes welcome the French adventurers with admiration and awe. Any sense of political unrest in the Sahara, like any reference to mechanical difficulties that slowed the journey down, are conveniently edited out of the fifty-minute documentary. But, as Peter Bloom notes, the film, in its efforts to promulgate the Citroën and French names, oversimplifies the actual relationship between camel caravans and the caterpillar cars. Bloom argues that the salt caravans depicted in the opening of the film were actually a response to French territorial expansion that altered the grazing patterns of livestock and access to water, shifting the entire political economy of the region. Thus, the "rapid communication" that the trans-Saharan crossing sought to achieve would also have rapidly deleterious effects for the landscape as well as for the tribes that inhabited the region.

On the trans-African journey, or *la croisière noire,* which took over a year and a half to complete, there was much less emphasis on beating the clock and more emphasis on geographic unity, on showing the French expedition traversing the entire length of the African continent (Bloom 2008, 91). In fact, here Haardt and Audouin-Dubreuil seemed more concerned with stopping and preserving time before they propelled it irreversibly forward. Their journal is filled with the knowledge that the motorization of West Africa was inevitable and that it would irreversibly change the landscape through which they were passing. They are proud to be part of the civilizing mission, but they admit that the progress they bring is destroying the same civilization that they are attempting to capture on film and in their journal. In one of their numerous hunting expeditions, they take along 135 African porters and sedan chairs and extol the charm of traveling in "safari fashion." While they somehow miss the point that railways and motorized travel make human porterage retrograde (even though it was often no worse than the forced labor of road building), it is not lost on them that the same manner of traveling that nourishes their bourgeois primitivism will soon become outdated. Haardt and Audouin-Dubreuil conclude their journal with a tone of nostalgia: "Our white cars have only been the advance guard; the faithful worshipers of Boula-Matari were not wrong in believing them to be heralds of a new era. The old world is suffocating: in its conquest of space it is annihilating distance—and also the charm of the unknown" (1924, 308).

What neither the book nor the film divulge, though, is the fact that the journey was part of Citroën's larger plan to expand his empire in Africa. At the time, Citroën had wide-ranging ambitions that went beyond simply cornering the automobile market in West Africa—he wanted the name of Citroën to become synonymous with the progress of Africa, a progress made possible by French industrialization. During the interwar years

Citroën advertised heavily in colonial journals and attempted to compete with the popular Fords in the African colonies.[15] He also had plans to establish European tourism in Northern Africa and even had land purchased to set up luxury hotels and tourist camps.[16] But in 1924, after Citroën had already invested substantial money in his tourism project, Colonel Dinaux, who was in charge of southern Algeria, informed him that there were too many security threats and that he could not guarantee the safety of the tourists. It was later revealed that Dinaux had exaggerated the level of instability in the region, most likely, as Alison Murray argues, because he did not believe that motorcar travel was appropriate for the desert. In a 1921 report entitled "L'automobilisme au Sahara,"[17] written three years before Citroën's proposal reached him, Dinaux wrote that the sight of the cars struggling to get over sand dunes would be humorous and potentially humiliating to French officials. He also believed that the camel was the only sensible means of transport in the Sahara and that anything else would cause a rift between colonial administrators and the natives. Without the approval of Dinaux, Citroën had to abandon his tourism project. He consequently focused a

Figure 1. Citroën half-tracks, or caterpillar cars, in the Sahara, 1923. Copyright Citröen Communication/DR.

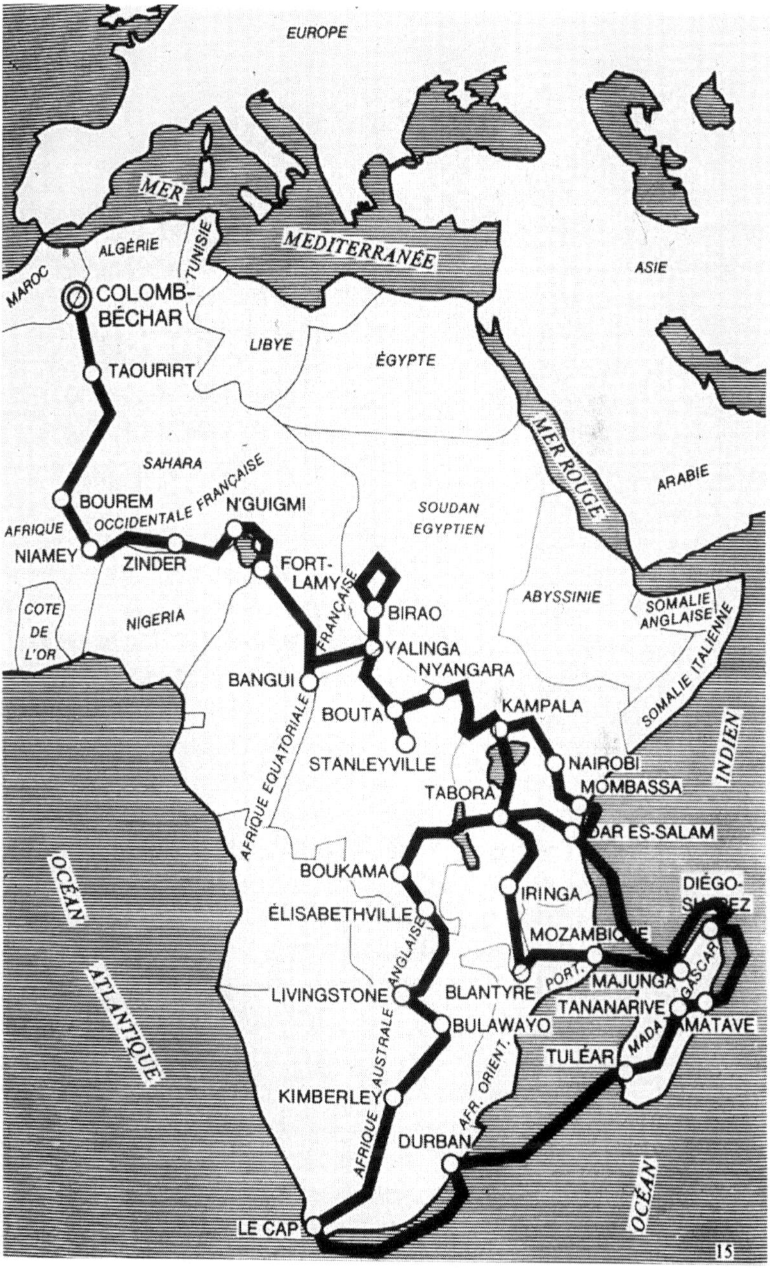

Figure 2. Map of the Croisière Noire itinerary, 1925. Copyright Citröen Communication/DR.

Figure 3. Diagram of the half-track, 1926. Copyright Citröen Communication/DR.

tremendous amount of energy on preparing for the *croisière noire,* which could make up for the loss of symbolic capital and did not rely on long-term security (Murray 2000, 106). Citroën had to prove that his cars would not, as Dinaux feared, become suspended in motion—that they would, on the contrary, become mobile symbols of France's industrial progress and global power.

Of course, Poirier's film does not position the trans-African trek as the massive publicity stunt that it was, nor does it allude to any of the objections raised by Colonel Dinaux and other skeptics. Furthermore, European viewers would have no way of knowing that the journey was arduous, full of breakdowns, and completely dependent on African guides, porters, and thousands of poorly paid conscripted road workers.[18] In an effort to make the Citroën half-tracks into conquering, civilizing heroes, Poirier and his postproduction team edited out anything that might contradict the grand narrative of colonial triumph. Moreover, by juxtaposing the technology of European manhood with partially nude, often dancing, and disproportionately female natives, colonialists not only sexualized Africans; they also made them appear less threatening, less capable of rebellion at a time when, as Peter Bloom notes, uprisings were actually quite common. Like many other colonial films that depicted the arrival of European technology in Africa, *La croisière noire* portrayed an unproblematic, smooth victory over space, time, and nature that in reality never happened quite like it did on screen.[19]

Indigenous Transporters; or, The "Cultural Hero"

Although the Citroën films and other colonial documentaries depicted Africans as primitive and unaffected by modernity, the few comprehensive studies that exist of early West African road transport show that it was often African businessmen who were pioneers in the motorcar industry.[20] While the colonial state acted on different rationales at different moments, Africans did not need to wait for any official decisions as they developed tactics that would allow them to control their own mobility. During the nineteenth century, when the colonizers replaced Africa's traditional internal trading networks with the railroad and shipping systems that facilitated trade for European firms, they also displaced many African traders and offered mainly subordinate positions to native businessmen. In turn, they created an export economy that provided few opportunities for Africans to establish themselves as entrepreneurs. But road transport was one of the rare exceptions (Hawkins 1958, 5).

While many foreign trading companies owned vehicles to transport their goods, they did not generally operate transport services for the public, nor did they establish their own garages (Hawkins 1958, 46). As motorized transport became more common, African men were therefore quick to take advantage of the new business opportunities by owning, driving, and maintaining buses and taxis and opening their own garages. As Sara S. Berry argues, jobs in road transport were important because they provided some of the only paths for self-employment and upward mobility available to a class that did not have high levels of formal education. Berry describes how mechanics could begin as apprentices and eventually work up to running their own small maintenance business specializing in, for example, "panel beating, welding, or electrical work" (1983, 4). But while mechanics were somewhat limited in what they could earn, importers could become quite successful. In Nigeria, for instance, some of the earliest innovators in the transport industry were Nigerian businessmen like W. A. Dawodu and Dr. Obasa. As early as 1913, Dawodu was operating transport services in northern Nigeria around Kano, and a few years later Obasa was running the only passenger bus and van service in Lagos. In 1915 Dawodu imported the first Ford cars into Nigeria and was converting light Model T Fords into commercial vans by building stronger bodies onto the chassis. That same year Dawodu's firm established an agency in Lagos where cars, mainly Fords, could be bought, sold, and repaired. By 1920 his firm was one of the largest vehicle importers, general mechanics, and builders of car and truck bodies in Nigeria (Drummond-Thompson 1992, 222–23).

Immediately after World War I, the introduction of lightweight Fords into West Africa shifted much of the debate as to whether cars could and should be promoted in the colonies.[21] The Fords proved to be much more suitable to West African conditions because they did not destroy the existing roads and they could more easily travel on roads that had not yet been surfaced. They also had the advantage of being equipped with pneumatic tires that were easier on the road than the solid tires used by European cars, and by 1923 almost 75 percent of the 550 cars imported into British West Africa were Fords (McPhee 1971, 118). Suddenly, the cost and hassle of maintaining both motorcars and roads dropped significantly, and motorcars were able to travel into areas that were not yet serviced by the railroads. Because motorcars opened up new circuits of trade that did not directly compete with old routes, they were no longer seen as a threat to the railway (118).

Philip Drummond-Thompson argues that it was in large part the Africans' eagerness to import American cars that gave them the competitive advantage over European firms. In Nigeria, the colonial government as well as many European trading firms were under contract to purchase British automobiles. But the American cars were cheaper and more durable, and spare parts were more readily available. Furthermore, thanks to the Congo Basin treaty of 1920 that allowed American and British cars into British West Africa under the same conditions, American cars were able to remain cheap and competitive. Therefore, African entrepreneurs such as Dawodu who imported American Fords, Dodges, and REOs along with American Firestone tires were able to operate cheaper services than their European competition. In the 1920s, Nigeria and the Gold Coast (present-day Ghana) imported twice as many cars as French West Africa, in part because of the unimpeded efforts of indigenous importers who brought over American cars (McPhee 1971, 118). But even in the French colonies where Fords were subject to high taxes, they were highly competitive with French makes like Citroën and Renault.[22]

Moreover, Yves Hazemann argues that indigenous transporters in the French colonies also flourished because they were able to provide flexibility that larger companies were not. Like the Nigerian transporters, they could vary their routes, their schedules, and the types of goods they transported on a moment's notice, and they often carried both passengers and cargos at the same time. Thus, in both the French and English colonies, small indigenous transporter companies or individuals operated the majority of the mass transportation for both people and products.[23] These transporters were financially successful because by waiting until they could travel with a vehicle loaded with as much cargo and/or as many people as possible, they ensured that each trip would yield a maximum profit. They were also able to benefit from earning a daily profit rather than a wage. While African wage laborers were affected by the global depressions and the strains on colonial finances, transporters and drivers were able to adjust to shifting conditions and continue to profit (Hart 2016, 67).

As indigenous transport flourished during the interwar years and beyond, driving became a prestigious profession, especially, it seems, in the British colonies. In Ken Saro-Wiwa's *Sozaboy*, for instance, the main character, Mene, is an apprentice driver living in a small town in Eastern Nigeria. He comes of age in the final years of colonialism and, just before the Biafaran war begins, he becomes an apprentice driver for a lorry named Progress. Mene describes how his mother, unable to pay his secondary school fees, advises him to learn to drive. In what Saro-Wiwa calls "rotten English," Mene recounts, "My mama say that if I am apprentice to this driver, after some time I will get my own licence *[sic]* and then I can get my own lorry to drive. And if I save my salary and my chop money, I can buy my own lorry and then I will be big man like any lawyer or doctor" (11). And indeed, after becoming an apprentice, Mene was "prouding plenty" (12) as he practiced his English with drivers and cosmopolitan passengers in the motorparks and bought books with his food money. Despite all the bribes they had to pay to government officials and police who stopped traffic, Mene and his master are quite successful and happy until Progress breaks down and, a short time later, the war takes over the region.

Likewise, drivers in Ghana during the late colonial period were often seen as cultural heroes (van der Geest 2009, 261). Sjaak van der Geest discusses how Ghanaian drivers, who were usually fashionably dressed, were often associated with the "good life"—they had money, women, and, most of all, mobility (266). He writes,

> The secret of a driver's success lay in his shuttling back and forth [between city and village]. At home [in the village], he was surrounded by an aura of the seething atmosphere of the city. His urbanity was evident in his manners and in the commodities he had at his disposal: clothes, electronic goods, alcoholic drinks and cigarettes. On the other hand, in the city he represented "the good country life" about which city people continued to muse

> nostalgically but to which they never wanted to return. He brought goods to the city from the village, food from the farm, (more or less) undiluted palm wine, presents from rural family members and, most importantly, the latest news. His car both brought him fortune and embodied the fortune he had already found. (261)

Indeed, in *The Boy Kumasenu* (1952), the first feature film made by the Gold Coast Film Unit, the famous Afro-jazz drummer Guy Warren plays a cool and cosmopolitan lorry driver named Yeboah.[24] The film's narrator emphasizes Yeboah's status by stating, "The lorry drivers' swagger told of the town . . . and their tongues spoke a language half foreign to Kumasenu." The sketch van der Geest paints and the image of the hip lorry driver have gradually been replaced with much more ambivalent representations now that drivers earn much less and are associated with a lower, sometimes criminal, class. However, for several decades, driving provided many Africans with an opportunity to live an enviable, albeit sometimes dangerous and unpredictable, life.

Although some Africans were nervous about the erosion of traditional culture and were often just as fearful as the colonizers about the corruptive and disorderly effects of increased motorization, it was clear that many West Africans sought to develop and democratize motorized transportation with or without the blessings of the Europeans. Jennifer Hart claims that attempts by the colonial government to regulate the ways that Ghanaians used motorcars actually strengthened the power of the drivers by professionalizing driving and creating a need for drivers to form unions and associations. The 1934 Motor Traffic Ordinance, she writes, reflected an increasing British concern about road conditions and the behavior of African drivers who were responsible for public safety. The ordinance made offences out of acts like driving without a light, overloading, and speeding and, most importantly, instituted a new licensing process. Potential drivers were required to demonstrate literacy (in order to read road signs as well as the ordinance itself), but "issues of health and physical fitness, height, disposition (i.e., 'nervous'), language (i.e., ability to speak English), and intelligence (or seeming lack thereof) heavily influenced such examinations" (Hart 2016, 85). What this did was effectively change and regulate who could enter the driving profession. And while it excluded many would-be drivers it also elevated the respectability of drivers who, in the wake of the ordinance, capitalized on their prestige in order to create unions that would protect drivers' interests and push back against regulations that impinged on their autonomy.

Though the Motor Traffic Ordinance and ensuing professionalization of drivers was in some ways unique to Ghana—Hart describes how licenses from neighboring countries were not accepted because regulations were not as strict—throughout West Africa automobility provided African workers in the transport sector with the opportunity to fashion their identity and articulate their autonomy. This was the case even in the French colonies where the tendency was not to legitimate indigenous transporters but rather to de-professionalize them and make them less competitive. As Hazemann argues, after World War I, France wanted to make it more difficult for the African businessmen to compete with the Europeans and *assimilés* (Lebanese and Syrians) and therefore cut Africans' access to bank credit and the chambers of commerce (1992, 212). This resulted in an informalization of economic activities and meant that indigenous business transactions were conducted entirely within local markets and were not the object of colonial surveillance (213).[25] In 1936 the lieutenant governor of French West Africa created a committee for the coordination of transport that excluded all indigenous transporters. The committee then granted the most lucrative routes to European transporters who operated on fixed itineraries and disallowed access to the indigenous transporters who operated on the more popular (and profitable) flexible and on-demand schedules. But as was the case in Ghana, the drivers and transporters enjoyed a certain amount of power, and by 1937 they were able to pressure the lieutenant governor to reverse his decision. Thus, despite the differing colonial attitudes toward indigenous transporters, African subjects asserted their rights to automobility and insisted on motorizing in a way that suited their own needs. Of course, as I'll explore at length in the following chapter, this did not mean that driving was without its dangers and anxieties, nor did it mean that motorcars always functioned with the speed and consistency with which their drivers hoped.

"Language as Asphalt" and Infrastructural Longing

As I have been suggesting, the process of motorization was intimately linked to the larger project of modernization. However, for most of the period of colonization, neither France nor Britain was entirely convinced that they should be investing large amounts of resources into improving infrastructure or creating the conditions for automobility in their African colonies. Frederick Cooper notes that even as late as the 1920s and 1930s both France and Britain rejected proposals to invest in infrastructure and decided instead that it would be more beneficial to rule over more "traditional" societies (2005, 145). However, by the 1940s both European powers began to realize that the legitimacy as well as the profitability of imperialism was becoming harder to sustain.[26] They came to believe that both of these problems could be addressed by adopting a developmentalist approach to colonialism. By socializing and urbanizing the African work force and by investing in large infrastructural projects, the Europeans believed that they could morally and financially reinvigorate colonialism. The imperial project, they finally decided, would indeed be a modernizing one.

During the post–World War II period, colonial governments in West Africa prioritized spending on transport infrastructure and, in a decisive turn from earlier policies, began to prioritize road building. Transport investment after World War II accounted for 40 percent of the French colonial budget and 30 percent of British expenditure, and in the period between 1945 and 1960 both the number of motor vehicles and the number of tarred roads grew tenfold (Hopkins 1973, 282–83). Colonial policymakers in West Africa began to adopt what Rudolf Mrázek calls, in the context of the Dutch Indies, a "language of asphalt," a language that speaks in terms of technology and speed and that relies on the road as both a literal measure of progress and a metaphor of teleological development.

In a 1957 report on the development of road networks in West Africa, M. Georges Gayet, the inspector general of overseas France, speaks in asphalt language as he proudly measures how far France has come in developing road infrastructure for its West African colonies. Following up on a series of studies presented at the International Congress of Roads held in Dakar in 1952, Gayet is pleased to report that new technologies for paving roads, along with revenues from a new gas tax, have enabled France to improve the circulation of transport vehicles on three important itineraries: the coastal route from Dakar to Cotonou, which transported 80 percent of French West African export products; the itineraries that fed the four railway networks of French West Africa; and routes that allowed better access to hunting reserves, cottages, and hotels that Europeans enjoyed in their leisure time. Thus, the selected routes were intended to improve the overall profitability of the colonies and make colonial exploitation a more enjoyable and leisurely pursuit. Here, asphalt language is a familiar mixture of what Mrázek calls "jargon, vacation language, and twaddling modernity" (2002, 30). Gayet's report therefore shows how development projects, while undertaken with a language of universalism and in the spirit of incorporating Africans into Western modernity, were often still exclusionary despite African's participation in automotive culture.

The colonizers, however, did not have a monopoly on the language of asphalt. Though Africans were not monolithic in their desire for roads and motorization—in many cases, the practices of forced labor, especially within the French colonies, created ill will toward roads and road transport—Africans often advocated for more and better infrastructure than the colonial government was willing to provide. As Hart notes, Ghanaians during the middle colonial period sometimes carried out maintenance on roads and built feeder roads in defiance of colonial governments. In one instance villagers even spent £47,500 to hire an Italian contractor to build roads connecting their village to major roads, markets, and ports (Hart 2016, 52). Zan Semi-Bi notes that in Ivory Coast after forced labor was abolished in 1946, many villages that were constructed along the roadside moved away from the road so that villagers could return to agricultural practices. But during the decades of decolonization and immediate post-independence, as Ivory Coast became more integrated into the global economy, the same villages that withdrew into the forest began demanding available road infrastructure.

Furthermore, during the period of decolonization, anticolonial advocates seized on the language of asphalt and advocated for modern infrastructure that would ameliorate daily life for the people. In his famous polemic, *Discourse on Colonialism* (1950), Aimé Césaire argues that, contrary to what the Europeans claimed, colonialism was actually serving as a *roadblock* to modernization. Césaire writes, "The proof is that at present it is the indigenous peoples of Africa and Asia who are demanding schools, and colonialist Europe which refuses them: that it is the African who is asking for ports and roads, and colonialist Europe which is niggardly on this score, that it is the colonized man who wants to move forward, and the colonizer who holds things back" (25). Similarly, Frantz Fanon sharply criticizes the disparity between the European sections of colonized cities and the native quarters by calling attention to infrastructural inequalities: "The settlers' town is a strongly built town, all made of stone and steel. It is a brightly lit town; the streets are *covered with asphalt*. . . . The native town is a crouching village, a town on its knees, a town wallowing in the mire" (1963,

39, emphasis added). Though Fanon criticizes the post-independence national bourgeoisie who hide their "mediocrity" behind "buildings which have prestige value at the individual level" or behind "chromium plating on big American cars" he passionately advocates for infrastructure that is beneficial to the masses (176). Likewise in "The Role of Culture in the Liberation Struggle," Amilcar Cabral argues in favor of "democracy . . . literacy, the creation of schools and health services, leadership training for persons with rural and urban laboring backgrounds, and many other developments which impel people to set forth upon the *road of cultural progress*" (211, emphasis added). Roads, whether used literally by Césaire and Fanon or metaphorically by Cabral, were part of a forward-looking and modernizing rhetoric, co-opted from the colonialists, but this time linked unambiguously to an appeal for universal rights.

Asphalt language was also part of a larger infrastructural longing and technopolitical rhetoric used by African (and Afro-Caribbean) intellectuals who were arguing that colonialism could not be consistent with an ideology of progress and that both modernization and technological development were needed in order to right the wrongs of decades of colonial neglect. For instance, Ousmane Sembene's novel *God's Bits of Wood* (1960), a fictional account of the 1947 Dakar-Niger railway strike in which Sembene took part, expresses a machine-based future in which technology works for and not against African subjects. As the strikers gather at the railroad stations to pass time, they begin to realize that the railway is a machine that belongs to them. Despite the fact that it was originally a form of colonial domination, that tribal lands were seized and workers exploited and mistreated in its construction, the younger generation of strikers, as Marian Aguiar notes, imbue the railway "with new meaning in the context of an anticolonial struggle" (2003, 284). Sembene writes,

> Something was being born inside them, as if the past and the future were coupling to breed a new kind of man, and it seemed to them that the wind was whispering a phrase they had often heard from [the strike leader] Bakayoko: "The kind of man we were is dead, and our only hope for a new life lies in the machine, which knows neither a language nor a race." (76)

Here the railway—but also technology more broadly—is celebrated as "a new, modern way of being" (Aguiar 2003, 286). Moreover, the workers understand that because they can shut down an entire transportation system, they are particularly poised to disrupt the flow of exports on which the French colonial economy depended. As they mobilize around the technology of the railway, they claim their rights as employees and citizens in the same way that the Ghanaian drivers did when they formed unions and protested the 1934 Motor Traffic Ordinance, demanding inclusion in a world of technological modernity.

Of course, despite aspirations, independence often brought with it a new set of exclusions, and it gradually became clear to most West Africans that the road to development would be neither smooth nor even. African leaders rarely made the infrastructural changes necessary to improve automobility for all. For instance, Hart writes that Kwame Nkrumah believed that drivers were important for the national economy, but he did not invest in roads, preferring larger industrial projects and leaving many feeder roads that connected villages to major roads in poor and unsafe conditions. Léopold Sédar Senghor spent a sizeable sum improving Dakar for the 1966 First World Festival of Negro Arts, building new hotels, museums, and government buildings in line with negritude aspirations of the time (Melly 2013, 385). But what this meant in practice was that he would simply contain the poverty and inequality that existed throughout the city from the visitors who came to the festival (385). Tourists would travel along the seaside Route de la Corniche into the elevated center of the city but see very little of the dusty, unpaved streets that made up the bulk of Dakar's popular neighborhoods. Likewise, in Lagos, the newly independent government inherited from the British a bifurcated city in which wealthy enclaves had received the lion's share of infrastructural investment while much of the city was neglected (Gandy 2006, 375). In the post-independence era, "the combined pressures of political instability, accelerated rates of migration and the destabilising effects of oil wealth" caused an already unstable Lagos to further deteriorate (374). But, as Matthew Gandy points out, even had post-independence leaders advocated for better planning policies, they would still have had trouble implementing them since there were very few Nigerians with the necessary technical and administrative experience: there were only thirty urban planners in the entire country and only one engineer trained to oversee the city's entire water system (378).[27]

The difference between the infrastructural dreams of decolonization advocates and the reality of independence can be seen in the affective distance between Sembene's 1960 *God's Bits of Wood* and his 1976 novella *Niiwam*. While *God's Bits of Wood* celebrates the railway workers as the vanguard of a new, albeit double-edged, modernist consciousness, *Niiwam* underscores the painful experience of postcolonial urban migrants suddenly transporting themselves through the city. *Niiwam,* made into a film by Clarence Delgado in 1988, tells the story of a father who has just arrived in Dakar from his village with his sick baby. After his son dies at the "Native Hospital," the father is shocked to discover that the cemetery is located on the opposite side of the city from the hospital and that he must have money to take transport there. A poor man at the morgue takes pity on the father and pays his bus fare. Much of the story deals with the degradation the father feels as he rides a rickety bus with the corpse of his son in his arms.[28] Even as early as 1963 in his first short film, *Borom Sarret*—which I will be discussing in detail in chapter 3—Sembene highlights the lived experience of inequality and degradation the urban poor faced when they were not privy to modern forms of transportation. Though automobility and the language of asphalt certainly provided Africans with opportunities to claim their position as modern global subjects, in the decades following independence it became clear that these citizens would need to orient themselves within infrastructures that were as profoundly unstable and contradictory as they had been during the colonial era.

Progress and Its Hum

The title of this chapter, "The Hum of Progress," is intended to recall Citroën's introduction to *Across the Sahara* in which he quotes his expedition leaders, Haardt and Audouin-Dubreuil (see my epigraph), who have equated the hum of their motors to the "song of progress, the rhythm of human effort chanting its victory over the elements" (13). The reader will by now understand both the irony and the arrogance of this victorious claim, given the fact that the Citroën treks, unlike indigenous transporters, were only tangentially concerned with modernizing Africa and not at all interested in providing any benefits to the people inhabiting the landscapes they traversed. The progress that they speak of, then, is a European one. But what I am interested in is the unintended implication of the twice-repeated word "hum."

A hum is different from a song in that it has an indistinct, droning noise and is, by definition, devoid of lyrics.[29] In *God's Bits of Wood,* Sembene uses the hum of the machine to denote the distortion and confusion associated with modernization: "All of the contradictory emotions he felt were still revolving in Tiémoko's head, like the humming of a motor he could not stop" (87). The hum of progress I am referring to in the title of this chapter is therefore meant to undermine the clear and meaningful "song of progress" that Citroën believed had chanted its victory over the untamed African landscape. The hum of progress, to me, underscores the indistinct, contradictory, and "noisy" nature of progress both in the period of colonization and in the equally muddy and emotionally complex postcolonial age. Moreover, for anyone who has spent time riding in cars, vans, or trucks in West Africa, it goes without saying that noise is an overwhelming part of the travel experience. Rattling mufflers, ageing suspension, sputtering exhaust, misfired engines, not to mention the shouting of roadside vendors who thrust their goods through the windows, often coalesce to form a chorus of indistinguishable noises and hums. For those traveling in collective transportation the noise level is intensified by touts, the conversation of very proximate fellow passengers, and loud, "staticky" music.[30] It is within this amalgam of hums, noise, and static that I situate the following chapters of this book.

A growing body of criticism has taken to celebrating African cities and streets as places "of manifold rhythms, a world of sounds, private freedom, pleasures, and sensations" (Mbembe and Nuttall 2004, 360). These critics have commendably sought to extricate Africa from narratives that position African cities as backward, exploited, and unmodern, and they have pointed to a number of ways that African subjects may stylize themselves and participate in the rich and sophisticated dynamics of global modernity. However, as these scholars well know, and have in fact spent much time analyzing, daily life in West Africa is extremely overdetermined: freedoms and pleasures do not always come easily. Amid the "manifold rhythms," the pulses of cosmopolitan delight, the sounds of hiplife or *mbalax* music blasting from clubs of youth wearing Pumas and knock-off Prada are the noises of clattering mufflers, screeching brakes, generators being fired up after another power failure, and men and women unable to find formal work hawking tissues or plastic combs on the streets. Thus, while it is important to note the dynamism and positive energy that shapes African social spaces, it is also important to note that daily mobility can often be severely limited both in the city and in rural areas. The question then becomes: how does one stylize the self in such a context? Or, to put it differently, what kind of narratives are created in this atmosphere? What types of meaning are fashioned amid all this noise?

Automobility is just one of many narratives of self-stylization available to West Africans today. But there is perhaps no other techno-object that has been as central to how West Africans navigate their complicated, affective relationship with modernity and no other object as deeply entangled in colonial-era conflicts about infrastructure and modernization as the automobile. Postcoloniality and the ascendance of neoliberalism have neither resolved nor condensed these ambivalences; they have only multiplied and complicated the already existing paradoxes of modern automobility. What remains consistent, however, is that the automobile continues to shed light on the dialectics of inclusion and exclusion and mobility and immobility that characterize African subjects' relation to global modernity and that it continues to be many things at once. In the various aesthetic objects I analyze in the remainder of the book, the automobile remains a "leading object" through which West Africans create meaning within and above the muffled hum of progress.

· CHAPTER 2 ·

"No Danger No Delay": Wole Soyinka and the Perils of Driving

I want to consider the ways in which the accidental converges with . . . contingency. It is important to recognize that the differentiation of the accidental and the contingent, which takes place in and through the figure of the car, and on the road, constitutes a primary means of economically hierarchized subjectification in the current moment.

—Rosalind Morris, "Accidental Histories, Post-Historical Practice?"

The road waits, famished.

—Wole Soyinka, "Death in the Dawn"

As noted in the previous chapter, the road has historically provided many West Africans with ways to make a living and act as mobile and modern subjects. However, roads in the region are also notoriously deadly and dangerous. The World Health Organization reports that Africa, with Nigeria leading the way, has the world's highest fatality rate from road crashes. Though road safety is not typically the terrain of intellectuals, it would be difficult to find someone more committed to curbing the bloodshed and breakdowns on Nigerian roads than Wole Soyinka, a literary giant who also spent two years in prison after trying to broker a peace deal during the Nigerian civil war and who was famously exiled for speaking out against the Abacha regime. The Nobel laureate is not as well known for his long-standing commitment to road safety campaigns, which dates back to the late 1970s, but it was Soyinka who initially urged the creation of the Oyo State Road Safety Corps. Appalled by the number of lives being lost on Nigeria's highways, Soyinka used his fame to call attention to the poor construction and maintenance of roads, lack of law enforcement, shoddy vehicles, and hazardous driving practices.[1] "We are tired," he asserted, "of an environment polluted by the stench from slaughter and maiming on the road" (qtd. in Gibbs 1995, 473). Soyinka even patrolled roads as an Oyo State marshal until the corrupt government disbanded the corps in 1983. In 1988, when the military regime of Ibrahim Babangida established the Federal Road Safety Corps, Soyinka accepted an invitation to sit on the council and then to become the chairman. It was a rare and controversial move for such an outspoken critic of the government, but for Soyinka this type of cooperation was necessary and worthwhile (480).

During his years with both the Oyo State and the Federal Corps, Soyinka wrote review sketches and journalistic pieces on the dangers of overtaking, speeding, and improperly maintaining vehicles (Gibbs 1995, 470). But his preoccupation with death on the road both predates his safety campaign and indicates a much deeper philosophical problem than the ones he articulated as the public face of the Safety Corps. For Soyinka, the road, associated with his patron god, Ogun—also the god of metal, iron, creativity, new technology, and transition—is a site of both creation and destruction. The language of the road is therefore decisively *not* the language of asphalt that, as Mrázek argues, smooths over contradictions in its teleological pursuit of modernity. Rather, the road in Soyinka's work represents both the potential to move forward and the prevalence of roadblocks that thwart progressive movement. This is why Soyinka's road is not one that finds its full expression in road safety material but in the literary space of his poems and plays. The complexity and density of Soyinka's literary road can be understood by thinking of the road as what Mikhail Bakhtin calls a chronotopic device, a spatiotemporal matrix in which "time, as it were, thickens, takes on flesh, becomes artistically visible" and "space becomes charged and responsive to the movements of time, plot, and history" (1981, 84). Though roads are a common trope in Soyinka's poetry, his 1965 play *The Road* is the work that deals most directly and profoundly with the paradoxical symbolism of Nigerian roads. Here, Soyinka uses the theatrical form to set various chronotopes of the road beside each other, creating multiple temporalities and perspectives that are resistant to any single linear narrative.

First staged at the Commonwealth Arts Festival in 1965, *The Road* dramatizes the lives and deaths of lorry drivers, touts (drivers' assistants),[2] policemen, and various sorts of criminals on the roads and highways of the newly independent Nigeria. The play is set on the urban periphery and, as Ato Quayson suggests, "recognizable traces of Lagos, Ibadan, Port

Harcourt, Kaduna, and other big Nigerian cities are evident not in the specific details but in the general combination of hope and hopelessness among the peripheral urban social types central to the dramatization of the edge of the city" (2003, 146). Each night these characters come together to drink palm wine at the AKSIDENT store, a bar and spare parts shop set up in the carcass of a lorry and run by a man simply referred to as Professor. The central action revolves around Samson, a tout for the truck "No Danger No Delay," and his driver Kotonu, who have recently been involved in two road mishaps. The first accident occurs during the annual Driver's Festival of Ogun when Kotonu runs over Murano, a palm-wine tapper who was masked as a god. Unbeknown to Samson and Kotonu, who believe that the masked god mysteriously disappeared, Professor has discovered the half-dead tapper, arrested him in his transitional death phase, and employed him as a servant. Samson and Kotonu's second brush with death occurs when they arrive at a bridge moments after it collapses and kills all of the passengers in a truck that had just overtaken them. Traumatized by the two events, Kotonu has sworn to give up the road, but Samson is intent on convincing him to continue driving. Samson seeks the help of Professor, but Professor is too obsessed with his own quest for the enigmatic Word—some truth incarnate—to provide Samson with any help. Moreover, the death-obsessed Professor, who amasses spare parts for his store at accident sites, is happy to declare Kotonu unfit for the road. His intention is to install Kotonu in his AKSIDENT store to replace Sergeant Burma, the manager who recently died in an oil tanker explosion when his brakes failed.

What I argue in this chapter is that automobility becomes legible not only in the movement and desired movement of the drivers but also in the detritus of their accidents, in the fallen bodies, spare parts, wallets, or uniforms that Professor collects, as well as in the psychological debris that accumulates in the consciousnesses of the characters. This chapter is therefore not about automobility per se, but rather about how it interacts with its foil: suspended animation. If automobility is comprised of a system of cars, drivers, roads, and signs that becomes the foundation for a culture of mobility, suspended animation is what occurs when the system is disrupted, when mobility becomes temporarily paused or frozen. However, in Soyinka's play, suspended animation becomes both the impediment and precondition to any type of progress: the road serves as a temporal holding zone that can unleash both death and positive transformation. Soyinka therefore creates a new language of the African road, one in which the shocks of modern technology enable both destruction and the conditions for the survival of the auto-mobile subject. Thus, I argue that the road also serves as the paradigmatic postcolonial time-space, one composed of the swings, inertias, and "meaningful acts" (Mbembe 2001, 6) that determine how subjectivity is formed in systems conditioned by and contingent on accident or breakdown. *The Road* therefore reveals the limitations of narratives of automobility that link the motor vehicle to a civilizing progress and to unfettered autonomous mobility, and it also underscores the fact that existing theories of technology and disaster need to be modified in order to better suit an African context.

The Technological Accident

What theories of new technologies and modes of production often have in common is that they presume that the technologies about which they are theorizing function properly.[3] Thus, whether one is talking about Henry Ford's mass production of Model Ts, the postmodern flood of consumer gadgets into public and private realms, or the new types of social organization engendered by the Internet, these theories only make sense when the technologies on which they are centered actually work. One might expect that histories of technology focused on sub-Saharan Africa would take a different approach, given the penchant for various types of breakdown and states of disrepair. However, by and large, this has not been the case.[4] For instance, Daniel Headrick's *The Tentacles of Progress* (1988), a study of how the massive transfer of technology from European powers to their colonies ultimately failed to enable industrialization, discusses many of the unsuccessful projects of technological development, but rarely mentions the failed technologies themselves. Headrick, like Walter Rodney before him, provides an impressive amount of evidence as to *how* Africa was "underdeveloped" without ever addressing how Africans lived and experienced this underdevelopment through everyday technological objects. Even Manuel Castells, who discusses technological inequalities in the information age, does not address the fact that it is, as Larkin suggests, often the slowness of an Internet connection or the malfunctioning of a computer—and not necessarily scarcity or absence—that shapes the African subjects' daily encounter with technology. Thus, while there are theories aplenty about the lack of technological development in sub-Saharan

Africa, relatively few address the embodied experiences of technologies that are often unreliable. Theories of development and underdevelopment alike fail to recognize the frustrating and shocking experience of technology, opting instead for studies that measure either the success or lack of technological progress.

For Soyinka, by contrast, the technology of the motorcar is always experienced alongside its uncertainties. His work therefore offers us a way of understanding how postcolonial subjects react to and are formed by what Paul Virilio calls the "immanent" or "integral accident." For Virilio, each technological invention produces not only new forms of movement but also its own localized integral accident:[5] "To invent the sailing ship or steamer is *to invent the shipwreck*. To invent the train is *to invent the rail accident* of derailment. To invent the family automobile is to produce the pile-up on the highway" (2007, 10). For Virilio, then, technological progress simply leads to quicker and more catastrophic accidents. And yet, he argues, the rhetoric of modernization and globalization deny the occurrence of the accident: the positivist ideology of progress, in its various guises, sweeps the potential for calamity under the carpet. What Virilio suggests is that these denials come at a very serious cost. But what he overlooks is that, due to the different ways people across the globe experience technology, some cultures are much more forthright about the frequency and ubiquity of accidents. The prevalence of the car crash or breakdown in African film and literature is a case in point.

Wolfgang Schivelbusch, in his analysis of early railway trauma, provides a useful model to begin to understand how the motorcar accident, as an integral accident, becomes a part of the Nigerian psychic landscape. According to Schivelbusch's account, in the initial years of the railway, travel was marked by an acute awareness of the latent destruction involved in this new form of technology. However, Schivelbusch argues that the fear of the ever-present disaster remained only until the railroad became a part of normal, daily life. Activities like reading in the train as well as new forms of panoramic perception eventually created an additional psychic layer, or an industrialized consciousness, that allowed old fears and anxieties to recede. These new activities formed what Freud would call a stimulus shield, a protective layer of consciousness, which acted as a preventative mechanism to buffer the effects of trauma.[6] Then, it was only the accident—the interruption of normal functioning—that would reawaken the repressed memory of danger and violence. Thus, as the train journey became smoother and more seamless, the accident had a more catastrophic, unexpected effect.

For Schivelbusch, the traveler who sat reading felt more secure because his attention was focused on an independent object rather than on the technological aspects of the journey. Likewise, the improved technology of the train, like the upholstery that eliminated vibration and jolts, made it easier to forget the possibility of derailment or collision. The car, of course, underwent parallel changes in the postwar period: softened suspensions, individualized sound systems, and climate control helped to create a feeling in which the driver was sealed off from the rest of the world. All of these developments helped to isolate the driver from the potential dangers of driving. It was no coincidence, then, that, as Jeffrey Schnapp argues, works like Andy Warhol's Death and Disaster series in the 1960s and Jim Dine's 1959 Car Crash pastels came about at precisely the moment when Americans could feel safer in their automobiles. These works, like other romantic celebrations of the car crash, restored the risk and thrill to driving. They reminded one of the original dangers of driving, dangers that the automobile industry works hard to have consumers forget.[7]

It should come as no surprise, then, that the car crash is not romanticized in countries where the threat of the accident has remained more visible and ever-present. While the type of analysis Schivelbusch instantiates is useful in understanding the way that transportation accidents leave their imprint on the psychic landscape of the subject, there is a dissonance when one is discussing accidents on African roadways. The condition of roads and vehicles—which since the writing of *The Road* have arguably worsened—makes it impossible to isolate oneself from the jolts of travel, and the experience of traveling in one's own private cocoon is reserved for a very small minority who will still hardly be as isolated as their Western counterparts. The lack of grade-separated highways, functional traffic signals, and speed limit enforcement means that colossal traffic jams, vehicles dangerously weaving in and out of traffic, and pedestrians successfully and unsuccessfully dodging cars are almost always a part of an urban driving experience in Africa. In Nigeria car accidents are one of the leading causes of death, especially for less economically advantaged young men like those portrayed in *The Road*.[8] Furthermore, wreckages that are slow to be cleared form a part of the landscape in both urban and rural West Africa, while cars that are repaired with recycled or makeshift parts often stall and clatter along the road. Far from being denied, as Virilio suggests, or repressed and compartmentalized, the commotion and violence of travel is a dominant and much-discussed part of the experience.

In *The Road* Soyinka uses the setting of the AKSIDENT store to give shape to some of the ways that accidents and disorder are very much a part of an everyday driving experience. The shop itself is an emptied-out *bolekaja,* or mammy wagon. A *bolekaja* is a midsize wood axial lorry, usually made from a Bedford chassis, and retrofitted with wooden benches for passengers by African carpenters.[9] Although they were eventually banned and replaced in the late 1970s by larger *molue* buses, during the immediate post-independence period *bolekajas* were a very common form of collective transportation and were how most Nigerians experienced automobility.[10] Because the *bolekaja* had only one wooden door at the back, passengers, who were often squeezed in to maximize profitability, would have to climb over each other to enter and exit. The experience of riding in a *bolekaja* was certainly not often characterized as a pleasurable one. In *The Road* the *bolekaja* is the form of transport that is denigrated by the characters of the play as the least prestigious type of vehicle to drive.[11] Say Tokyo Kid, a thuggish lumber transporter, refuses to drive a *bolekaja* because he says that he does not want to die with "passenger piss running on ma head" (27). The noble way to go, he boasts, is carrying timber: "Carrying timber ain't the same as carrying passengers I tell you. . . . You carrying rubbish. You carrying lepers. The women tell you to stop because they're feeling the call of nature. If you don't stop they pee in your lorry. And whether you stop or not their chirren mess the place all over" (26). Soyinka himself calls the *bolekaja* a form of "transportation torture on four wheels" (1988, 250), not simply because it is unsafe, highly prone to catching fire, and usually illegally operated, but also because it entails riding "with humans crushed against one another and against market produce, sheep, and other livestock, suffocated by the stench of rotting food and anonymous farts" (251). Tellingly, the meaning of the word *bolekaja* translates into "come down, let's fight."[12]

And yet the history of indigenous forms of transport like the *bolekaja* indicates that there is a more complex meaning system at play, one in which danger and disorder are mixed with ingenuity and creative adaptation. As Jennifer Hart writes, "For many African drivers and passengers, the hybrid vehicle—the product of both foreign manufacturing and local construction—symbolized the economic creativity and autonomy of the African entrepreneur, physically transforming foreign technologies to serve local economies rooted in African mobility practice" (2016, 69). The setting of the *bolekaja* for Professor's AKSIDENT store is therefore particularly dense. On the one hand, the *bolekaja* evokes the chaos and unpleasantries of everyday road travel and attests to the mayhem and disorder of both life and death on the road.[13] On the other hand, the transformation of a passenger lorry, which has already been transformed by local mechanics, into a store and drinking venue emphasizes that the *bolekaja* is the site of meaning making, entrepreneurial opportunities, and economic autonomy. That it is filled with goods gleaned from accident sites—windscreen wipers, springs, pistons, children's toys, cigarette holders, and trousers—captures the fact that the creative and lively entrepreneurial spirit of transport work often becomes intimately intertwined with death and danger. These same contradictions are also evident in the character of Salubi, an excited and ambitious driver-in-training who finds and even proudly wears the blood-stained uniform of a deceased driver. While in the West innovations like smoother roads, air bags, and sound systems, as well as a less direct encounter with human mortality, make it possible for drivers to forget the danger of the accident, in Africa, the constant reminders of accidents create a state of continued and palpable anxiety. And yet, in *The Road* it seems to be this very anxiety that prepares the drivers emotionally and that makes survival and creativity possible.

The Road therefore affords a certain understanding or theorization of the accident in post-independence and contemporary Nigeria where many of the driving conditions remain as precarious as ever. As Caroline Levine argues, turning toward fictional works to theorize the social is "to be faithful to the roots of the word *theory,* which comes from the Greek word for 'a looking at,' 'spectacle,' or 'contemplation.' *Theoria* entails the possibility that one might be able to extrapolate generalizable rules about the world from the experience of a spectacle" (2015, 133–34). Moreover, Levine notes that certain fictional forms have an advantage over sociological works that often "isolate one pattern at a time for analysis" because narrative forms are particularly well suited to express "multiple forms operating at once" (134). What Soyinka's play does, then, is create a spectacle that sets in motion the multiple and concurrent experiences of and reactions to Nigerian road accidents. By providing these different vantage points, Soyinka theorizes the complex time-space of the road through his drama and allows his audience to "look at" and "contemplate" the overlapping affective experiences of road users.

"Death in the Dawn"

Because *The Road* builds on many of the themes and affective modes adumbrated in Soyinka's poetry collection *Idanre* (1967), it useful to begin there. Of particular importance is "Death in the Dawn," which was penned in 1960, five years before *The Road*. "Death in the Dawn" lays the foundation for a view of the technological accident as a negative indicator of progress and also begins to point toward the type of hardened consciousness one develops in the wake of these accidents. As a preamble to the poem, Soyinka describes the event that inspired it: "Driving to Lagos one morning a white cockerel flew out of the dusk and smashed itself against my windscreen. A mile further I came across a motor accident and a freshly dead man in the smash" (6). "Death in the Dawn" begins with an injunctive: "Traveller, you must set out / At dawn" (6), enjoining the reader to become a fellow traveler, to experience the event as a co-witness to the destruction. The poem opens, like Soyinka's journey, at dawn, a time of hope and promise, a time filled with the potential for productivity and action. It is the time for "racing joys" and "processions on grey byways" (6); it is the hour when marketplaces set up and people begin to stir for another day. Yet it is precisely at this "holy hour" that the cockerel's "perverse impalement" smashes into the poet's windshield. Unfortunately, the cockerel is not, as the traveler might have hoped, a sacrifice that will appease the hungry god of the road but instead "a futile rite" that only whets the road's appetite. A mother prays that her child never walk "when the road waits, famished"—a line repeated in Soyinka's famous "Idanre" poem and in *The Road*. But it is to no avail. The cockerel serves as a warning sign for the far more insidious crash that the poet witnesses farther down the road. The collision with the bird therefore symbolizes a challenge, or impediment, to "the wrathful wings of man's Progression" (7).

The final line of the poem addresses the dead man the poet sees in the crash: "Brother, / Silenced in the startled hug of / Your invention—is this mocked grimace / This closed contortion—I?" (7). Most critical readings of the poem assume that Soyinka is pondering his relationship with the dead driver and wondering whether he too, a fellow traveler of the road, is not inching toward death.[14] The fraternal salutation draws Soyinka away from the position as a detached witness and makes him and his readers all comrades-in-arms, all victims of the machines that humans have invented. However, what I would like to suggest is that the "mocked grimace" and "closed contortion" is not necessarily the surprised expression of a man freshly torn from life but instead, or maybe even as well, the twisted metal of the car itself. In this reading Soyinka would be proposing an identification between the poet and the crashed automobile and shifting his focus toward the way in which the technological apparatus too has become the victim of its own invention. If I am correct in recognizing the poet's identification with the mangled automobile, then the poem is not a tale of man against technology but rather a reflection on an entire system of roads, drivers, and automobiles—a system of automobility—that destroys itself. The crisis, in other words, generates from within the system itself, and perhaps this is what Soyinka means when he writes and repeats the line, "The road waits, famished."

Furthermore, if the poet has identified with the shattered shell of the car, this will no doubt have serious implications for his shell, or "shield." Like the body of the automobile, the poet's consciousness or psychic shield has been badly damaged, and the crisis of the automobile accident has become interiorized. The poem ends with a question mark, which I argue is as much an identity crisis—a fear that man and machine have become one—as it is a question about the effects of technological failure on the psychic process itself. Soyinka's play *The Road* essentially picks up where "Death in the Dawn" leaves off—it opens at daybreak, in the aftermath of accidents too numerous to count, and it weaves together the lives of characters who piece themselves together despite the fact that moments of danger and destruction threaten their very existence.

The Road of Life and Death

When *The Road* begins, Samson, the tout for the lorry "No Danger No Delay," awakens in the motor-park that is situated beside Professor's AKSIDENT store and the church where Professor was once a lay reader. While the other drivers, touts, and thugs sleep peacefully on benches or on the floor amid worn-out tires, mangled bumpers, and other rubble, Samson watches Murano, the mysterious palm-wine tapper, perform his daily ablutions. After Murano sneaks off to begin collecting palm-wine for Professor, Samson wakes Salubi, a would-be driver who is desperately waiting for Professor to forge him a license. The two begin enacting a parody where Samson, standing high on a table, pretends that he is a millionaire and Salubi is his personal driver. Just then Professor returns from an accident site carrying a road sign bearing the word BEND. Thinking that he has lost his way and that Samson is a real millionaire, Professor promptly leaves for another accident site, this time taking Kotonu with him, despite Samson's protests that Kotonu be kept away from accident sites after two traumatizing road accidents have left him psychologically unable to drive. When Professor and Kotonu return, Samson tries to convince Kotonu to return to driving "No Danger No Delay," and he unsuccessfully pleads with Professor to help him.

The dramatic action of the play is interspersed with call-and-response-style banter, praise-singing, boasting, satirical police chases, flashbacks, and a funeral dirge. The climax occurs at Professor's bar when Samson and Kotonu begin to suspect that Murano was the masked god that they ran over during the Driver's Festival, an annual Ogun ritual. To satisfy Samson and Kotonu, Professor instructs Murano to try on the mask of the *egungun* spirit that he was wearing during the Driver's Festival and to perform the ritual dance. However, to wear the mask and invoke Ogun out of season is sacrilegious, and the revelers at the bar assume that Professor is plotting something diabolical. As is the case in Soyinka's *Death and the King's Horseman* (1975), irreverence toward the *egungun* mask invites death. Many of the characters implore Professor to stop Murano's dance, but when he refuses, a frenzied and inebriated Say Tokyo Kid deals Professor a fatal stab. As Professor dies, he warns the audience of the necessity to "be even like the road itself" (96), a line to which I will return later.

When *The Road* was performed on Nigerian stages during Soyinka's tenure at the Road Safety Corps, local critics and audiences focused largely on its literal meaning, seeing its emphasis on accidents as lessons about overtaking, speeding, and the need for proper road signs.[15] Outside of the context of Soyinka's safety campaign, however, many critics have focused on the spiritual quest of Professor and its allegorical meanings. For instance, Ato Quayson suggests that Professor's quest is shaped by two contradictory notions of time that can be seen to parallel Dipesh Chakrabarty's idea of enchanted time, or the nonlinear time of the gods, and disenchanted time, the time of homogeneous scientific historiography. Quayson argues that Professor's quasi-Christian teleological quest for the Word is coupled with his embrace of the Yoruba belief system that adheres to cyclical time. To him, "Professor mirrors in his consciousness the contradictory temporal frameworks that shape postcolonial transition" (2003, 150). And though these contradictory temporalities exist for the drivers and touts as well,

Quayson's reading places the chronotopicity as well as the allegorical meanings of the play almost exclusively within the time that Professor occupies. However, in order to understand the complex time-space of the postcolonial road, one must also look at the chronotopes of the drivers, touts, and thugs attempting to survive the ordeals of the Nigerian road.

For Bakhtin, the chronotope of the road is a decisive one in the history of literature. The road, a particularly precise articulation of the unity of space and time, is the site of adventure, chance encounters, and social heterogeneity. He writes,

> On the road the spatial and temporal series defining human fates and lives combine with one another in distinctive ways, even as they become more complex and more concrete by the collapse of *social distances.* The chronotope of the road is both a point of new departures and a place for events to find their denouement. (1981, 243–44)

The road, as we saw in the previous chapter, is therefore particularly well suited to metaphorical expressions. Soyinka's original title for the play, "The Road of Life," captures perhaps one of the most common metaphors of the road: the road as an expression of the course of one's entire life. However, Soyinka's decision to shorten his title to a more ambiguous one underscores the way in which *The Road* contains a constant slippage between the geographical road and the metaphorical quests of the road's users. Thus, the chronotope of the road that Bakhtin describes as the time-space of chance encounters and literary turning points becomes in Soyinka's play a chronotope of the modern African road, a time-space overdetermined by motorcars, accidents, death, spiritual journeys, and survival and experienced as a bodily reaction to forms of contingency.

For Professor, the road is a place for chance encounters that become meaningful coincidence. Professor believes that all road accidents are teleological, happening precisely at the right moment in order to provide him with some clue along his journey to discover the one true Word, which the reader or audience member comes to understand is also the essence of death. In addition to acquiring spare parts for his store, he collects scraps of paper, football pools, or road signs (sometimes still standing), seeing them all as miraculous chance "signs" that set him forth on the right path. Thus, when he calls his trips to the crash sites "business trips," he is referring both to his business of selling the detritus he finds and the business of finding what he calls "redemption." He says to Kotonu: "Come then, I have a new wonder to show you . . . a madness where a motor-car throws itself against a tree—Gbram! And showers of crystal flying on broken souls" (10–11). To him, the driver and the passenger had a reason for fleeing up the tree: to provide Professor with the BEND sign he finds near the site. He therefore denies that the car crash had any "accidental" qualities, for to him the event is purposeful and replete with meaning:

> You would think, to see it, that the motor-car had tried to clamber after them. Oh there was such an angry buzz but the matter was beyond repair. They died, all three of them crucified on rigid branches. I found this growing where their blood had spread and sunk along plough scouring of the wheel. Now tell me you who sit above it all, do you think my sleep was broken over nothing, over a meaningless event? (11–12)

In Professor's world, the accident is therefore more like the preindustrial natural disaster, an event often seen to be the result of outside forces rather than immanent breakdown.

But for the drivers and touts, the road is not a time-space where "actions lie outside . . . consequence" (Bakhtin 1981, 91). Rather, accidents are events contingent on unsafe driving, shoddy automobiles, poor infrastructure, and lack of road safety. The chronotope of the road that the drivers and touts experience results, then, from a politically and historically determined contingency that is, as Rosalind Morris suggests, both distinct from and intertwined with the notion of the accident. With a focus on South Africa and the rampant crime of carjacking, Morris insists on distinguishing what happens as the result of mere technological breakdown (the accident, or car accident in this case) with what happens as a reaction to complex and often unjust historical events (the contingent). People respond to an accident, she says, by trying to prevent it, but contingency "solicits management—of risk and of the costs of accommodating oneself to it" (2010, 599). Contingency, then, is what helps navigate the complexities and indeterminacy of criminality in a place like South Africa, where poverty and the legacies of apartheid lead to high rates of carjacking. But in Soyinka's work the accident is always contingent, always at least partially criminal because it is the result of a structural neglect for road safety and infrastructure. The accident is neither meaningful, as Professor suggests, nor arbitrary, but something more sinister—"not just any arbitrariness, but arbitrariness as human and contingent violence" (Mbembe 2001, 13). What *The Road* does, then, is dramatize how different characters accommodate themselves to these forms of contingency.

The Ogunian Road

In Yoruba mythology, it is the story of Ogun—the god of the road—that provides the model for the psychic preparation needed to face danger and violence. Soyinka goes the furthest in describing his version of Ogun's tragedy in the poem "Idanre," which was written at about the same time as *The Road.*[16] An abbreviated version of the myth is as follows: Ogun, the "Primal mechanic," builds the town of Ire in order to bring the worlds of man and the divine closer together. The town's inhabitants ask Ogun to be their king, and after originally declining, he accepts their offer. However, when the king is absent, the people of the town decide that they must relocate in order to escape drought and disease. When Ogun finds them, he slaughters his subjects in a mad, drunken rage. After sobering up, Ogun is left with the shocking truth of what he has done and the task of restoring order so that he might prevent further violence. In "The Fourth Stage," Soyinka writes that Ogun "is saved only by channeling the dark torrent into the plastic light of poetry and dance" (1976, 160). Thus, Ogun breaks the cycle of violence and retribution by admitting his tragic flaw and bridging the abyss of damage and ruin through his creative will.[17] Soyinka explains that Ogun continues to enjoy palm wine as a reminder of his error and as a constant challenge to his "exercise of will and control" (159). The road in Soyinka's play is therefore an Ogunian road: a road that unleashes both destruction and the psychic strength necessary to survive it.

This ability to accommodate so well to accident and contingency has historically been inscribed, quite literally, on the bodies of vehicles themselves. In Nigeria slogans, like the "No Danger No Delay" of Kotonu and Samson's lorry, are typically painted on cars and trucks as a sign that the drivers have special power and that however lackluster a given vehicle might appear, it has been divinely endowed with the ability both to overcome danger and to produce wealth. Olatunde Bayo Lawuyi explains that in Nigeria the slogans painted on vehicles are important for creating a sense of confidence in the driver as well as assurance to potential passengers. He writes that common slogans like "Unlimited promotion," "The struggle continues," or "The world is hard" reflect both the precarious nature of motorcar travel in Nigeria as well as the sense of struggle and endurance of road users.[18] In *The Road* "No Danger No Delay" is a fitting slogan for Samson, who gives the truck's name as his address. Throughout the play Samson maintains that danger is surmountable, that the near miss at the bridge was an act of providence, and that squandering time, or delaying, is a waste of money. At Professor's bar, he expects his wine glass to be filled promptly: he expects others to act without delay just as he would. Samson therefore gladly and willingly submits to the speed and chaos of life on the road. Salubi, who is anxiously waiting for a forged driving license, and Say Tokyo Kid, who boasts about the type of lumber he carries, articulate a similar attitude. All of these characters embrace the risks of the road and, much like Ogun, seemingly welcome challenges. For the drivers and touts, the chronotope of the road is an Ogunian chronotope, one that Bahktin would refer to as "everyday survival."

However, throughout the play, the everyday survival of accommodating oneself to the contingency of road life often means accepting that death is an ineluctable part of daily life. The list of drivers and friends the drivers and touts have lost to the road seems endless:

> Where is Zorro who never returned from the North without a basket of guinea-fowl eggs? Where is Akanni the Lizard? I have not seen any other tout who would stand on the lorry's roof and play the samba at sixty miles an hour. Where is Sigidi Ope? Where is Sapele Joe who took on six policemen at the crossing and knocked them all into the river? . . . And Saidu-Say? Indian Charlie who taught us driving? (21)

But in an Ogunian fashion, these fallen friends do not deter or traumatize most of the drivers and touts; rather, they become heroes, the subjects of praise-songs. Sergeant Burma, the late manager of Professor's store and a fearless oil tank driver, is particularly admired for his ability, in Kotonu's words, to "protect himself" against the trauma of losing so many friends. It is a skill he learned while fighting in Burma and one that proves useful to the battlefield-like conditions of driving in Nigeria. Kotonu remarks: "Sergeant Burma was never moved by these accidents. He told me himself how once he was stripping down a crash and found that the driver was an old comrade from the front. He took him to the mortuary but first he stopped to remove all the tyres" (21). The drivers and touts in *The Road* therefore react to the shocks of road life by attempting to survive at all cost, a task that often requires a position of detachment, aloofness, and humor.[19] Samson, for instance, tells Salubi that his breath "stinks so much" that he would be an effective bodyguard: "When the police bring their riot squad with tear-gas and all that nonsense, you will open your mouth and breathe on them. That is what is known as counter-blast" (7). The characters in *The Road* use their sharp tongues, wit, and swagger to demonstrate not only the toughening of their psychic stimulus shield but also their willingness to channel destructive energy into creativity and playfulness. It is therefore important to note that both Kotonu and Murano, the characters least capable of surviving the road, are the only ones isolated from the mockery and witty banter of the play.

Infrastructures of Anxiety

While most of the drivers and touts occupy a chronotope of everyday survival, Kotonu and Murano show that the road can also be a time-space of suspended animation or arrested time. Kotonu, who is "tired of feeling too much" (20), knows that he lacks the indifference and bravado of Sergeant Burma and the other drivers, and without this Ogunian exercise of will, he teeters on the brink of madness. After running over Murano during the driver's festival, Kotonu panics and tells Samson that the engine of his truck is stalled, even though he is not inside the truck and not experiencing any problems with it. Kotonu's misperception of the stalled engine foreshadows the mental state that, after his second accident at the bridge, will eventually prevent him from driving "No Danger No Delay." Like the poet in "Death in the Dawn," Kotonu identifies with the paralyzed motorcar. Samson therefore becomes furious when Professor drags Kotonu along to accident sites, fearing that further exposure to traumatic scenes will only result in increased anxiety and prolong his driver's state of paralysis.

Throughout the play, discussions of movement and mobility are punctuated with tropes of death, inactivity, and immobility. This is evident in the language used to describe car crash victims suspended in a tree or Professor's following report of the lorry that overtook Kotonu and Samson on the bridge: "It dragged alongside and after an eternity it pulled to the front swaying from side to side, pregnant with stillborns. Underline with stillborns" (56). The image of a truck filled with stillborns, with those who are dead at birth, captures, perhaps better than any other, the notion of automobility that is pregnant with its own demise. These stillborn passengers, who failed to make it across the bridge alive, become permanently suspended in their act of animation. And like the stillborns inside the truck, the time of the play too has suspended itself—Professor's broken watch (that still tells time) marks the hour of the nightly evensong at his bar, and flashbacks to the accidents occur seamlessly integrated into the forward progression of the play. In one case a flashback is even said to have occurred "about an hour later" (55). Likewise, the play is preceded by Soyinka's notes to the producer and a brief explanation of the preface poem, "Alagemo," which is meant to help explain the significance behind the *egungun* dance. Soyinka writes: "The dance is the movement of transition; it is used in the play as *a visual suspension of death*—in much the same way as Murano, the mute, is a dramatic embodiment of this suspension. He functions as an arrest of time, or death, since it was in his 'agemo' phase that the lorry knocked him down" (n.p., emphasis added). Thus, Murano's state of "arrested time" between life and death becomes a metaphor for the drivers and touts whose daily encounter with deadly car accidents suspends them between the world of the living and the world of the spirits.

And while Murano is quite literally suspended between life and death, Kotonu's arrested time is experienced as a psychological condition. Though for Samson "No Danger No Delay" was a slogan that described his boldness and love of speed, for Kotonu the name takes on a more ironic meaning and highlights his inability to overcome his anxiety about the danger of fatal road accidents in the way his comrades have. Freud would describe Kotonu as someone who was experiencing an inhibition of locomotion, a neurotic state that paralyzes his own "motor apparatus" (1959, 5). And though the applicability of Freud's theories to an African context have been widely and contentiously debated by literary critics and anthropologists, Margaret Field argues that anxiety, insecurity, and mental stress are not the "prerogative of 'over-civilized' societies" (1962, 13) of the West. In 1956 Field interviewed 146 mental health patients in rural Ghana and was so struck by the large numbers of drivers among them that she began to collect lorry inscriptions and to interview the drivers about what they meant. She concluded that while the lorry inscriptions reflected the bravado of drivers, as Lawuyi suggests, they also revealed the many anxieties and insecurities that drivers had about driving: they were concerned about the risky investment they made in their vehicles, the potential envy of others who may use witchcraft against them, and, of course, the dangers of accidents. Kotonu's paralysis and refusal to drive therefore reflects the fears and inhibitions that many West African drivers at the time may have had despite their bluster. Although the play is full of characters who, like Ogun, "exercise will" and have built up a psychic shield in order to become auto-mobile subjects, *The Road* is very much a play about the fragility of the subject and the infrastructures of anxiety that undergird daily life on the road. The various chronotopes of the road dramatized in the play speak to road users' multiplicity of experiences and to the different ways that one might adjust to the precariousness of life and death on the road.

"Be the Road"

What seems to concern Soyinka in *The Road* and throughout his work is the cycle of postcolonial violence that keeps subjecting the body to shock, that leads over and over again to states of paralysis. In his poem "Idanre" Soyinka offers a theoretical way out of such cycles by describing Ogun's road as a Möbius strip. He then offers the following definition of this bounded and twisted strip: "A mathe-magical ring, infinite in self-creation into independent but linked rings and therefore the freest conceivable (to me) symbol of human or divine (e.g., Yoruba, Olympian) relationships. A symbol of optimism also, as it gives the illusion of a 'kink' in the circle and a possible centrifugal escape from the eternal cycle of karmas that has become the evil history of man" (90–91). It is within this context that I would like to situate Professor's final speech as he lay dying from Say Tokyo Kid's fatal stabs. Professor advises the drivers and touts who have come to drink at his bar to

> be even like the road itself. Flatten your bellies with the hunger of an unpropitious day, power your hands with the knowledge of death. In the heat of the afternoon when the sheen raises false forests and a watered haven, let the event first unravel before your eyes. Or in the dust when ghost lorries pass you by and your shouts your tears fall on deaf panes and the dust swallows them. . . . Breathe like the road. Be the road. Coil yourself in dreams, lay flat in treachery and deceit and at the moment of a trusting step, rear your head and strike the traveller in his confidence. (96)

If the road is indeed a Möbius strip, the suggestion to be like the road is not just a recommendation to internalize the chaotic world of the road; it is also advice to find the kink in the system, to escape treachery at all costs, and to seize the opportunities the road might provide.

Though the road might be deadly and dangerous, it is also, of course, a source of livelihood and a conductor of life for a vast number of Nigerians, and it has profound symbolism for an emerging nation trying to stamp itself as modern and independent.[20] The road is therefore an enabler of automobility as much as a source of destruction: it links together families; it enables pan-African trade; it is the lifeblood of a nation in motion. Historically, the drivers and touts that occupy Nigerian motor-parks during this period are those who have left their villages with the hope and expectation of earning incomes, often to send back home to their families. All of these aspects of the road are present in Soyinka's play as well, woven through the banter and praise-songs that take place among the drivers, touts, policemen, and thugs who pass through Professor's bar. As Biodun Jeyifo suggests, there is an ironic hope in the message that "if the road, as literal highway for commerce and travel and as metaphor for the journey through life, is destructively treacherous, to 'breathe like the road,' to 'be even like the road itself' is to live without illusions, to become equal to the destructiveness of the road" in order to survive its contingency (2004, 229). And it is this ironic hope that provides the kink in the Möbius strip, the opening to move forward, even if by Soyinka's own accounts the kink offers up only an illusion of escape.

In his later work, Soyinka turns toward Sembene's *God's Bits of Wood* and Amilcar Cabral's "National Liberation and Culture" as texts that offer viable cultural solutions that reverse the cycle of colonial and postcolonial stagnation. He admires in both works the insistence on cultural autonomy, on searching for progressive solutions within one's own culture, but he also notes that for these authors part of cultural autonomy is opening oneself to the possibilities technology might afford. Soyinka admires in Sembene's novel about the 1947 Dakar railway strike, discussed in the previous chapter, that there is "a passive technological phenomenon which must be dominated and exploited by the collective will, forged in the pre-eminence of an organic community," and he notes that for Sembene "the railway is translated into the pulse of that community" (1988, 130). I would argue that the role Soyinka ascribes to the railway in Sembene's novel is the exact role he assigns to the road in his own work. *The Road* can therefore be read as a theorization, or "contemplation," as Levine suggests, of how a technological matrix can be utilized, despite setbacks and complications, by the creative and collective will of a group of people. Professor's advice to "be the road" is, after all, advice to make the properties of the road one's own, to be dominant instead of passive. The antidote to suspended animation, or rather the solution that emerges from it, is not automobility in its liberalist avatar but rather a cultural autonomy that would reshape or transform automobility along its own lines.

In the end, then, if a man of the road wants to survive, it might mean fixing his truck with the carburetor of one he just crashed into, wearing the uniform of a fallen friend, or buying his children toys scavenged from an accident. This is clearly no exuberant celebration of a life of informal labor and no stamp of approval for the horrid conditions of Nigerian roads, but it is an acknowledgment that ruins may be pieced together for the sake of survival. Thus, layered over Soyinka's eschatological vision of an urban periphery living off its own debris is the dramatic action of people who know how to prepare themselves for the worst and who can, perhaps, emerge for the better.

· CHAPTER 3 ·

Moving Pictures, Mired Cars: The Automobile in African Francophone Cinema

What counts is that the mobile camera is like a general equivalent of all means of locomotion that it shows or makes use of—aeroplane, car, boat, bicycle, foot, metro.

—Gilles Deleuze, *Cinema 1*

What goes on in the windscreen is cinema in the strict sense.

—Paul Virilio, *War and Cinema*

In an early scene of Abderrahmane Sissako's film *Heremakono* (*Waiting for Happiness*, 2002), the protagonist, Abdallah, paces around an empty bush taxi that is stalled in the Mauritanian desert en route to the coastal town of Nouadhibou. The hood of the car is propped open and the roof is loaded with the baggage of its passengers who wait patiently in the shade of a small adobe building. After completing his circle around the car, Abdallah sits down in the driver's seat and turns off the radio, abruptly silencing the hypnotic desert music that the audience assumes to be extradiegetic. He gazes emptily through the open passenger door at his fellow travelers resting in the shade before laying his head on the steering wheel in a gesture of impatience and defeat. The driver, who was enjoying a cigarette with the other passengers, looks back at Abdallah for several minutes and finally approaches to examine the engine. He guesses that the problem is "*le ratement*"—the car simply misfired. He explains: "That happens to a car when spark plugs get wet or gas is cut. Sometimes it goes click and tap tap. *Ça va*." His nonchalant reassurance that it is okay *(ça va)*, or literally, "it goes," is a reminder of the regularity of these mishaps and an indicator of his faith that the car will again be able "to go." In the next shot, seen from behind the front windshield, the taxi is indeed on the move, steadily driving through the desert past camel pens and lax checkpoints. Only the driver's malfunctioning visor, which constantly flips down and dumps out his papers, recalls *le ratement* of the previous scene. This sequence is typical of an African Francophone cinema in which various perspectives of time are set side by side and framed within each other, where mobility and immobility become two sides of the same coin, and where technology often misfires.[1]

At the end of the film, which is a slow-paced poetic meditation on temporality and daily life in Nouadhibou, Abdallah, who had been visiting his mother, meticulously packs his suitcase and prepares for his departure. Again, we see the taxi from the beginning of the film driving down the main road of Nouadhibou. As before, it is first seen in motion from behind the windshield, and the driver is still experiencing problems keeping his papers from falling out of the visor. But when Abdallah leaves Nouadhibou, the taxi does not take him away. The car appears to be functioning well, and there seems to be no apparent reason why Abdallah would not be able to secure a place, why the car that brought him to Nouadhibou at the beginning of the film would not ferry him away at the end. However, instead of waiting at the taxi park, a nearly expressionless Abdallah walks out into the desert, away from the road, and sits down next to a giant sand dune: Sissako leaves the job of the automobile unfinished. What makes the final image of Abdallah sitting on the dune so unsettling and so striking is that it subverts the viewer's expectations. Abdallah simply sits there with his packed suitcase and a total disinterest in the car that should, logically, take him away.

This chapter examines the way that African art cinema, which emerges largely out of Francophone countries, utilizes the automobile in unexpected ways, in ways that challenge its role as both a status symbol and as a simple means of transportation. According to Gilles Deleuze, traditionally the movie camera acts as "a *general equivalent*" to the forms of transportation that it films: like a moving vehicle, the cinematic shot communicates or "translates" space by reproducing the continuity of space and time through movement (1986, 22). Indeed, this is the way that the vast majority of films utilize the automobile, from early cinema, to colonial documentary, to contemporary Hollywood and Nollywood films. But the African Francophone filmmakers I discuss here seem to both acknowledge the affinity between the cinema and the automobile and, at the same time, open up other possible relationships between the two moving technologies.

Figure 4. Heremakono. *The bush taxi stalled in the desert. Abdallah rests his head on the steering wheel.*

Figure 5. Heremakono. *"I think it misfired." The driver diagnoses the breakdown for Abdallah.*

My focus is primarily on two *auteurs,* the Senegalese filmmaker Ousmane Sembene, often called the father of African cinema, and the Cameroonian Jean-Pierre Bekolo, whose postmodernist and eclectic style is typically positioned as a challenge to Sembene's social realism.[2] In particular, I focus on Sembene's *Xala* (1974), a national and sexual allegory about El-Hadji Abdou Kader Beye, a corrupt Mercedes-driving businessman who loses his ability to have an erection,[3] and *Quartier Mozart* (1992), Bekolo's absurdist farce about Cameroonian gender politics and a neighborhood riddled with stasis. In both films, the automobile faces a similar fate: in *Xala,* El Hadji's Mercedes becomes undriveable and is pushed off screen by policemen who have come to repossess it; in *Quartier Mozart* the mise-en-scène is littered with abandoned and broken-down automobiles. Though both films seem to complicate cinema's equivalence with the automobile, they mark different moments in postcolonial life and different aesthetic reactions to forms of precarity, instability, and patriarchal power. Sembene's film, made a decade and a half after independence, is representative of what Kenneth Harrow calls a "politics of engagement" where the failure and impotence (*xala* means the curse of impotence) of the national bourgeoisie are critiqued along Fanonian lines. Bekolo, by contrast, creates a layered and at times bizarre pastiche about the imaginative forms of mobility and self-invention available for youth, and young girls in particular, during the era of structural adjustment. As is the case in *Heremakono,* moving cars in these films are both integrated into the cinematic space and removed from it.

As products of industrial capitalism, both the car and the cinema are mechanisms of mobility, displacement, and modern consumption that, as Kristin Ross argues, have instantiated similar forms of subjectivity and spatio-temporal consciousness. Over the past several decades, several scholars in media and cultural studies have been interested in underscoring the connections between the technology of cinema, the corporeal experiences of modernity, and transportation systems such as the railway, streetcar, and automobile (Beckman 2010, 9). However, as Karen Beckman argues in *Crash: Cinema and the Politics of Speed and Stasis* (2010), what is often overlooked in such scholarship is "modern media's equally complex engagement with stasis" (9). Exploring the close alignment between the automobile collision and cinema, Beckman emphasizes the contradictory ways that subjects not only experience modernity but also fantasize and fret about its dangers and pleasures. Although in this chapter I extend my discussion beyond the crashed automobile, I share with Beckman the desire to continue to think about the historical and perceptual links between the moving image and the moving vehicle while also challenging the scholarly discourse that emphasizes "movement above film's other qualities" (5).

What I argue is that *Xala* and *Quartier Mozart* participate in a larger African Francophone cinematic tradition that, like the crash films discussed by Beckman, engages the possibilities and difficulties of movement in different forms, tempos, or directions. In both films cars become mired in different ways and for different reasons: they are delayed, stalled, stuck, or undriveable. But these moments of stasis or suspension open up "potentially productive temporal and spatial uncertainties, in spite of the motorcar's privileged position in patriarchal sexual structures" (Beckman 2010, 15). And it is these uncertainties, uncertainties about the past, present, and the future, that allow African filmmakers to not only register disillusionment with the false promises of development and modern automobility but also reflect on the heteropatriarchal social structure and class system that have mired or muddied the postcolonial period. Moreover, what the filmmakers discussed here do is decouple the moving vehicle and the moving image that had been aligned in West Africa during the colonial moment.

Colonial Cars, Colonial Cameras

As was the case in Europe and the United States, in West Africa both the cinema and the motorcar arrive nearly simultaneously at the beginning of the twentieth century. In 1900, the same year that the governor of French West Africa made the region's first official automobile drive in present-day Mali, a foreign merchant projected the Lumière film *L'arroseur arrosé* (*The Waterer Watered,* 1895) in a Dakar marketplace.[4] However, while the *New York Herald Tribune* as well as newspapers in France, Belgium, Germany, Russia, and South America enthusiastically reported on the first "autocar through French West Africa,"[5] little attention was given to the traveling merchants who began to tour films throughout West Africa just five years after the Lumière brothers debuted their *cinématographe* in France. And yet, during the colonial period, the motorcar and the cinema became mutually dependent technologies that often enabled and reinforced one another. In many documentaries the motorcar and the movie camera were conjoined in colonial expeditions. In the Citroën films I discussed in chapter 1, the roaming half-tracks, because they were equipped with cameras, could capture a culture that had supposedly been unmoved by technological progress and transport that "fixed" culture back to the modern metropole where "the automobile was the symbol of European modernity" (Bloom 2008, 69). Moreover, filming Africans in their "natural" habitat—which, of course, could only be reached thanks to the motorcar—manufactured their docility and, as Bloom argues, reinforced the unlikelihood that they would cause unrest or disrupt the process of colonization. Without the movie camera, the Citroën expeditions would not have been able to communicate their triumph in the grandiose way that they did, and, likewise, without the half-tracks to take them through the African hinterland, the cameras would have been unable to capture the movement and speed of this conquest.

Likewise, Patrice Nganang notes that in many French colonial documentaries, cameras were mounted at the front of a ship, car, or train, and he suggests that such positioning made the filming of Africa a part of its physical conquest. As in the case of the Citroën treks, cameras were almost always present in expeditions into unknown territories, and they allowed audiences in France to travel to distant lands and feel as if they were participating in the colonizing process. Furthermore, according to Nganang, several of these documentary films were titled *La France en marche (France on the March),* and they showed Frenchmen using various modes of Western transport, deploying their heroic machinery in order to spread the benefits of civilization throughout Africa. Colonial cinema, therefore, relied on the motorcar to bring the camera to distant places, while the motorcar relied on the cinema to make its conquests known to the European public.

But it was not just in documentary production that cars and cinema depended on one another. During the interwar years, missionaries used motorcars to tour the African countryside with Bibles as well as film and slide projectors. Furthermore, merchants, who had been traveling with copies of popular commercial films since the turn of the century, found their task made easier with the advent of the automobile. After World War I, George Weekes, a British businessman, brought a cinematograph outfit and truck to Nigeria and started to travel around to villages projecting films outdoors or in courthouses. After the shows he found that he could also charge the audience for a ride home, and he became one of the first Europeans to establish regularly scheduled transport services throughout southeast Nigeria (Drummond-Thompson 1992, 224). Likewise, Brian Larkin notes that it was not uncommon for the African staff of the mobile cinema vans of the Colonial Film Unit to furtively use the vans as taxis to transport people between the cities and towns they visited (2008, 96). Though according to the journal *Colonial Cinema,* which was published by the unit, the vans were charged with the crucial task of "carrying enlightenment and education" to rural areas ("Vans" 1952, 92), the African staff found ways to use the cinema vans for their own entrepreneurial purposes.

However, while West Africans, as discussed in chapter 1, were quick to enter the transport business—importing vehicles, operating commercial truck companies, and stocking spare parts—and challenge European automotive hegemony, many decades would pass before Africans would start making their own films. As N. Frank Ukadike writes, "Cinema came to Africa as a potent organ of colonialism" (1994, 31), and because of its power of influence as a visual medium, it proved to be an extremely adept way to introduce Africans to the ideals and aesthetics of foreign cultures.[6] In the French colonies, where the 1934 Laval Decree had been implemented, anyone wishing to make a film in Africa was required to submit a script as well as a list of people involved in the production process to the French authorities (Diawara 1992, 22). According to Manthia Diawara, this policy insured that the cinema would not have any sort of revolutionary role in the colonies, and it also discouraged any would-be African filmmakers from entering the industry. In the British colonies, the Colonial Film Unit, which was established in 1939, did enlist African help in film production after World War II. However, here the goal was to make documentaries about British ways of life and promote Western practices of farming, hygiene, and industry. The colonialists decided that their messages would be better received if Africans were participating in the making of the documentaries.[7] But as was the case in the French colonies, Africans in the British colonies were not filming their own stories. Thus, in both the French and British colonies, the degree to which Africans could participate in filmmaking was limited and partial, and neither colonial power adequately invested in cinematic infrastructure.[8]

After independence the French and the British took very different tracks when it came to the development of cinema. The French Ministry of Cooperation, in an effort to form binding economic ties with its ex-colonies, began to actively fund films in Francophone West Africa and in 1963 formed the Bureau of Cinema to facilitate technological and financial support. This financial support, along with the cultural influence of the French New Wave filmmakers, led to a robust art film culture. Many filmmakers from Francophone colonies traveled to study filmmaking in France or Russia. The Anglophone postcolonies, devoid of such support, produced fewer films and did not develop their own industries until the 1990s. The low-budget video films they made, which I'll discuss in the following chapter, were much more commercially oriented and geared toward local audiences than the Francophone films. But in the immediate postcolonial decades Senegal became one of the hubs of African cinema, and one of the most prominent filmmakers to emerge at that time was Ousmane Sembene. Sembene's first film, *Borom Sarret* (1962), was the first to receive financial support from the French Ministry of Cooperation and is considered by many critics to be the first professional film made by a black African in Africa. Before turning to a detailed discussion of *Xala,* Sembene's most famous film and the first he made without any help from the Bureau, I want to briefly discuss *Borom Sarret,* a nineteen-minute short about a horse-cart driver who loses his cart. While colonial cinema was linked perceptually and historically to the motorcar, modern transport, and forward movement, *Borom Sarret,* I argue, inaugurates a postcolonial cinema that not only expresses the simultaneity of various experiences and forms of modernity but also uses the cinematic form to open up new relationships between transport technology and cinema.

Cinema and *Mégotage*

While Sembene did receive funding from the French to make *Borom Sarret,* the infrastructure needed to make a celluloid film in postcolonial West Africa was—and still is—virtually nonexistent. In order to make the short, which was filmed by three people using nonprofessional actors, Sembene had to start his own production company, Domireew, meaning "the country's child," and build partial production facilities in Dakar. (All of the post-production work was completed in Paris where the film was postsynched in French.) In a play on the words *bricolage* and *mégot,* or cigarette butt, Sembene called this form of shoestring filmmaking *mégotage* because scraping together the financing for a film was akin to piecing together a cigarette using random butts (Murphy 2001, 71).

It is perhaps not surprising, then, that the first African film is itself a reflection on the infrastructural inadequacies and inequalities of the postcolonial moment. The protagonist of the film is a *borom sarret,* a horse-cart driver, or wagoner, who struggles to earn a daily living in a newly independent Senegal. The wagoner lives in the Medina, a working-class neighborhood of Dakar, and as the opening credits roll, Sembene layers the continuing sound of the prayer call over shots of a local thoroughfare. For half a minute, cars of various makes along with minibuses, motorbikes, and a handful of bicycles and pedestrians steadily traverse the screen.

In these images of Dakar, shot on location, the absence of horse-carts is conspicuous and especially paradoxical given the title of the film. Therefore when the audience sees the wagoner hitch his horse to his cart in the hopes of earning enough money to feed his hungry family, it is clear that in Dakar the horse-cart has already been surpassed by motorized transport and that the type of passengers the wagoner attracts will be required to pay very little for the experience. Beyond the sandy, pedestrian-filled streets of the Medina, automobiles, taxis, and buses dominate the road, and those with means gladly choose these modern motorcars over the slow and jerky discomfort of the horse-cart, which Sembene emphasizes by using the horse-cart as a dolly for the camera. The positioning of the camera on the horse-cart recalls, of course, the placement of the camera on the front of ships, trains, and Citroën half-tracks in the colonial cinema. However, here the camera does not film the conquering of exotic, unknown territory, nor does it signify the unobstructed triumph of man over nature. Rather, it films a crowded market, an everyday scene in Dakar, and forces the viewer to experience the market through the bouncy shots and awkward framing that come from the movement of the horse-cart, a lower-class and nonmodern form of transport. And like Sembene, who sees filmmaking in postcolonial Africa as *mégotage,* the wagoner, whose cart consists of a wooden platform set on a car axle and two tires, makes use of whatever equipment is available. Sembene is therefore not only filming Dakar's urban poor but also rewriting the historical relationship between cinema and modern transport by predicating his film on the conjoining of cinema with the horse-cart.

After the wagoner foolishly hands over his morning wages to a *griot,* or traditional singer, he is approached by an upwardly mobile Senegalese businessman who needs to be transported to his new neighborhood. The businessman is headed for the Plateau, the former colonial administrative center where Europeans and Senegalese elites reside. Although horse-carts are forbidden in the Plateau, the businessman persuades the penniless wagoner with good pay and promises of connections. As the wagoner enters the Plateau, the camera offers a slow panoramic view of the European-style high-rises and government buildings towering over the trees. In this clean and modern neighborhood where shiny cars drive down tree-lined streets, the noise, smell, and sight of a horse-cart is an unwanted reminder of the poorer, grittier, and less modernized city below the Plateau.[9]

As the clearly out-of-place wagon encroaches on the modern city, it is evident that the *borom sarret* is circulating in a system that is not designed for him. Not surprisingly, he is unable to pass through the streets of the Plateau unnoticed, and as his passenger hurries into an automobile without paying his fare, the wagoner is stopped by a police officer. He must then hock the cart in order to pay his fine. As he is leaving the Plateau with his horse (sans cart), he stops at a traffic light meant for automobiles, for those who have the means and the right to go anywhere they choose. Ejected from the center of his city, the wagoner nonetheless remains subject to its rules and regulations. When he looks up at a tall apartment building that contrasts so much to his own home, the viewer can catch a glimpse of an Air France sign outside one of the retail shops below, but boarding an airplane is so outside of his realm of possibility that the camera only lingers for a brief moment.

When the wagoner returns to the Medina, he must break the news about his day to his hungry wife. When she finds out, she calmly hands him their child and heads for the door, promising him that they will eat that night. Before she leaves she must turn away two *talibey,* or street children who beg for food and collect money for the religious leader who shelters them. Thus, as the wife leaves, presumably to sell her body, the only resource she has, we see that it is not simply the wagoner's child who is hungry. The same system that suffocates Dakar's working poor also prevents them from fulfilling their religious obligation to give alms and from looking after the country's children, for whom Sembene named his production company. The film, which begins with images of modern traffic, ends by insinuating that the wagoner's wife will have to participate in one of the oldest forms of traffic. Whereas colonial cinema so often filmed "progress" on the move, sub-Saharan Africa's first film, made in a country without the infrastructure to produce its own films or, for that matter, any other goods, was very much about a progress that was partial, limited, and seemingly stalled for those not part of the postcolonial elite.

Xala and the Facade of Autonomy

While *Borom Sarret* depicts the impossible lives of those who are not auto-mobile, those without cars as well as those without economic self-determination, Sembene's *Xala,* made over a decade later, turns its attention to the likes of the businessman who duped the wagoner. In *Xala* Sembene's aim is to expose the corruption and greed of the Mercedes-driving Senegalese comprador class. The protagonist of the film, El Hadji Abdou Kader Beye, is a member of the prestigious Businessmen's Group, which in the opening of the film is celebrating the appointment of one of its members as president of the Chamber of Commerce. As the businessmen are assembled, El Hadji invites them to the wedding celebration of his polygamous marriage to N'Gone, his third wife. However, when El Hadji attempts to consummate his marriage that night he discovers that he has been struck with the *xala,* the curse of impotence. He initially blames his first two wives, whom he suspects of jealousy. When he cannot confirm their guilt, his search for a cure and for the source of his *xala* begins to consume him. Eventually, El Hadji's physical impotence becomes an economic impotence—he loses his business customers and his overspending catches up to him. When it is exposed that El Hadji has paid for his wedding by selling off the National Food Supplier's rice, which had been intended to help those affected by a recent drought, El Hadji's Mercedes is repossessed and he is expelled from the Businessmen's Group.

To date there has been much criticism and debate surrounding this now-canonical film, and it has inspired many rigorous analyses. What follows is an attempt to read *Xala* as a film that is just as much about automobiles and (im)mobility as it is about postcolonial elites, polygamy, or what Sembene calls "the double fetishism" of the commodity and animist practices.[10] Reversing the notion that cars are the bearers of progress and development, Sembene instead uses the automobile to draw attention to the facade of autonomy and progress that has been erected, so to speak, by the postcolonial patriarchy. Sembene therefore extricates the automobile from its Fordist narratives and places it instead in a state of suspended animation, a state in which it symbolizes postcolonial "impotence," or a temporal impasse, instead of postcolonial modernity.

As the film opens, El Hadji's Businessmen's Group ceremoniously ousts the French members of the Chamber of Commerce to a dancing and cheering crowd. Given that after World War I France cut African businessmen's access to bank credit and the Chamber of Commerce so that they would have trouble competing with the Europeans and Lebanese and Syrian *assimilés* (Hazemann 1992, 212), the claiming of the Chamber of Commerce by the Senegalese group is an important event. However, as the businessmen take their seats around the table that the colonizers had occupied, the previously ejected Frenchmen reenter through the back door and hand the Senegalese men attachés filled with francs. At the same time, Sembene has an offscreen narrator, in the style of a colonial newsreel, state: "We chose socialism. The only true socialism. African socialism. Socialism on man's level. Our independence is complete." The actions on the screen are therefore meant to undercut the party line. What the audience hears may be one thing, but what they see is that Senegal's independence is anything but complete. Sembene makes no secret of the fact that the French financially back the Senegalese economy and that the national bourgeoisie are impotent and incapable of making changes that would improve life for the vast majority of Senegalese.

Once El Hadji loses his Mercedes, those responsible for placing the curse come forward—they are a group of beggars who have situated themselves outside of El Hadji's office. Annoyed by their music, El Hadji had called them "human rubbish" and used his friendship with the president of the Chamber of Commerce to have them expelled from Dakar. But, as they later reveal, they are also El Hadji's kinsmen, and years earlier they had been duped by El Hadji, who appropriated their inheritance and sold the rights of their village land with falsified documents. The *xala* they place on El Hadji is to exact revenge for his original misdeed. They offer to remove the curse only if El Hadji agrees to undress, place N'Gone's wedding tiara on his head, and allow them to spit on him. Feeling that he has no other choice, El Hadji consents.

Throughout the film, the trope of *xala,* of impotence and immobility in different guises, is repeated in the cinematic language to remind the audience that despite outward appearances these elites do not embody Senegalese independence—their actions, in fact, stall and thwart the very progress they pretend to represent. For instance, as the businessmen exit the Chamber of Commerce, a red carpet is imperially unfurled down the stairs, but it falls just short of opening up all the way. Here, Sembene seems to be making a pun on the French word *défilement,* which means both unwinding (as in the unwinding of the carpet) and the projection of a film's progressive static frames. After the unfurling of the carpet, each of the businessmen enters his own chauffeur-driven automobile. In the logic of modernization theorists like Walt Rostow, who argues that mass automobile consumption is the sign of a truly developed society, this action would seem to indicate the pinnacle of modernity, the true sign that individuals in a society can be completely autonomous. But as they enter their automobiles, the Senegalese businessmen carry the attachés stuffed with French money, and this, Sembene suggests (and elaborates on in his film *Guelwaar*), is the true face of development. In the same scene Sembene further mocks this narrative of progress with another quick gag as one of the Mercedes starts and then jerks to a stop so as not to hit the president's black Ford. In both of these early gags, the usual *défilement* of the moving image is interrupted. Increasingly throughout the film, these types of impediments will reveal that the businessmen are not the agents of autonomy and postcolonial progress that they appear to be. Driven around by chauffeurs and funded by the French, they are actually anything but the modern, self-sufficient individuals fulfilling the promises of automobility.

Défilement is also related to the word *défilé*, or parade, and, fittingly, in the shot sequence following the incomplete *défilement* of the red carpet, the businessmen begin their motorcar parade to El Hadji's wedding. In the exaggerated two-minute, police-escorted *défilé* of the businessmen's luxury automobiles, Sembene satirizes the Senegalese upper class by calling attention to its automobilic excesses. Then, if this *défilé* were not enough, a few scenes later, the film contains another equally long and perhaps noisier procession of N'Gone's bridal motorcade that makes its way around the Place de l'Indépendance, where the wagoner from *Borom Sarret* was fined for bringing in his horse-cart, and through downtown Dakar, passing both a Renault dealership and a Mobil petrol station as crowds look on. At the end of the line of cars is El Hadji's wedding gift to N'Gone—a light blue two-seater car perched backward on top of a trailer and decorated with ribbons.

A number of scholars have commented on the multiple ways that these opening scenes reference Jean-Luc Godard's film *Weekend* (1967), a film that stages endless car crashes in an effort to satirize the absurdities and paralysis of the French bourgeoisie.[11] While *Xala* never approaches the nihilism of *Weekend,* which stages car crash after car crash, and gridlock after gridlock, Godard's skewering of the auto-mobile elite and Western capitalism echoes throughout Sembene's film. Indeed, the cacophonous and drawn-out motorcar parades of *Xala* certainly owe something to Godard's infamous eight-minute tracking shot of traffic that his protagonists encounter on their way to their weekend getaway. And at El Hadji's wedding reception, "weekend" becomes a joke, as two characters playfully compete to win the attention of a young girl first by promising her a Mercedes and then a weekend villa. This prompts the men to ask each other, "How do you say 'weekend' in English?" and a servant, a *gorjigen,* or a man who dresses as a woman, responds, "'Weekend' is 'weekend.'" The "weekend" joke—followed by a gag in which the *gorjigen* turns to the camera and drawls the English word "shit" in a baritone African American accent—draws attention not only to the intertextual presence of Godard's film but also to Sembene's ambivalent relationship to foreign culture. While the film satirizes French financial assistance—which this time Sembene rejected in favor of a coproduction between Domireew and the Senegalese-backed government production company—it does not sever itself entirely from foreign influence.[12] Whereas *Borom Sarret* makes visible the *mégotage* of Senegalese filmmaking, *Xala* highlights Senegal's deeply tangled and often complicated relationship to French and Western influence. As Karen Beckman argues in her discussion of *Xala,* Sembene's invocation of Godard and

Figure 6. Xala. *The businessmen, assisted by a Frenchman, each enter their own chauffeur-driven automobile.*

Figure 7. Xala. *The businessmen's motorcade as it leaves the Chamber of Commerce.*

Figure 8. Xala. *N'Gone's motorcade around the Place de l'Indépendance as the opening credits roll.*

his repetition of similarly staged traffic scenes from *Weekend* suggest a dialectical approach to French culture: *Xala* pays homage to Godard while, at the same time, implicating him in the critique of other foreign commodities (2010, 217). This complex relation shows Sembene borrowing from the critical stance of French New Wave cinema but also working through types of movement and automobility that are particular to a postcolonial and post-independence context.

"Impotent Stasis"

Despite the initial gags and the excessive motorcades, the automobiles at the beginning of *Xala* are by and large aligned with the forward movement of the film, translating space and time and acting, as Deleuze suggests, as a "general equivalent" to the camera. Automobiles transport characters to their destination, and much time is spent showing El Hadji in his Mercedes collecting his first two wives to take them to the wedding party. As the wives fight over who will sit next to El Hadji (this is resolved by showing El Hadji smashed in the backseat between them both while the passenger seat remains empty), other guests arrive at the party in their respective automobiles. However, after El Hadji's failure to consummate his marriage, the automobile becomes one of several signs of a mired postcoloniality; it becomes part of the stalling and suspension of the film's plot and semiotics.

According to John Mowitt, Sembene's reflexive devices throughout *Xala* work to highlight "the 'impotent' stasis" (2005, 110) of the postcolonial present. In Mowitt's detailed reading of the shot sequence that reveals El Hadji's impotence, the failed act of copulation is mimed and repeated in the semiotics of the film. Mowitt points out that while El Hadji prepares himself for N'Gone, he stands in front of a bathroom mirror, reflected by his own moving image. But N'Gone, as her aunt instructs her on how to be a docile and subordinate wife, is framed by a triad of black-and-white photographic stills of herself. In other words, while El Hadji, as husband, is associated with the moving image, his bride is reflected in the atemporal and immobile image of the photograph.[13] But Sembene follows El Hadji's exit from the bathroom with a false match-on-action cut to the next morning when the aunt arrives to confirm N'Gone's deflowering. This shot sequence, therefore, skips the attempted consummation and, as Mowitt argues, literally *suspends* the act of copulation (113). When the unsuccessful couple is discovered, Sembene again organizes his shots and frames around the atemporal stills in the bedroom, but this time he includes the now impotent and immobile El Hadji who is sitting on the bed in shame.

Mowitt concludes his shot-by-shot analysis as El Hadji leaves the villa and the soundtrack, interrupting the forward motion of the film, plays the music and muffled conversations from the previous night. But in order to understand how automobiles are also integral to the suspension of progress, how they enact a certain impasse, I want to analyze the shot sequence that follows El Hadji's exit. After leaving N'Gone's villa, El Hadji stands outside the gates staring dejectedly into the headlights of the parked wedding gift, which can only be driven once he confirms his bride's virginity.[14] When N'Gone's motorcade arrives at her villa on the night of the wedding, the blue two-seater is parked suggestively on its trailer—it is a sign of the "ride" that will occur on the wedding night, a sign that is confirmed by the camera's cut to N'Gone's car key just as El Hadji's jealous second wife snaps off the head of the figure on the wedding cake. However, the morning after the failed consummation, it becomes clear that the wedding-gift car will not become part of the forward, continuous movement of the film. As El Hadji gazes at the parked car, it is framed in a shot that is nearly identical to the one when the car first arrives at the ceremony. Rather than moving forward, this repetition, like the soundtrack, brings the film back to the previous night's impotence.

From this point on, the parked wedding car seems to be associated with El Hadji rather than with N'Gone. When El Hadji stares into the headlights of the parked car, he is in fact looking at a reflection of his own failure. El Hadji therefore no longer faces himself as a moving image as he did when he examined himself in the mirror on his wedding night. Instead, he becomes feminized like the small, pastel-colored car wrapped in bows. (This, of course, also foreshadows the final scene of the film when the beggars persuade El Hadji to undress and wear N'Gone's wedding tiara). Later in the film, when he is temporarily cured of the *xala,* El Hadji returns to N'Gone's villa to take his bride's virginity. Before entering the home, he kisses the car's ribbon and pats its front tire. Confident that his virility is restored, he feminizes the car and attempts to reintroduce his separation from it. However, his confidence is premature, for N'Gone is menstruating and El Hadji is turned away. Soon after, El Hadji's *xala* is returned when the marabout who had removed the curse tries to cash El Hadji's check and finds that it has bounced.

Moreover, with the arrival and rearrival of the *xala,* cars in general are no longer associated with a triumphant independence as they are during the opening motorcades. As El Hadji is driven to his office after his failed wedding night, the band of beggars hobble through the same streets—some using crutches, the polio victims with shriveled legs using their hands and knees. El Hadji's shameful "morning after" drive is therefore set alongside the victorious yet imperfect march of the beggars who have successfully enacted their revenge. But here the violence of the automobile and the vulnerability of the beggars become apparent when their advance is interrupted by the sound of a car striking down a pedestrian. At the scene of the accident, a blind man is robbed of the money he has collected from his fellow villagers to buy much-needed supplies during the drought. The thief, a Monsieur Thieli, is the one who will replace El Hadji when he is expelled from the Chamber of Commerce as the cycle of theft, violence, and corruption continues. No longer a symbol of progress and autonomy, *Xala's* automobiles become linked to various forms of impasse.

Alternative Mobilities; or, Rama's Moped

Because of its allegorical structure, the plot of *Xala* is largely about El Hadji's downward mobility and the accompanying loss of his status, material goods, and wives. But his daughter, Rama, interrupts El Hadji's story and offers the film a very different model of mobility. Tellingly, Rama is both the one character who challenges El Hadji throughout the film and the one character who is associated with an alternative form of mobility: a moped, or motor scooter. Rama, from the beginning of the film, acts as the quintessential foil to her father. While El Hadji insists on speaking French, she speaks to him in Wolof, telling him, "All polygamists are liars." While he guzzles Evian water, which he also uses to wash down his Mercedes, she says that she prefers local tap water. And while he dresses in Western suits, she alternates between trendy bell-bottoms and African boubous. In a story that focuses so much on revealing the impotence and immobility of the Senegalese patriarchy, Rama, especially as a young, educated woman, "is a loaded sign of what is realizable" (Adesokan 2011, 71).

Rama, then, seems to be the only character in the film who represents an alternative to the mired present. Her bedroom has posters of anticolonial heroes like Samory Touré and Amilcar Cabral, but there's also one of Charlie Chaplin. This suggests that the revolutionary past, one that El Hadji, a

Figure 9. Xala. *"A car . . . Here are the keys." N'Gone's mother shows off her wedding gifts.*

Figure 10. Xala. *N'Gone's car perched on its trailer during the wedding reception.*

former revolutionary, so egregiously betrays, might coexist with a different type of future. As Françoise Pfaff argues,

> Rama is not attracted by the luxurious automotive machines of the Western world. She only uses the aspects of Western culture that can serve in daily life—education and modern technology—and does not confer on imported goods the same fetishistic quality as her father. In spite of the concise development of her character, Rama's function in the film is trenchant. Sembene visually stresses her independence of mind as well as her independence as a character by presenting her alone in many more shots than the other female characters. (1982)

In this way, the moped-driving, slightly androgynous Rama also acts as a foil to her age-mate N'Gone who, like the wedding car that she is associated with, serves mostly as a feminized object of exchange, fetishized like the other commodities in the film and dependent on others for her value. Rama presents not just another option of mobility but also another model for Senegalese womanhood. Scooters, therefore, become important marks of an auto-mobility or self-mobility that is de-linked from the liberal *automobility* embodied in El Hadji's often phallic Mercedes.[15]

And just as the motorcade at the beginning of the film links *Xala* intertextually to Godard's *Weekend,* Rama's scooter points to another film that *Xala* appears to be in dialogue with: Djibril Diop Mambety's surrealist masterpiece *Touki Bouki* (1973). Released the year before *Xala, Touki Bouki* stars Myriam Niang, the actress who plays Rama, as Anta, and Magaye Niang, the actor who plays Thieli, as Mory. In *Touki Bouki,* a Senegalese *Easy Rider* meets *Bonnie and Clyde,* Mory and Anta cruise around Dakar on Mory's motorcycle, which is adorned with a zebu's skull and horns. The young, rebellious couple—he from the village, she from a poor neighborhood in the city—spends much of the film hustling and scheming in order to get enough money to move to Paris. In this film, then, the motorcycle, as is often the case in West Africa, becomes a means of transport more accessible to the non-elite and, especially with the horns attached to its handlebars, becomes the decisive sign of bridging the traditional with the modern in a way that privileges neither.

Furthermore, as is the case in *Xala,* the motorcycle in *Touki Bouki* serves as a form of mobility that is associated with youth and their frustrations

Figure 11. Xala. *Myriam Niang as Rama.*

Figure 12. Touki Bouki. *Myriam Niang as Anta.*

with the present, while cars become both the object of parody and markers of violence.[16] In one scene Mory and Anta steal a Citröen convertible adorned with an American flag and, in a fantasy sequence, parade around Dakar like royalty. Overly obsequious bystanders line the streets, and Mory, who drops his pants at one point, lavishes in the attention. Here the car is lightheartedly mocked, but when it comes time for Mory to join Anta on the boat that will take them to France, the camera cuts to a Mercedes being lifted onto the boat. The Mercedes becomes foreboding as it is juxtaposed with Eisensteinian images of animals being lead to slaughter, and Mory decides to run away rather than join Anta and risk everything for the elusive good life in France. Though Anta leaves for Paris and Rama makes Senegal her home, both of Myriam Niang's characters are androgynous-looking, motorcycle-riding iconoclasts who seem intent on paving their own paths. They are women constantly on the move and challenging norms. In the novella version of *Xala,* which Sembene wrote as he was piecing together finances for the film, Rama drives a Fiat, not a moped. It is possible, then, that Sembene gave Rama the moped after casting Niang in order to establish a link between her two characters.

As Pfaff argues above, Rama's moped shows that she can pick and choose which types of Western modernity suit her, and she is neither totally anti-Western nor, especially in her opposition to polygamy, a traditionalist. Unlike her father who forgets his revolutionary past and seems to be stalling the Senegalese future, Rama, transgressing gender norms and zipping around Dakar on her scooter, may be a way out of the current rut. But *Xala,* unlike Sembene's *Faat Kiné* (2000), which I will be discussing in the final chapter, is ultimately not too concerned with mapping out future possibilities or giving women positions of prominence. Rama remains a minor character who, at the end, stands by her father in the face of his humiliation by the beggars. The film is, above all, a critique of the patriarchal national bourgeoisie who have become mired in an unsustainable present. And it is El Hadji's Mercedes, to which I now turn, that becomes the unequivocal symbol of this mess.

The End of the Mercedes

As the audience continues to follow El Hadji on his fall from grace, the protagonist's movements are increasingly staggered and less aligned with the security of the Mercedes. The forward and teleological automobility that characterizes the film before the *xala* (driving to the wedding, driving to pick up his wives, driving to the office, etc.) is replaced by a quest that leads El Hadji to nothing but dead ends. When he travels to villages to find a cure for his *xala,* the lack of drivable roads means that he must leave his Mercedes behind and travel by horse-cart, when he returns to Dakar he crisscrosses the city in his dirty car to his three wives' villas looking for somewhere to rest, and upon the advice of a traditional healer he crawls (like the beggars) toward N'Gone with a fetish in his mouth.[17]

In *Postcolonial African Cinema* (2007), Kenneth Harrow argues that the story of El Hadji is typical of a filmmaker who sees "History" as moving toward progress: in this reading El Hadji's downfall, as well as his "day of reckoning" (18) with the beggars, paves the way for positive change. As should be evident by now, my reading of the film suggests that *Xala* is more about stalling, stuttering, and an insurmountable present than what Harrow describes as a "sense of a movement forward" (18).[18] However, where I find Harrow's analysis of Sembene invaluable is in his insistence that we push past forms of reading that see the commodity fetish simply as a symptom, as something to be decoded and then discarded. Here, Harrow positions himself against Laura Mulvey who reads the sexual and commodity fetishism in *Xala* through what he calls "the language of concealment and of revealing, of the burial of meaning or desire in an invisible depth that can be plumbed for meaning and brought to the surface" (44).

Mulvey argues that the clothing, language, briefcases, and, of course, automobiles in *Xala* serve as a carapace or a protective shell that the postcolonial "upper crust" uses in an attempt to camouflage its corruption and neocolonial collusion.[19] Thus, when El Hadji's Mercedes—the "literal material of the carapace" (1994, 526)—is taken away, it can no longer protect him from the truth of his original crime against his kinsmen. When he receives the news of the Mercedes's repossession, an officer brings him his chauffeur's stool from inside the shop. Mulvey writes, "The stool is like a shrunken, or wizened, version of the proud object of display. It is a trace of, or a memorial to, the Mercedes and its meaning for El Hadji" (526). El Hadji is therefore downgraded from a moving Mercedes to a parked two-seater, to a squat stool. Mulvey's argument is certainly key to understanding how the objects in the film mimic El Hadji's downward mobility, and her analysis can be extended to the final freeze-frame of the film: El Hadji's completely paused and naked body being spat on by the beggars is literally without carapace and without motion. But as Harrow suggests, there is a danger here in treating the commodity fetish as pure deception, as something "false and irrelevant" rather than as "surface in its own right" (2007, 44–45).[20]

What I want to focus on, then, is not what happens to El Hadji when the carapace is removed but, rather, what happens to the car/carapace when *it* is removed. In other words, I want to track the Mercedes itself in order to fully understand how *Xala* produces an ambivalence about the tropes of mobility offered up in the postcolonial era. The officer serving El Hadji with the notice of the repossession asks the three uniformed policemen who accompany him if any of them knows how to drive a Mercedes. They each respond with an assertive, military style, "No, sir." The three officers then position themselves behind the Mercedes and proceed to push it down the street. The camera zooms in on the mosque toward which they are headed and eventually cuts the Mercedes out of the frame, leaving only a close-up of the mosque's phallic minaret. In its final act, the Mercedes becomes both undrivable and irrelevant. It is not decoded but simply removed, not unlike the car in *Heremakono*. Instead of allowing the car to establish the continuity of the film by showing characters logically moving from place to place, Sembene suggests that the automobiles of the postcolonial elite serve as a blockage, or a jam, that has to be removed. As the Guinean filmmaker Flora Gomes says about postcolonial society in general, "We have to stop because we started poorly. . . . Just like when you build a house, if you feel that something is not going right, it is better to stop or else the house will fall down" (Ukadike 2002, 106). In *Xala,* it is better for the car to stop, to disappear, than to continue driving in a direction that will lead down a flawed road.

As El Hadji and his loyal chauffeur walk away from the shop after the Mercedes's repossession, the mosque's minaret again protrudes in the background. Then, several seconds later, the phallic walking stick of the beggar replaces the image of the phallic mosque. It appears that it is the beggar, a member of the *lumpenproletariat*—the class Fanon famously places at the forefront of a revolutionary national consciousness—who is the last phallus standing. In *Xala* the liberal demand for automobility is compromised by the fact that it depends on the immobility of the masses; for as we discover at the end of the film it is only through depriving his kinsmen of their inheritance, and in fact turning them into beggars, that El Hadji can become a member of the Mercedes-driving class. But it would be too simplistic to state here that the void created by the removal of the neocolonial Mercedes is simply filled or fixed by the insertion of the less-mobile outcasts into national life. As Akin Adesokan reminds us, the beggars are not exactly heroes: when they storm El Hadji's home, attack his maid, and raid his refrigerator, they show that "the poor are no less susceptible to consumerism" and not always kind to each other (2011, 76). And though Rama is the character that receives the most sympathetic treatment, when the beggars humiliate her father she seems to align herself with him, shedding tears at his treatment, rather than with the "outcasts."

In the final shots of the film, El Hadji is stripped naked as the beggars hurl their spittle on his body. The film ends with a freeze-frame—El Hadji's torso, covered in dripping saliva, is paused or frozen for eight seconds as the word *fin* appears in red letters on the screen and the soundtrack continues the collective spitting noises. The final scene, then, leaves us with another blockage, or jam, for there is, I'd argue, no foreseeable path forward: the ending speaks to the immobility of not just the postcolonial elite in the form of a frozen El Hadji but also the *lumpenproletariat* who end their battle with a win that still leaves them powerless. They have been able to shame El Hadji and occupy his home, but they are clearly not the new revolutionaries. And as the novella version of *Xala* suggests with its final image of the policemen readying their rifles outside of El Hadji's home, the beggars are still subject to the same law and order.

Though it's typical of French and Francophone films to end with a frame that reads *fin,* the *fin* or ending of *Xala* again recalls Godard's *Weekend,* where we find several "final" frames, one of which reads *Fin De Conte* (end of story) and another of which reads *Fin de Cinéma* (end of cinema). In Beckman's reading Sembene engages Godard's repetition of ends and "weekends" by creating a cinema that stages the "coming after" of decolonization. She suggests that N'Gone's two-seater, facing backward on the trailer (reversing a similar shot from *Weekend*) suggests "the possibility of simply moving in other directions and at different speeds" (2010, 218). What I am arguing is that the ending of *Xala,* like the image of the backward two-seater perched on a forward-facing truck, bears the weight of opposing movements. On the one hand, Sembene has offered alternative visions of mobility in the form of the beggars walking, Rama's scooter, or even El Hadji's horse-cart ride to the marabout. On the other hand, the film hardly offers a set path forward, and the removal of El Hadji's Mercedes seems to lead, above all, to a stalemate, to a question mark as to how to proceed. The ending of the film—which both freezes time and moves the soundtrack

Figure 13. Xala. *Modu, El Hadji's chauffeur, prepares to wash the Mercedes with Evian water.*

Figure 14. Xala. *The Mercedes is repossessed and pushed away by three officers.*

forward—is typical of this paradox, a paradox that explores both the possibilities and impossibilities of moving in "different directions and at a different speeds."

Postcolonial Polyrhythms

Sembene begins *Xala* with a moment of hope, a moment when it was possible to establish a postcolonial nation that would not simply mimic the structure of the colonial state. However, as El Hadji's various betrayals to the Senegalese people are revealed to the audience, the tropes of thwarted progress become increasingly evident. In Jean-Pierre Bekolo's film *Quartier Mozart* (1992), the moment when a different future was possible has long been forgotten: stasis is the point of departure. Amid Bekolo's fast-paced and disjointed style of editing, dissonant soundtrack, and disorienting jump cuts, any signs of economic development are already worn out and in disorder. The cars once occupied by Cameroon's postcolonial elite, and even increasingly by the middle class, are almost entirely incapable of physical movement; they are quite literally misplaced, appearing abandoned at the side of the road rather than as a part of modern traffic flow. After all, Bekolo's film takes place in a country where cars have come to be called *congelés,* or frozens.[21] But whereas the Mercedes in *Xala* was removed because it was on the wrong track, *Quartier Mozart* also uses its automobiles as sites of self-invention and imagination.

Quartier Mozart sets the precedent for other African films that have repurposed the car: Jean-Marie Téno's *Clando* (1996), about a Cameroonian man who turns his private car into a taxi; Jean Odoutan's *Barbecue-Pejo* (2000), in which a Peugeot in Benin, after failing as a taxi, is mined for its engine block, which is used to grill and sell corn; and Dominique Loreau's documentary *Divine Carcasse* (1998), where an old family car imported into Cotonou passes through many hands until it is turned into a Fon god. The cars in these films, as is the case with those in *Quartier Mozart,* are not hitched to a fixed meaning and are quite far from embodying the liberal ideology of automobility. Like Roberto Schwarz's misplaced ideas (see introduction), these misplaced automobiles, transplanted and transformed in a new context, become sites for creative adaptation. But what is unique about *Quartier Mozart* is that Bekolo also uses cars to reflect on the bodily feelings of incoherence in Cameroon during times of economic crisis. *Quartier Mozart* demonstrates how the inherently paradoxical lived time of globalization and postcoloniality is seen and felt as a multiplicity of speeds, rhythms, and tempos. And where *Xala* takes us to the impasse of the *fin,* Bekolo, whose career is "implicitly connected to the phenomenon of globalization" (Adesokan 2011, 109), explores what living and filmmaking in the wake of what the *fin* might feel like.

The film is set in Mozart, a working-class neighborhood of Yaoundé, during a period of widespread economic collapse in the early 1990s. During the time that Bekolo was filming, Cameroon was also experiencing a period of political unrest, and the film was released just after a five-month general strike (called the Ghost Town Movement) attempted to bring down the corrupt government of Paul Biya by shutting down cities and neighborhoods like Mozart.[22] The strike failed, however, and economic conditions continued to worsen. The failed political movement seemed to be reflected by an overall atmosphere of deterioration. Achille Mbembe and Janet Roitman describe the state of affairs in the 1990s as follows:

> Today, Yaoundé's roads are in near total disrepair and dilapidation. Central avenues are as bad as streets in peripheral neighborhoods. Many roads that were paved a few years ago are now paths of beaten earth. They are broken up by sections that juxtapose efforts of resurfacing with potholes, crevices, and precarious ditches. Most traffic circles are nothing more than a heap of old tires or empty, rusted barrels.
>
> The traffic lights no longer function. Some are still intact but no longer light up. Due to the absence of maintenance, vandalism, or, most often, traffic accidents, others have either toppled over, exposing their massive cement base, or lean dangerously over the *ad hoc* sidewalk or over the road itself. Although they are still there, sometimes in the very spot where they were erected, they are now masses of useless "traces," outliers of bygone days. (1996, 159)

Until the mid-1980s, Cameroon had experienced one of the highest rates of economic growth in sub-Saharan Africa. In Yaoundé, a powerful middle class strove to create a city with visible markers of modernity—paved roads, traffic circles, skyscrapers, and foreign automobiles. But in the 1980s and 1990s, the World Bank's push toward the free market in Cameroon resulted in a liberalization of the importation of used vehicles and an influx of very old and poorly functioning cars and trucks. Mbembe and Roitman argue that in the wake of economic crisis and structural adjustment, these distinctive signs of modernity, now in ruins, were indicative of the "instabilities, shortages, constraints, and blockages . . . [that] bring about several types of incoherence" (171). Cars in Cameroon, they argue, became barely drivable, with missing windshields and doors, defective joints, and faulty soldering as par for the course. Automobile transport was therefore no longer characterized by a relative certainty that one will arrive at a destination safe and on time; rather, it became one of the ways that the Cameroonian subject of the 1990s experienced the disjointed nature of urban life (160–61).

However, unlike Mbembe and Roitman, who see the car simply as a figurative object, as an emptied-out sign referring to nothing more than its former power and status, Bekolo invents new uses for the *congelés*. Rather than using the car as a form of continuity editing, a way to visually connect disparate places in the mind of the viewer and move the film forward, Bekolo uses images of nonfunctioning modes of transportation—often tied to witchcraft and magic—as a way to privilege interruption and nonsynchronous spatio-temporal formations, reanimating and reimagining the possibilities of postcolonial life. Bekolo—only twenty-six years old when the film was made—turns his attention toward the younger generation, who must, given the political and economic crises, envisage a very different type of auto-mobility than what one might have hoped for in the euphoric days just after independence. While the neighborhood of Mozart itself is riddled with images of abandoned, broken-down, and immobile vehicles—clear signs of its overall inertia—the youth of the neighborhood find ways to enact a comical, informal, and imaginary form of mobility that does not depend on the cinematic alignment of speed, capitalism, and progress.

Quartier Mozart is a farce about the sexual politics of Cameroonian teenagers who are preoccupied with the types of things that concern all teenagers—sex, beer, soccer, popular culture, and parental authority. But it is in no way a typical coming-of-age "teen flick," and Bekolo satirizes this Western genre by peppering his film with jokes, puns, and clichés about "scoring" and "climaxes" that make fun of the teen flick's teleological and heterosexist presuppositions. The protagonist of *Quartier Mozart* is Queen of the Hood, a brazen and curious young girl who asks a local witch, Maman Thékla, to transform her into one of the neighborhood guys. She says that she wants to "rip off the houses' roofs with one blow" in order to catch a glimpse of what happens in the private spaces of the neighborhood, and she articulates her desire for magical sex reassignment as the wish "just to see." In essence, Queen wants to become an active viewing subject in a social space where, as the female characters note, girls are considerably less free to move about and must conform to different social standards than boys. Maman Thékla agrees to transform Queen into My Guy, a neighborhood stud who seduces Samedi, the daughter of Mad Dog, the corrupt police chief. The witch Thékla then transforms herself into Panka, a man who arrives in Mozart and shocks all by his ability to make a man's penis disappear by shaking his hand. After finally convincing Samedi to sleep with him, My Guy fumbles to find his lube and in a very anticlimactic and totally obscured sex scene is chased away by Mad Dog before the audience is able to tell whether he actually succeeds in achieving his goal. When My Guy leaves Samedi's house, he is picked up by Panka, who has become a taxi driver and guard to Mad Dog. My Guy is then transformed back into Queen of the Hood and Panka again becomes the witch Thékla. The film returns full circle to show Queen and Maman Thékla sitting right where they were before their transformations. Despite a claim in the tongue-and-cheek introduction to the film that things will never be the same in the neighborhood of Mozart, nothing has ostensibly changed for Queen or any of the other residents of Mozart.

In this sense the film rejects a teleological, heterosexually normative linearity, or what Jack Halberstam calls a "hetero-temporality," in favor of a queered temporality that reflects the layered polyrhythms of postcolonial life where change and stasis are endlessly enmeshed.[23] Throughout the film, the humorous and baffling plot is paired with a filmmaking style full of stops and starts, jerky camera movements, and a sometimes dissonant soundtrack. More in the style of Mambety than Sembene, Bekolo uses jump cuts, photographic stills, and false match-on-action shots to continually disrupt the continuity of the film and to create an unruly rhythm. Sounds don't always match up with images, and Bekolo, in fact, compares himself to a DJ who puts his finger on the gramophone in order to stop the record from playing normally. And as Harrow notes, "Bekolo wants us to move at a rapid-fire pace through the scenes in which the question of dealing with modernity in a postcolonial, global age can best be posed . . . at the site of a wrecked hulk of a car" (2007, 100). Abandoned cars, stopped cars, and wrecked cars serve as nodes throughout the film where movement becomes stasis and stasis becomes movement.

Beginning with the opening sequence of the film, in which Bekolo knits together several unrelated events, non-moving cars punctuate the rhythm of Bekolo's storytelling. As *Quartier Mozart* opens, Bekolo, who also narrates the film, introduces the audience to the various characters, including Queen of the Hood. We see Queen of the Hood talking back to Atango, the tailor, and then conversing in the dark with the witch Maman Thékla, who tells her tales of "traveling" as a man. Thékla has "known all sorts of women . . . Japanese, English, American" and has concluded that what she prefers most of all is "to be a woman but in a man's body." As the two talk, the narrative digresses, and the narrator/filmmaker tells a story about a woman who lost her husband when he died suddenly in his car at a stop sign after having just returned home and surviving a plane crash. This is the first stopped car in the film: the narrative pauses here to tell the story of the woman's husband, but, tellingly, these characters never reappear; the story is simply temporarily interrupted by a random death at a stop sign. Bekolo stops and then restarts.

After the widow's story, there is movement again: Queen and Thékla are on the move, invisibly spying (through magic) on Atango having sex with a girl who is describing an outfit she wants him to make. After the spying adventure, Queen is also ready to travel in a man's body. The camera then combines stasis and movement in a single shot, focusing on the wheels of a pickup truck being towed or pushed by something unseen. As a cloud of fog envelopes the truck, Bekolo narrates the transformation that is taking place in the dark and inside the truck, "I see the witchcraft happening. You see it too? She's become a man . . . I see it all here in Mozart." As Bekolo narrates, Queen emerges from the driver's seat as My Guy, a muscular young man who is taking stock of his new body and searching for clothing. The body of the truck, while remaining momentarily fixed, becomes the site where Queen acquires a new, more mobile body. But then the truck is removed, and the camera shows the audience the two feet of an unknown person pushing it. Continuing his voice-over narration, Bekolo asks, "Where are they taking that car?" but instead of answering the question, he declares, "I'm going to sleep, to take a break." Again, like the automobiles throughout the film, the storyline moves at its own unique tempo. It stops and starts; it suspends itself midway and needs to be tugged or towed in order to continue. If Bekolo, like Sembene, is exploring the options for "different directions" and "different speeds," he does so in a consistently tongue-in-cheek manner.

Figure 15. Quartier Mozart. *Queen of the Hood (top) before her transformation and My Guy (bottom) after the transformation.*

Figure 16. Quartier Mozart. *A man dies suddenly at a stop sign.*

Figure 17. Quartier Mozart. *Queen of the Hood emerges from the pickup truck as My Guy. The narrator claims to "see it all" despite the obscured nature of the scene.*

Knowing, Seeing, Moving

Because Queen of the Hood's conversion into My Guy occurs in an abandoned pickup truck, Bekolo invites the analogy between My Guy's newly acquired masculinity and the figure of the automobile. However, this analogy is immediately undercut as the truck is removed and it becomes clear that it does not belong to My Guy and is not available for his use. We are certainly not in the realm of American films like *American Graffiti* or *Rebel without a Cause* where teenage boys cruise around town in their cars. The truck therefore remains an ironic and ambiguous symbol of My Guy's newfound mobility, and it never returns to the story. The question "where are they taking that car?" becomes unimportant because the film does not engage the viewer at the level of cognition. Rather, *Quartier Mozart* forces the audience to submit its sensoria to the incoherence of the film.

What Bekolo seems to be doing is confronting the audience with the limits of the knowing/seeing/moving modern, post-Enlightenment subject. As Caren Kaplan writes, "Light, sight, and travel become structuring concepts for this . . . subject, a subject that is arguably generically masculine, raced, propertied, and individualised in a legal as well as political, psychological, and philosophical sense" (2006, 401). But in *Quartier Mozart,* "light, sight, and travel" as well as the individualized masculine body and rationality in general become destabilized. The bodies that travel are female bodies—Maman Thékla's and Queen's—and they travel only because they have access to witchcraft, not to property, passports, or modes of transport. And although the story is full of references to being able to see, or accessing hidden or private worlds—such as Queen's desire "just to see" and Bekolo's claim to "see it all here in Mozart"—the film seems to be more about the impossibilities of seeing and knowing. In fact, while the opening sequence allows Queen of the Hood, through the magic of cinema, the ability to, as Walter Benjamin famously put it, "calmly and adventurously go traveling" (1968b, 236), much of the sequence is shot in dark spaces with very little lighting. The low lighting, combined with the zigzagging plot, the sleeping narrator, and the jarring soundtrack, forces the audience to deprioritize vision as a way of interacting with the film.

The viewing experience Bekolo creates, then, supports Vivian Sobchack's assertion that although vision is typically understood to be the dominant way in which we understand cinema, we actually "see and comprehend and feel films with our entire bodily being" (2004, 63). For

Sobchack, vision has had a "hierarchical sway" over the other senses, but the camera and the male gaze do not necessarily need to have an overarching mastery over its object (63). When Bekolo, the male narrator, falls asleep on his audience rather than explaining the plot and when he allows a young girl to occupy the body of a teenage boy, he seems to be undercutting this overarching mastery in potent ways. And when these moments are coupled, as they so often are, with the immobile cars, Bekolo places the moving, male gaze under suspension.

Moreover, when cars do move and work in *Quartier Mozart,* it is only the corrupt and vitiated patriarchal figures who have access to them, as was the case in *Xala.* Mad Dog, the corpulent and physically abusive police chief and father of Samedi, who happens to resemble the Cameroonian president Paul Biya, uses his car to pull over a man in a wheelchair and confiscate his identity papers. His haranguing of the less mobile is clearly reminiscent of El Hadji's, and Mad Dog's troubles with his newly polygamous family show that, like El Hadji, he has also overextended his patriarchal power. The priest, another dodgy figure, takes his car to bless Mad Dog's polygamous marriage. Even Panka (the former Maman Thékla, who can now make penises disappear with his handshake) drives a taxi once he starts working for Mad Dog and almost immediately becomes an irresponsible, abusive husband.

But as Bekolo subverts male power and hegemonic ways of seeing and knowing, he also foregrounds alternative points of departure and instantiates new types of mobility. Broken-down cars, which do not produce the same types of meaning as functional cars, become sites of play, imagination, and satirical performance. In a scene midway through the film we see Samedi's younger brother and Queen of the Hood making out, or playing hide-and-seek as they euphemistically call it, in the back of an abandoned car. Here, My Guy approaches the car hoping to give Samedi's brother a note to pass to her, since Samedi's father has restricted his daughter's ability to move about the neighborhood. However, My Guy is taken aback when he sees Queen of the Hood there and, in an intimidating manner, chases her off screen. Since My Guy and Queen are supposed to be the same person, the inconsistency of them appearing together disturbs the narrative and temporal logic of the story. This moment of confusion stands as is, without any explanation, and becomes another instance where the multiply gendered body of My Guy/Queen is juxtaposed next to the body of the immobile automobile. But here, the hulk of the car also becomes

Figure 18. Quartier Mozart. *Mad Dog pulls over a man in a wheelchair for exceeding the speed limit down a hill.*

Figure 19. Quartier Mozart. *My Guy and Queen of the Hood face off at an abandoned car.*

Figure 20. Quartier Mozart. *A neighborhood girl writes rumors about My Guy and Samedi on the windshield of a car.*

the place where a different form of communication is initiated: the very low-tech, but tried-and-true practice of note passing. In *Quartier Mozart* messages are communicated both through modern technology and, because that technology isn't always working, or available, or even necessary, through informal word-of-mouth networks. In fact, Bekolo seems to be implying that a different form of movement sustains the neighborhood when a gaggle of women at the well declare, "Mozart moved last night!" whenever something rumor-worthy occurs in the neighborhood.

Furthermore, in a scene later in the film a neighborhood girl approaches another deserted vehicle and, using her finger, writes, "My Guy and Samedi did it" in the dirty windshield. Since the spreading of rumors is in direct violation of Mad Dog's order that My Guy keep his relationship with Samedi quiet, the windshield of the car becomes a way to counter the authority of the corrupt and patriarchal police chief. The windshield, rather than aligning the camera with the movement of the automobile as it typically does, acts as a stationary screen, or windscreen, where the characters (like the filmmaker) can circulate information without having to answer to local or state authority. Thus, Bekolo rejects the often-used graphic match between the windshield and the camera viewfinder—such as that described by Virilio (see epigraph)—in order to produce an entirely different form of movement. If the cinematic apparatus is a "cinematograph," literally the writing or graphing of movement, or kinesis, Bekolo uses film to re-graph movement.

Fordism out of Place

Like the DJ that he imagines himself to be, Bekolo selects the sounds and images that reflect the multiple and often confusing rhythms of urban Cameroonian life, rhythms that include gossip, rumor, banter, remixes of American pop music, and brawls that are informed just as much by working technology as they are by abandoned and retooled technology. Jonathan Haynes, borrowing the language of Arjun Appadurai, suggests that the characters of *Quartier Mozart* inhabit a "post-modern globalized mediascape" (1999, 27). To a certain extent, there seems to be a case for such an argument. The local teens mock global perceptions of Africans as starving and barbarous, and their popular culture savvy seems to be a direct response to those who only see Africans through the lens of underdevelopment. The young Cameroonians discuss Denzel Washington, Lady Di, and Princess Caroline of Monaco, and they point out that Michael Jackson stole his "Wanna Be Startin' Something" lyrics from the Cameroonian Manu Dibango's "Soul Makossa." Likewise, the various forms of hip-hop music played throughout the film reflect the multiple directions of musical influence across the Atlantic and show that global cultural flows are not a one-way street. In today's parlance, the characters in *Quartier Mozart* might be described as Afropolitan, people for whom "cultural mixing" and "the interweaving of worlds" has always been an African "way of belonging to the world" (Mbembe 2007, 28).

And yet I would argue that *Quartier Mozart* actually complicates the "modernity at large" theory espoused by Appadurai and refashioned by Afropolitan boosters who lay claim to fluid identities and to a locality that is contextual and relational instead of spatial. What is missing from *Quartier Mozart,* in fact, is anything that would physically connect the neighborhood to the outside world. Despite mention of a plane crash and a brief shot of telephone wires in the opening sequences, there are no images of airplanes, telephone calls abroad, or references to emigration. The neighborhood of Mozart is bound heavily by space and is not so much "shot through with . . . realities of having to move or the fantasies of wanting to move" (Appadurai 1996, 33–34) to different global locales as it is "shot through" with tropes of immobility, breakdown, and accidental death. It presents a Cameroon in which access to global fashions and media are often at odds with access to the types of physical mobility necessary to be part of what has been labeled the global Afropolitan class, a Cameroon that despite considerable economic improvement still exists today.

Quartier Mozart therefore compels the audience to think beyond totalizing narratives of globalization and instead reproduces what it might feel like to inhabit a world that experiences post-Fordist life in a Cameroon steeped in incongruities. In this respect, Bekolo seems to be in agreement with many postcolonial scholars and feminist theorists of modernity who argue that global capitalism "is filled with contradiction and contests for interpretive power," that different bodies live and experience late capitalism in different ways (Kaplan 1996, 154). Along these lines and referring to the oft-repeated and totalizing script that globalization is about the "penetration" of capitalist social relations to all corners of the world and all aspects of life, the feminist geographers Julie Graham and Katherine Gibson (writing under the pen name J. K. Gibson-Graham) challenge this master narrative by provocatively asking, "How might we get globalization to lose its erection?" (1996, 126–27). What I argue is that Bekolo's film, though less explicitly focused on the loss of erection than *Xala,* provides a playful and comical answer to Gibson-Graham's provocation. Of course, at the level of its loose narrative, we have a neighborhood where women can turn into men and men can make penises disappear with a handshake. But what I also want to underscore is that this challenge to global capitalism and to Fordist and post-Fordist relations also occurs at the level of *Quartier Mozart's* form.

In her book *Fast Cars, Clean Bodies: Decolonization and the Reordering of French Culture,* Kristin Ross argues that it is not just the car and cinema that have a shared historical and perceptual framework but also cinema and the overall paradigm of Fordism. Ross writes,

> In production, cars had paved the way for film; now, film would help create the conditions for the motorization of Europe: the two technologies reinforced each other. Their shared qualities—movement, image, mechanization, standardization—made movies and cars the key commodity-vehicles of a complete transformation in European and consumption patterns and cultural habits.
>
> Much of that transformation involved a change in perception, a change in the way things were *seen.* (38)

I've already commented on the way in which Bekolo uses framing, lighting, and the immobile car to re-graph movement and visual perception. What I also want to emphasize is that Bekolo plays with the still and moving images in a way that highlights the limits of film's historic relationship to Fordism.

Departing from the typical format of the *moving* image, Bekolo chooses to compose an entire scene in the film with still black-and-white photographs. This is the scene where My Guy is courting Samedi at a dance, a scene that one might think to be particularly charged with movement. Since there is no dialogue here, each photograph contains a brief caption. Most of the time the captions match the action, narrating the progression of My Guy's advances. But some are actually statements that have no relationship to the plot and instead directly speak to the nonlinearity of time that the film constantly evokes. One caption, for instance, reads: "A boy died the day he was born." Here, the photographic stills (frozen images) like the frozen cars *(congelés)* disrupt the usual *défilement* of events and images and point to the boundaries of film itself.[24]

By substituting the continuous moving image with a series of photographs, Bekolo calls attention to the fact that in motion picture film, each frame is a continuous photograph broken into a number of discrete samples, or frames per second. Media theorists like Lev Manovich have argued that the most likely reason that film has these discrete levels is because film itself emerged as a result of Fordist assembly-line production. The assembly line relied on two principles: the standardization of parts, and the separation of the production process into a set of simple, repetitive, and sequential activities (Manovich 2001, 29). Manovich suggests that film therefore follows the logic of the factory in that it requires standardization of both time (frames per second) and of image (in terms of size, frame ratio, and contrast). But, as I've been discussing, *Quartier Mozart* works against this notion of sequence and standardization and in this way creates a cinema in which capitalist mobility, mass consumption, and progressive movement are all "misplaced," or out of sync, with Cameroonian reality. Here, imagination, self-reinvention, and informal networks seem to be the only "preconditions for take-off."[25]

Moving On

Much less interested in a cinema of engagement, and much more interested in pushing the formal limits and boundaries of African cinema, Bekolo experiments with form in order to find new ways to express the postcolonial subject's encounter with global modernity. Unlike Sembene, Bekolo does not dwell on the historical past, nor does he provide the audience with characters, plot, or dialogue that seem committed to any explicit or easily discernable political agenda. Rather, *Quartier Mozart* is a mischievous, and in the end inconclusive, exploration of a cinema and technology in which movement and stasis are continually entangled. And while *Xala* is typical of a filmmaker who remained committed to both a social realist style and critiques of patriarchal power structures, *Quartier Mozart* seemed to be a launching pad for Bekolo, who went on to experiment formally with conceptual films like *Aristotle's Plot* (1996) and *Les Saignantes* (2005) that address questions about what filmmaking should look like in Africa. But both Bekolo and Sembene, despite their differences in generation and style, are combative filmmakers in their own ways, and both make films dedicated to critiquing postcolonial patriarchy, corruption, nepotism, and global inequalities. Moreover, both deploy cars satirically and critically in order to contemplate the paradoxical forms of mobility and modernity that circulate in the postcolony. Automobiles in their films are not aligned with progress, speed, masculinity, or autonomy, but with the various feelings of uncertainty that make up the postcolonial modernity African subjects inhabit.

Certainly, though, not all Francophone films open up the relation between the moving picture and moving vehicle in identical ways, and not all, in fact, would even be able to neatly fit into the admittedly flexible category of art film. But what Francophone African filmmakers do typically make visible are the failures of development narratives that, as James Ferguson argues, have themselves "de-composed." Moussa Touré's road trip movie *TGV* (1998) is an instructive case in point. On the one hand, *TGV* is a film seemingly more focused on entertainment than *Xala* or *Quartier Mozart,* and though, as all good road trip movies do, it does have numerous breakdowns and comical mishaps, the film does not appear to undercut the alignment of the car and the camera. Many shots of the Senegalese landscape are predictably seen through the windshield or the side of the bus, and the linear narrative begins with the characters boarding their bus at a station on the outskirts of Dakar and ends with them reaching their final destination in Conakry. On the other hand, the rickety bus they've boarded is named *TGV,* after the French Express Train, and the slogan on its side, "Plus Vite Que TGV" (Faster than TGV) can only be taken as an ironic statement about the vastly different types of travel available in the postcolony. Likewise, when the bus leaks from the rain, the driver, in a move that reminds viewers of both the *mégotage* of Senegalese filmmaking and the *bricolage* of Senegalese road trips, hands out chewing gum to the passengers and asks them to plug up any holes. And when *TGV*'s driver gets lost, he turns to a French ethnologist who arrogantly believes that his map of the area from the eighteenth century will still be sufficient. Thus, even a seemingly straightforward road trip movie like *TGV* critiques narratives of development and underdevelopment: Touré mocks not just the slowness and precariousness of traveling in Senegal, but also the belief that Africa is unchanging and static.

Of course, there are still many Francophone films where cars, whether they are Mercedes-Benzes, Peugeot 504 taxis, or local buses, function just fine, where they get the characters from point A to point B without much fanfare. But what I am suggesting is that the filmmakers I've discussed in this chapter participate in a cinematic tradition that contemplates and complicates the relationship between movement and stasis and that uses film as a way to meditate on the particular forms of progress, travel, and gendered mobility available and blocked off in the postcolonial decades. Bekolo might be the most blunt in his disregard for linearity and his critique of teleological time—a placard in his futuristic *Les Saignantes* set in Yaoundé in the year 2025 where "nothing has changed" reads, "How can you make an anticipation film in a country that has no future?"—but he is not the only one for whom modernity is a contradictory affective experience. Films like Mambety's *La petite vendeuse de soleil* (1999) and *Hyenas* (1992), Moussa Sene Absa's *Tableau ferraille* (1997), Joseph Gaï Ramaka's *Karmen Gei* (2001), Sissako's *Bamako* (2006), Gahité Fofana's *Un matin de bonheur* (2005), and, more recently, Olivier Delahaye and Dani Kouyaté's *Soleils* (2013) or Philippe Lacôte's *Run* (2014), to name just a few, also all showcase the complex and paradoxical ways African subjects insistently participate in global modernity that both includes and excludes. Francophone films therefore tend to deconstruct the idea that modernity "is a universal *telos*" (Ferguson 2006, 178) and question the extent to which Western forms of temporality or capitalist consumption work in an African context. By contrast, Anglophone video films, to which I turn in the following chapter, tend to view modernity and the automobility that accompanies it as something that is still both achievable and desirable. In these video films, based on an entirely different production model and made in an entrepreneurial spirit that has not been part of the Francophone tradition, modernity is not something that once existed, or was once promised, but rather something to be obtained by individuals who can work the system to their advantage. Nollywood's critique of automobility and teleological narratives therefore takes a very different form and necessitates a deep engagement with the possibilities opened up by popular culture.

· CHAPTER 4 ·

The Return of the Mercedes: Upward Mobility, the Good Life, and Nigerian Video Film

If one had to choose a single image to express the culture of the [Nigerian] videos, it would undoubtedly be a Mercedes Benz, which appears ubiquitously as the symbol of the desired good life, the reward of both good and evil, the sign of social status and individual mobility.

—Jonathan Haynes, *Nigerian Video Films*

"Oh man, we're good. That's why I'm driving a Hummer."

—*Boys Cot*

IN GET RICH OR DIE TRYIN (2005), the semi-autobiographical film about rapper 50 Cent's rise to fame, 50 Cent (Curtis Jackson) plays Marcus, a young gangster lured into the life of crime after his mother is killed in a drug deal gone bad. The film chronicles Marcus's life on the streets of New York until he eventually makes it big as a star. As he defeats his enemies and rises to the top of his game, Jackson/Marcus, who acquires an iconic Mercedes-Benz S500, equates his upward mobility with automobility. In the film and then again in his song "Poor Lil Rich," he boasts: "In the Benz on Monday, the BM on Tuesday, Range on Wednesday, Thursday I'm in the hooptay, Porsche on Friday, I do things my way: Vipe or Vette, I tear up the highway." In *Darker Than Blue: On the Moral Economies of Black Atlantic Culture* (2010), Paul Gilroy reads *Get Rich or Die Tryin* and the above lyrics as symptomatic of the waning of contemporary African American political life. For Gilroy the type of attitude expressed in *Get Rich or Die Tryin* typifies the way that cars, which during the United States civil rights era and its immediate aftermath were linked to the freedom to travel and to compensation for material deprivation, have now come to undermine the idea of a public good and public citizenship. Using a range of examples from African American popular culture, Gilroy argues that the automobile can be read as an ur-commodity that gauges the shifting terrain of the black American "moral economy" and black America's compromised relationship to consumer culture and to the commodity form.[1]

Though African forms of popular culture do not figure into Gilroy's narrative, he does link car culture to a shared black Atlantic politics. He writes, "Car culture may now become a way of foreclosing the possibility of any substantive connections between the privileged caste of U.S. blacks and other less fortunate groups, both inside their own society and among the 'third world' folk who live within the veil of scarcity defined, if they are lucky, by the alternative transit technology of the bicycle" (40). While I find Gilroy's analysis of the political pitfalls of what Raymond Williams calls "mobile privatization" to be very astute and particularly useful in considering how the negative aspects of American automobility become global exports, ultimately I think he articulates an unfortunately common and oversimplified view of "third world" automobility and consumerism. I see two significant problems with Gilroy's assessment here. First, for most African subjects, especially the majority of those who live in urban centers, private cars and the pleasures of automobile culture are everywhere. Bicycles may be alternative transit technologies, but most who use them consider themselves unlucky, especially outside of more bicycle-friendly cities like Ouagadougou, Burkina Faso. Second, Gilroy fails to consider the possibility that Americanized car culture is both appropriated by the transnational black community and transformed by it, that consumer capitalism outside of the Global North might be simultaneously coveted and critiqued. For instance, Nigerian hip-hop star Olu Maintain borrows from 50 Cent's "Poor Lil Rich" in the video for his hit song "Yahoozee" when he walks down a line of luxury automobiles each with a vanity plate imprinted with a different day of the week. But, as I'll be discussing below, when Afam Okereke samples "Yahoozee" in his video film *Boys Cot* (2007), which is about young, unemployed boys in contemporary Nigeria, cars are not only celebrated and flaunted but also associated with the failings of the formal economy and the breaking of social bonds. While the automobile in *Boys Cot,* like the forms of criminality the boys turn to, does indeed offer individual and private solutions to collective problems, there is not, I argue, a foreclosure of critiques in the way that Gilroy and other skeptics of popular culture suggest. What this chapter offers, then, is an examination of the moral economy of popular car culture on the "other" side of the black Atlantic, the side often overlooked in Gilroy's writing.

Nollywood and the Global Subject

I focus my discussion of popular representations of car culture on the widely consumed and highly visible Nigerian or Nollywood video films that have, as Matthias Krings and Onookome Okome put it, "become a truly pan-African affair" (2007, 1). Despite the fact that the movies are decidedly low budget, a UNESCO report finds that Nigeria is now the world's second-largest producer of feature-length films, just after India. Originally distributed on VHS cassettes, Nollywood films are now viewed on VCDs (video compact discs), on DVDs, or streaming online.[2] In part because of what Brian Larkin calls "infrastructures of piracy," Nollywood films are easily available and highly popular across the continent and the African diaspora. In African communities across the globe, Nollywood stars have become household names and the stars themselves have become the very modern and mobile subjects that the films so often project.[3]

What Nollywood typically refers to are the English-language video films (inaugurated somewhat ironically by the Igbo-language *Living in Bondage*) that are produced in Southern Nigeria and that have been influenced by West African forms of popular culture like Onitsha market literature, concert parties, traveling theater, and highlife music.[4] Though my focus here is on the Nigerian film industry, critical discussions of Nollywood often link it to the smaller English-language Ghanaian film industry that began slightly before the Nigerian industry and, despite different challenges and vicissitudes, follows similar production and distribution models, addresses similar themes and moral dilemmas, and now shares several actors, directors, and producers.[5] The regional and pan-African popularity of both of these straight-to-video industries has marked a significant change from the Francophone art films discussed in the previous chapter and has led to calls for new models of study, ones more appropriate for popular culture than auteur cinema. As Karin Barber has famously suggested, African popular culture ought to be understood as "the work of local cultural producers speaking to local audiences about pressing concerns, experiences and struggles that they share" (1997b, 2). And indeed, many scholars have followed Barber's lead by exploring the ways that Nigerian and Ghanaian videos turn urban legends into melodramatic stories that reflect the anxieties about everyday life where inflation and the cost of living have spiraled out of control and where one has to resort to inventive and often dubious means to acquire the consumer goods that these same movies often excessively parade. West African video films are particularly productive objects of inquiry, then, because they "allow their viewers to imagine what it means to be modern in an African way" (Krings and Okome 2013, 5) and to see this vision of African modernity on screens in their own homes. Accordingly, the Nollywood movies discussed here enable unique ways of tracing the paradoxical relationships that contemporary West African subjects have to cars and automobility.

Though Nollywood films emerge from older West African vernacular forms, they are also heavily influenced by global soap operas and telenovelas, and like those televisual media they often focus on the highly commodified world of the urban upper class. Although the production values of the videos might not be up to Western standards, the main characters themselves are dressed in the latest American, European, and African fashions and live in opulently decorated mansions, shop at expensive boutiques rather than in crowded markets, and seamlessly traverse cities in luxury cars and SUVs. Rather than highlighting the conditions of uneven development or rejecting the premises of capitalist mass culture, these films center on stories of upwardly mobile, auto-mobile individuals. Indeed, as Jonathan Haynes points out, nothing typifies the culture of video films as much as the Mercedes-Benz, or the flashy luxury car. Unlike the Francophone celluloid films that reject the glamorization of consumer society, video films thrive on the world of shiny, new things, a world where viewers can participate in the pleasures of global capitalism from which they are so often excluded. In the video films, then, the Mercedes exiled in Sembene's *Xala* makes a comeback.

However, in many Nollywood videos, the characters associated with luxury cars have often acquired their vehicles because they have engaged in cult worship, ritual murder, illegal organ trade, or fraud. Like the *wazimamoto* stories Luise White describes (see introduction) in which cars in the colonial context were rumored to be driven by vampires who worked for the Europeans, motorcars in these cases are associated with dubious labor practices and occult deeds. This suggests that the films are not a "forgetting" of the neocolonialist legacy, as critics of the melodrama genre suggest,[6] but rather a refashioning of continuing anxieties about work, the origin of wealth, and the gap between highly mobile subjects and those with less access to global flows and technologies. It also means that despite their commitment to entertainment, glamour, and popular consumption, Nollywood videos should not be understood as diametrically opposed to Francophone art films: though they proffer different critiques and solutions, they too are concerned with the misdeeds of the local elite as well as with the uneven flows of global capitalism.[7] Indeed, while video films may gleefully depict modern capitalist subjects, they also exhibit quite a bit of ambivalence about how one attains these capitalist pleasures, and they almost unilaterally condemn those who become part of commodity culture by trouncing on social codes integral to the welfare of the community at large. In this context they grapple with the task of determining how, in an economy of scarcity, one might become a global, self-sufficient and automobile subject without breaking the moral bonds of community and sacrificing human integrity.

As Nollywood filmmaker Bond Emeruwa argues in Franco Sacchi's documentary *This Is Nollywood* (2007), video films aspire to be a form of "edutainment," educative entertainment. This mission statement by one of the industry's leading practitioners suggests that even though the moral messages of the films might at times be obscured behind the glamour of Nigeria's elite or relegated to the last five minutes of a five-hour film, Nollywood filmmakers are not simply concerned with filming the outward signs of material success. What I argue in this chapter is that Nollywood films demonstrate how consumer objects—like the ubiquitous and paradigmatic car—allow the characters to become global subjects in a world where consumption, for better *and* for worse, has increasingly become the mode through which subjects forge their identities. Whereas the vehicles shown in (and sometimes removed from) the Francophone films are often linked to patriarchal power structures and to the stalling of progress, the cars in Nollywood films are both coveted and maligned, necessary and excessive at the same time. In other words, though the automobile may be associated with corruption, witchcraft, or the shady underworld, it also becomes a way for global subjects to define themselves through the ideals of automobility and a display of consumer goods rather than through the physicality of their poverty. Through a reading of *Living in Bondage* (1992), *Blood Money* (1996), and *Boys Cot* (2007)—three popular Nigerian video films[8] about the criminal and often occult acquisition of wealth—this chapter explores how tensions between desires for material wealth, or dreams of development, collide with pervasive feelings of uneasiness about heightened levels of conspicuous consumption amid widespread financial insecurity. Each of these films, then, utilizes the automobile as an object through which to contemplate the simultaneous attachment to and distance from the "good life," a term I use to describe the feelings of pleasure and emotional security that come from success in the capitalist economy.[9]

According to the often-repeated Nollywood origin story, Kenneth Nnebue's 1992 *Living in Bondage* is the film that jump-started the industry, paving the way for many films that would follow its generic formula: the film is a multipart melodrama about rich city-dwellers joining cults and engaging in witchcraft or ritual murders in order to achieve wealth. While *Living in Bondage* was certainly not the first Nigerian video film, the widespread and sweeping market success of Nnebue's film proved for the first time that a Nigerian televisual industry was able to exist autonomously without state or outside funding.[10] I start with *Living in Bondage* because of its canonical status—it is perhaps the most-written-about Nollywood film—but also because it initiated what I have elsewhere called the "occult melodrama," a popular subgenre of video film blending storylines that focus on witchcraft and spirits with melodramatic tales about love, the accumulation of wealth, and the precarity of the family structure.[11] *Blood Money,* starring the highly popular Zack Orji, is also considered to be a "classic," or canonical, Nollywood film and a paradigmatic occult melodrama.[12] Like *Living in Bondage, Blood Money* is a morality tale that focuses on magical money cults and the extent to which men will kill and sacrifice their friends or family in order to attain the material possessions they covet. As Carmela Garritano writes, the occult genre that *Living in Bondage* and *Blood Money* are a part of is so popular in part because it criticizes those who place a high premium on the accumulation of wealth over family and community and because it documents the "horrific transformation of human life into surplus value" (2012a, 61). Nigerian and Ghanaian occult films like *Zinabu* (1987), *Rituals* (1997), *Blood Billionaires* (2003), *Billionaires Club* (2005), and *Sika Mu Sakawa* (2009) therefore articulate potent moral critiques of neoliberal capitalism (51).

In the first decade of the video film industry, from the early 1990s to the early 2000s, occult melodramas were by far the most common type of film in Nigeria, often capitalizing on and dramatizing local rumors about the occult practices of criminals and wealthy men.[13] While many of these occult films are still being produced, the genre's dominance began to wane in the early 2000s. One type of film that became popular as the number of occult melodramas decreased, was the 419 (pronounced four-one-nine) film, a genre that emerges from the occult melodrama story format but focuses on different forms of criminality.[14] 419 is the Nigerian penal code for financial crime and is the colloquial term used to describe scam artists, forgers, impersonators, and money doublers. These types of criminals have become increasingly visible and active in the post-oil-boom economy and have gained global notoriety by using Internet technology to seek out victims across the world, sending out the familiar emails requesting various types of financial "help."[15] Like the protagonists in *Living in Bondage* and *Blood Money,* the young men of the popular 419 film *Boys Cot*—and I am also including the two-part sequel *The Return of Boys Cot* both of which I will simply refer to as *Boys Cot*—are trying to figure out how to make money and live the good life in an economy where education and hard work no longer add up to success and where the material satisfaction and stability they seek are elusive.[16] Rather than turning to blood money cults, they become involved in Internet scamming, which is available as an option because Internet cafés, laptops, and Blackberries—all tools they need—have become much more accessible. As Andrew Smith argues, stories about Internet fraud and occult rituals often operate according to similar logic: both reveal "hidden" and often obscured economic processes about how goods and values enter the world (2009, 39). Despite addressing different modes of criminality, then, all three of the video films deal, in quite similar ways, with the desire and difficulty of acquiring wealth and material objects in a world where the paths to such accumulation are neither clear nor righteous. But unlike *Get Rich or Die Tryin,* which ends with the triumph of the gangster-turned-rapper, the Nollywood films punish those individuals who have made their way to the top through dubious means. Thus, while the characters in the films struggle to obtain a certain standard of living—or a global "status," as James Ferguson would say—and the filmmakers strive to re-create this standard in the videos' mise-en-scène, Nollywood is full of stories in which the good life comes at a price too high to pay.

The Mercedes Returns: Nnebue's *Living in Bondage*

Kenneth Nnebue's Igbo video film *Living in Bondage* is, like Sembene's *Xala,* a Mephistophelian tale about the illegitimate accumulation of wealth in the postcolony.[17] However, unlike El Hadji, Andy Okeke at the beginning of *Living in Bondage* has not yet discovered how to make money in the complex world of the postcolonial city. Dissatisfied with the pay at his previous job, Andy attempts to go into business on his own, but he finds himself unable to garner wealth as his trading partners have. Each of the three friends with whom he does business has been able to acquire a Mercedes, and Andy, in his opening soliloquy, lists these friends and their cars and admits that he is desperate to own one. Then Andy runs into Paul, a former school friend driving by in a Mercedes, who takes Andy to a party at Ichie Million's home and introduces Andy to his "millionaire's club friends." Eventually, Andy is permitted to join their exclusive cult of Lord Lucifer and is informed that he must offer a blood sacrifice of the person he loves the most: his wife, Merit. Andy is shocked to hear that such a sacrifice is required, but each of the cult members reveals that he too sacrificed a loved one and that the loved one was quickly replaced by more friends, wives, and luxury cars like Mercedes, BMWs, and Pathfinders. Andy presents Merit to the cult, and she dies in a bloodletting ritual where her blood is given to the cult members to drink. Nnebue's message here could not be more explicit: those who get rich do so with the lifeblood of the most innocent. The film then jumps forward several months, and the audience sees that Andy has acquired the signs of material wealth: a mansion, fine clothing, and a blood-colored Mercedes. Several hours of the five-hour film are consumed with Andy enjoying the good life, frequenting fancy restaurants and hotels, and entertaining women. But Andy begins to be haunted by apparitions of Merit, and he eventually goes mad, tears off his clothing, and wanders the streets of Lagos digging through trash bins like a pauper. Luckily, Tina, a reformed prostitute, discovers Andy in the streets and brings him to church where he confesses his sins and is redeemed.

Living in Bondage displays the various anxieties about outward displays of wealth in what Jean and John Comaroff have appropriately labeled "occult economies." According to the Comaroffs, occult economies are those in which wealth, because it has been separated from formal, discernible labor practices, appears through seemingly supernatural or mysterious networks. Although occult economies begin in the colonial moment—when the circulation of new goods and values radically restructured indigenous economies—the Comaroffs use the term to describe the proliferation of occult reactions to a neoliberal economy structured on the flexibility of laborers, markets, and products rather than actual production or agriculture. In other words, an occult economy is one in which people "acquire vast fortunes without ordinary labor costs" (1999, 20), making wealth appear enigmatic or magical and leading to rumors that money and material objects are attained through witchcraft, vampirism, zombies, or cult rituals. The occult economy is a direct result of forced privatization, soaring food prices, inflation, and unemployment that have increasingly pushed African workers into the informal sector and made ways of earning money more and more opaque. In such economies, the clear and observable paths to wealth—education, government employment, salaried labor, production of agricultural exports—have been overshadowed, if not replaced, by the shady and underground routes that are beyond the ken of the regulated economy. The logics of witchcraft, vampirism, and occult fraud, which act as explanations for capitalist accumulation under such conditions, operate such that personal success is accomplished only through cheating, tricking, or somehow "consuming" the labor of unwitting innocents like Andy's wife.[18]

In Nigeria, the occult economy is also linked to the overnight oil boom of the 1970s that provided a sudden influx of wealth to a select elite who performed virtually no work and had nothing to do with the actual process of production.[19] In fact, as was the case in other African countries that experienced a period of economic prosperity in the 1970s, few average Nigerians were able to profit from the boom because jobs created for unskilled or semiskilled laborers were minimal. In the aftermath of the oil boom, as Nigerian currency became virtually worthless while the cost of living rose, wealth became even more distanced from formal and established modes of labor and production. As McCall points out, "The petroleum wealth that was supposed to capitalize the commercial development of Nigeria, found its way into private bank accounts, foreign real estate, and other destinations far from the persistent poverty, endemic corruption and socio-economic stagnation that plagued Nigeria" (2012, 13). Rising elites, benefiting from corruption and nepotism, were able to conspicuously display their prosperity, but the flood of wealth and new commodities in the midst of stagnation often appeared to be enigmatic and confusing, especially considering the fact that it did not seem to come from physical labor or production.

Nigerian audiences who eagerly watched *Living in Bondage* when it was first released were all living in an economy where luxury goods like the ones Andy desires were everywhere visible but increasingly unattainable. This is why, despite his despicable deeds, the audience can most likely sympathize with Andy's initial dilemma and the challenges he faces pursuing the good life. The problem with pursuing wealth in sub-Saharan Africa, they know, is that opportunities to become wealthy via legitimate routes are few and far between. Andy's wife Merit is well aware of this and tells Andy that his friends are only rich because they participate in money doubling schemes or drug-pushing. She would rather see them make do with what they have, but Andy identifies, above all, as a consumer whose existence is contingent on objects. For Andy, not owning an automobile is a source of what he describes as physical malaise: "My body is suffering" is a common refrain for the pre-rich Andy. Yet Andy does not appear to be suffering in any visible, outward manner. Merit has a decent-paying job as a secretary for Ichie Million, and she has even been able to borrow a substantial sum of money from her parents for Andy to start his own business. The couple dresses reasonably well, lives in a small but respectable apartment, and has sufficient food. They are quite far from the millions of Nigerians living in true poverty, and they are certainly not representatives of the *lumpenproletariat* eking out an existence in Nigeria's growing slums. What Andy means, then, is not that his body itself is suffering but that his ego is suffering. It is no coincidence that Ego is the name of the wife who replaces Merit, the one who "deserves" to be Andy's wife, and it is telling that Nnebue should play here on both the English meaning of "ego" and the Igbo meaning of the word, which is "money." When Andy replaces Merit with Ego, he is attempting to add to his self-worth, to increase his value. And Andy's choice to emphasize his corporeal misery is important in understanding his position as a consumer-subject in the neoliberal global economic order that has become the rule of the day.

Andy's body, I suggest, is suffering because he is failing to consume—to nourish his body—in the way that he believes a viable capitalist subject must. Cars become a particular obsession for him because they are the most visible and outward manifestation of the ability of his body to become fully integrated into consumer society. As Marshall McLuhan suggests, cars, like all technologies, are extensions of the physical body, "extensions of our physical and nervous systems to increase power and speed" (2001, 90). It is in this sense that Andy's Mercedes acts not as a carapace but rather as a prosthesis. In *Xala* the car is a carapace because it allows the members of the comprador class to "encase themselves in expensive consumer goods" (Mulvey 1994, 519)—it serves as a shell for some, while leaving others, like the beggars, completely vulnerable and open to the harsh realities of daily life. Likewise, it props up the facade of Senegalese autonomy and helps to perpetuate the illusion that independence has achieved its intended goal of allowing Senegalese citizens a slice of the consumer pie. But in *Living in Bondage,* everyone seems to know that the cult members get rich by appropriating the lifeblood of others; there is no gradual process of revelation here as there is in *Xala.* Merit, in fact, repeatedly rebukes the advances of the Mercedes-driving Chief Omego, whom she directly accuses of matricide, an act that Omego does not deem necessary to deny, and Andy's involvement in Merit's death is hardly a secret. The car, then, does not protect the body, nor does it camouflage the moral transgressions it necessitates. Rather, it serves as the visible sign of the often-invisible duplicity of its owner, and, at the same time, it works to integrate him into a world where these transgressions have become normal.

The prosthesis points not only to the way in which a body has been wounded or disfigured but also to the way in which it can constitute or reconstitute itself with and through material objects and technologies. Unlike the carapace, which is always only an outer shell, the prosthesis joins the body to extend its ability to function as a human. While I do not wish to trivialize or erase the very real disabled bodies that make use of prosthetics (not to mention the nonprivileged disabled bodies that often have to make do without prosthetics), the prosthesis serves as a useful way to understand how Andy inhabits the car as an extension of the self and relies on it to constitute himself as a "normal" consumer subject. Normal, of course, is always a highly unstable term, but for Andy it seems to indicate a certain standard of living that consists of owning a car and a house and knowing that one has a steady flow of income. As Charissa Terranova argues, the automotive prosthetic, which she reads as both a literal and figurative prosthesis, "transforms the technologically enhanced body" into an ambiguous self that "is at once mutilated and mechanically reborn" (2014, 58). Like a prosthetic limb, the Mercedes adds to or extends Andy's ability to participate in the sensuous world of consumer society and to reinvent himself by filling the wound created by his missing wages—wages he should have been able to obtain through honest work. It helps him to navigate a world in which subjects are defined by the objects from which they are simultaneously kept at arm's length. But at the same time, it makes him dependent on an artificial body: his self-worth is contingent on the possession of a machine. In other words, the Mercedes both extends Andy's agency and limits it. In the process of pursuing his dream of automobility, Andy loses his autonomy. Although he obtains a car, he becomes subject to the demands of the cult, and eventually he finds his own actions determined more by the ghost of Merit than by his own free will.

Despite its focus on Andy's initial exclusion from capitalist consumption, *Living in Bondage* is replete with multiple extended scenes depicting grandiose displays of wealth. The scene at Ichie Million's party, for instance, takes up sixteen minutes of screen time and contains very little dialogue. Here the millionaires gorge themselves on meat and dance to Oliver de Coque's song *Ana enwe obodo enwe* ("We Own the World"). By contrast, Andy's descent into madness under a highway overpass takes up only five minutes of screen time, and it does not occur until over four hours into the five-hour film. The plot advances the moral lesson that the personal accumulation of wealth, no matter what the given obstacles are, should not be pursued at the expense of others. However, the visual images of abundant wealth send a more ambivalent message: they place the conspicuous consumption of the urban elite on display and confirm the fact that there is indeed much money to be made in Lagos.

At the end of the film, when Andy and Tina both embrace the church, Nnebue intimates that another point of entry into bourgeois respectability

Figure 21. Living in Bondage. *"I hear they've all bought a Mercedes Benz each." Andy complains to Merit that his friends have Mercedes-Benzes.*

Figure 22. Living in Bondage. *"Is this your car?" Andy runs into his friend Paul and admires Paul's Mercedes.*

Figure 23. Living in Bondage. *"If you have money, everyone—the high and the mighty—will bow for you." Andy is persuaded to join the cult of Lord Lucifer.*

is possible. Although the audience is not sure whether the church will lead Andy to material prosperity, the narrative logic of the film—and of many Nigerian churches that now offer profit through prayer—certainly does not foreclose the potential for this type of financial redemption. Considering the fact that many popular Pentecostal churches in Africa now preach the "prosperity gospel" in which material wealth—often embodied in the Mercedes of the pastor[20]—can also act as the sign of moral righteousness, Andy very well might be able to regain at least some of his former status. What has come under attack in the film then is not the dream of automobility but rather the immoral method Andy has taken to pursue this dream. As Hyginus Ekwuazi argues, *Living in Bondage* charts the cultural shift in contemporary Igbo society in which the "atomized individual" is now prioritized above the community and capital is now accumulated at the individual level rather than as a collective (2000, 138). Andy's punishment—the madness that overtakes him when his individual aspirations become overinflated—is retribution "that, significantly, does not take place, as it would have in Western films, in a quiet corner, away from the rest of the world" but rather "is enacted coram populo—in full assembly of the community—upholding, thereby, the *collective* ethos of the people" (136). Being integrated into the church therefore signifies Andy's reentry into the community, and, tellingly, he's brought there in a collective van, the only non-private vehicle we see in the film.

The Dream of Development

It is perhaps not surprising that the first major Nollywood success is a film about how one acquires money in a post-oil-boom economy. Nollywood is predominantly a profit-generating enterprise that rejects the model established by African celluloid filmmakers who rely heavily on funding from governments or international agencies, exhibit primarily at film festivals and embassies, and do not expect to make much money from their filmmaking.[21] Nollywood video-makers produce films without foreign and state financing and they are therefore dependent on consumer tastes and the popularity of each film in a way that celluloid filmmakers are not. Though this is changing as the industry blossoms, initially Nollywood video-makers would hope to make just enough money from one video to be able to fund the next. And still today, they try to sell the bulk of their films in the first several weeks after release in order to recoup costs as quickly as possible and to stay ahead of pirates who will soon be selling cheaper copies. Their ultimate goal, then, is to make a film that will be immediately recognizable, popular, and profitable. If a film flops in the marketplace, or if pirates get an advanced copy, the film becomes a liability.[22] As Haynes writes, "The Nigerian films are always commercial calculations: if they do not make their money back, it is a disaster for the filmmakers, something that has not been true for much or most [Francophone] African cinema" (2014, 58). Like the characters in their films, many video-makers are often figuring out how to garner wealth, how to keep their heads above water, and how to do so in an economy driven by informality and illicit exchange. And, again, like the characters, video-makers often have to seek out individual solutions to collective economic problems. As McCall argues, the Nollywood video industry, like much of the Nigerian economy, is a "network of scattered informal economic activities and interactions held back from capitalization because the system depends on informal practices to produce and distribute its products" (2012, 11).

Initially, Nollywood was a reaction to economic crisis and the surplus of laborers—sparked by new circuits of capital and the global shortage of liquidity—that began to plague most West African countries in the 1980s.[23] According to Onookome Okome, Nigerian video films first emerged during the post-oil-boom economic collapse of the mid-1980s when Yoruba theater groups turned to the new technology of the VHS cassette in order to be able to continue performing during times when theater patronage was in decline (2007, 2). By recording their plays on video, or "canning" them, and selling cassette copies, they could generate enough profit to fund their subsequent performances. At the same time, economic hardships made it increasingly difficult for Nigerian state television stations to survive, and many directors and technicians who had been released from their positions turned to the widely available videocassette technology and began making low-budget films to sell or rent for a small profit (Haynes and Okome 2000, 57).[24] As both VCRs and VHSs became cheaper and security issues under military rule made it unsafe to attend cinemas at night, the Nigerian video film industry boomed, and today the success of the industry is a point of immense pride.[25]

Though video-makers often struggle with power outages, inadequate roads, slow Internet speeds, and other infrastructural impediments, they create a dream world where cities look and function like idealized images of Los Angeles, Las Vegas, or Dubai. As Garritano argues, "A split between narrative condemnation and visual desire structure the movies. Narratives denounce and punish the greedy or selfish protagonist, engaging the spectator as a moral witness, while a visual economy of pleasure that aestheticizes consumption addresses the spectator as a desiring subject" (2013, 11). Many films, in fact, will open by positioning the camera inside the protagonist's Mercedes or SUV as he or she passes by high-rises, fancy restaurants, large hotels, or wealthy neighborhoods like Lagos Island or Accra's Osu.[26] The camera often lingers on modern infrastructure and the smoothly functioning technologies that the characters own and operate. Roads are wide, gutters are covered, and cars are not constantly breaking down and sputtering. Amid what Andrew Apter describes as the "pervasive condition of verisimilitude and dissimulation" (1999, 287) of everyday life in West Africa, video-makers have constructed their own world of simulacra where the infrastructure is up to par with Western standards, where those who cheat the system are held accountable, and where modern Christian cosmopolitanism triumphs over witchcraft and sorcery. As noted film scholar Christian Metz argues, capitalist cinema is a dream code, a conscious fantasy that can be read and interpreted as the projection of the spectator's latent wishes. And though many of Nollywood's filmmakers may not have had access to the banks and formal centers of capital, they do, I argue, aspire to make movies that reflect the audience's capitalist desires.

For Metz one of the ways the cinematic apparatus participates in an economy of pleasure is by offering the viewer a glimpse of what is absent, but always desirable, thereby leaving the spectator in a state of heightened anticipation. Cinematic framing and camera movement, he suggests, reveal space to the spectator in a type of generalized striptease where the camera partially undresses its objects but always reserves and exercises the power to dress again. In video films where less attention is paid to the details of each shot composition, it is largely the setting that accomplishes these "veiling and unveiling processes" as directors alternate images of a glistening modernized city full of mansions, boutiques, and fancy cars with its seedy underside and spaces of cult worship, prostitutes, and uncollected trash. The camera therefore captures the spectators' very conscious dream of development while simultaneously showing it to be a chimera at best, a nightmare at worst.[27] In *Living in Bondage,* we see Andy in his mansion, Andy in his Mercedes, Andy at a lavish party, but we also get Andy trembling before the cult of Lord Lucifer and, at the end of the film, Andy digging through trash heaps under a bridge. In *Blood Money,* as I'll discuss below, the modern and the occult spaces are often folded into each other:

a zombie boy resides inside a beautiful mansion, cult members practice their rituals in a high-rise office building, and victims of occult murder are transported in the boot of the Benz. By reminding the audience of the coexistence of these two types of spaces, the video films "gamble simultaneously on the excitation of desire and its non-fulfillment (which is its opposite and yet favours it)" (Metz 1977, 77). In other words, the desire for goods, their simultaneous scarcity and visibility, and the spiritual compromises one must endure to attain them are precisely what makes these movies so popular and so reflective of the pleasures and moral anxieties that Nigerians navigate on a daily basis. Indeed, in the world of Nigerian video film owning a fleet of luxury cars and drinking the blood of a friend's wife do not appear to be contradictory: they are both a part of what it means to succeed in modern Lagos.

According to Brian Larkin, it is precisely this mixture of spiritualism and consumerism that makes the video film an entirely new form of cultural expression. Larkin emphasizes the fact that video films are about "stimulation not cultivation" (2008, 192), that they reject the didactic "developmentalist" films produced by both the colonial government and the nationalist postcolonial state. In fact, he argues that the most "rationalist" characters in the video films—the bankers, the businessmen in suits, and the government officials—are the most likely to be involved in occultism (192). Rather than addressing the viewer as one to be "uplifted," he points out that Nollywood hinges on "an aesthetics of outrage" where the narrative is organized around events that shock and outrage the viewer (172). Clearly, one can see this type of aesthetic at play in *Living in Bondage* when Andy, after initially drawing sympathy, becomes a moral pariah, an appalling example of greed. And yet while "stimulation" and moral shock are indeed crucial to the videos' aesthetics and to distinguishing them from other forms of media, I am suggesting that in the video films the seedy occult economies commingle with an economy of desire that is both rationalist and, in a certain sense, developmentalist. What becomes important is punishing individuals who have violated codes of morality not just by putting the individual ahead of the greater good but also by bastardizing modernity, by turning high-rise office buildings into spaces of cult worship, by using their Benzes to kidnap young children, or by transforming human beings into zombies.[28]

In other words, the films are not developmentalist in the sense that they show characters on some well-tread path to modernity, but they are developmentalist in the way that they project a "first class" standard of living that is attainable and, at the same time, threatened by those who pursue individual success at all costs. And though Nollywood films reflect the anxiety and anger about the way wealth is accumulated in a post-oil-boom Nigeria rife with unemployment, they also clear space for dreams of upward mobility and fantasies of the good life—a life filled with consumer goods, large homes, and working infrastructure. In this way, the videos illustrate the simultaneous resentment for and attraction to the new elite who parade through cities in luxury cars but are often suspected of illegitimate trade or occult activity.

The Boot of the Benz: *Blood Money*

One way to make sense of the contradictions inherent in Nollywood films is to place them in the context of local rumors and understand them as works of art that dramatize everyday stories that circulate in the marketplace, living rooms, and local tabloids. Ojiofor Ezeanyaeche's occult video *Blood Money* provides an indicative case study of the way in which the anxieties present in word-of-mouth stories, also called *fabu,* become the basis for successful films that resonate with local and regional audiences. Frances Harding argues that "'fabu' often focus on one mystery in particular: the changes in the lives of individuals which take them from poverty to wealth by 'unseen' methods, i.e., not through openly trading or farming, for example, or by good husbandry, but by means of exchanges and dealings invisible to the ordinary person" (2007, 10). Accordingly, *Blood Money,* set in Lagos, is a melodrama loosely based on local rumors of ritual murder and illegitimate wealth that crystallized during the famous Otokoto Saga. In September of 1996, the local news station in Owerri in southeastern Nigeria broadcast images of a worker at the popular Otokoto Hotel holding the severed head of a young boy. Several days later, the police found the rest of the boy's body buried at the hotel. The sudden death of the hotel worker in police custody (a possible cover-up for police involvement) and the discovery of the rest of the body at the hotel led to a series of riots in Owerri and a flood of rumors concerning the discovery of more human corpses at millionaires' homes and at a local church. The assumption was that these bodies had been killed in blood money rituals, rituals that had lead the murderers to wealth and prosperity.

According to the anthropologist Daniel Jordan Smith, the rioters in Owerri attacked only symbols of the young elite and the religious and state powers that were rumored to support them. They burned, among other things, fancy vehicles, the Otokoto Hotel, an upscale supermarket, expensive homes, and the palace of a local chief. The riots were seen largely as a purging of the "connected evils" of kidnapping, ritual murder, and the accumulation of illegitimate wealth through 419 crimes (2001, 804). Although it was widely known that the nouveaux riches of Owerri—like those throughout Nigeria—were 419 men, operating largely with either tacit or direct support of government officials and church leaders, according to Smith, the discovery of the headless boy at the hotel seemed to confirm long-standing rumors that these men were also involved in ritual murder and the trafficking of human body parts.

The storyline of *Blood Money* roughly follows that of *Living in Bondage,* but it also makes explicit reference to many of the rumors that exploded in Nigeria in the aftermath of the Otokoto scandal. For instance, Smith, who was doing fieldwork in Owerri at the time of the riots, describes rumors about a boy who died vomiting banknotes in his uncle's home and others about men who were temporarily turned into vultures so that their businesses could flourish. Both of these rumors made their way into the plot of *Blood Money,* which follows the story of Mike Mouka, a bank manager who, at the urging of his greedy wife, misappropriates money for a laundering scheme. When Mike himself becomes the victim of fraud and is unable to repay the money, the bank discovers his theft and threatens to send him to prison if he cannot replenish the funds. His only choice, it seems, is to join a blood money cult and commit unspeakable acts. Like *Living in Bondage, Blood Money* is a morality tale that focuses on magical money cults and the extent to which men will kill and sacrifice their friends or family in order to attain the material possessions they covet. But *Blood Money* is a darker version of *Living in Bondage.* Here, the dreamed-of good life turns into a nightmare, a world where human vultures, zombies, and ritual murderers inhabit modern city spaces and are supported by corrupt government officials who believe that, as a crooked police officer says, "today the ends justify the means." And in *Blood Money* the luxury car is not just an incarnation of upward mobility; it also acts as both a symbol of and a tool for illegitimate trade and occult activity.

Like the rioters in Owerri, *Blood Money* targets the outward signs, the specific *things* of the capitalist market, in part to express anger but also in part to create an alternative spectacle by calling attention to the excesses and horrors of the new elite. Smith quotes the following newspaper article that articulates one way in which the highly mobile 419 men are viewed in Nigeria:

> The result is that big designer and exotic cars were bought, huge magnificent mansions and castles were built in villages for rodents and insects because their owners were always either in Lagos or overseas. A new class of *"Nouveaux Riches"* emerged. They moved in convoys of about six cars on the largely untarred roads. The first, usually a jeep, often a Nissan Pathfinder followed by another jeep (this time either a Mitsubishi Pajero, Izuzu *[sic]* Rodeo or the American Cherokee), then the man in the Lexus brand of car followed by an American Limousine (carrying wife and children where he is married), escorted by two V-Boot Benz cars. . . . Whenever they spoke money was splashed. (2001, 815)

And in *Blood Money,* as is often the case in Nollywood films, shots of groups of criminals pulling up to a party, a meeting, or a club in their luxury cars appear again and again. What is implicit, though certainly not emphasized in the video's aesthetics, is that these parades often obstruct traffic on the road, that the mobility of the wealthy and corrupt cause the immobility of the ordinary people.

As *Blood Money* opens, we find out that Mike is desperately trying to figure out how to pay the bank back for the funds he "borrowed." He has already sold his two cars and is panicked that his boss will soon discover the missing money. In the next scene, the camera follows the Mercedes of one Chief Collins as he travels down Lagos's boulevards with high-rises prominent in the background. Eventually, Collins arrives at a morgue and the camera lingers in a low-angle shot on the Benz. The odd angle—it is rare in a film to see a car shot from such a position—establishes the Mercedes as an imposing figure, and would indicate to any viewer familiar with the reputation of 419 men that Collins is up to no good. And indeed, he waits in the car as his muscular driver heads in to the morgue to collect body parts: a heart, a liver, and lungs. When the organs are delivered to Collins, the Mercedes becomes a meeting room and a trading partner joins him in the back seat, gravely disappointed in Collins for not having procured human breasts. From the beginning, then, the Mercedes acts as a site of perverse mobility: Collins uses it not just to move through traffic but to traffic in human body parts. And when Collins and Mike are introduced to each other by their mutual friend, a corrupt police officer named Clem, Mike too joins his world of vulgarized capitalist accumulation. Because Mike is a friend of Clem's, Chief Collins offers to let Mike join his cult of "Vulture Men" and assures Mike that once he submits to the cult, he will not have any trouble repaying the bank. Like Andy Okeke, Mike is initially repulsed by the idea, but eventually he is seduced by the promise of riches and the good life. As a sacrifice to the cult, he first offers his own mother, whom he kills with a magical death cloth, and then he is turned into a vulture for three days while he feeds on human flesh.[29] At the end of the three days, Mike is turned back into a human and is told to bring the cult a young boy. The boy is transformed into a zombie that spews out an endless supply of fresh banknotes, and Mike is instructed to keep him locked away in a hidden room of his house.

As in *Living in Bondage,* several hours of the film are consumed with spectacles of Mike enjoying his newfound wealth. But while Mike accumulates cars and other material goods, the zombified boy, immobilized in Mike's mansion, becomes the antithesis of an autonomous, mobile subject. He is a complete automaton, the ultimate figure of alienated labor and of the disempowered victims of a rapacious capitalism. As Garritano writes, "The boy no longer speaks or moves, but exists as bare life and only to create money, which pools all around his small body. But one body is never enough, and the men must find other sacrifices to stave off poverty. Cultists prowl the city for disposable bodies, typically poor women who work as house cleaners, road-side merchants, or prostitutes, and they use their bodies in the rituals that produce their wealth" (2012a, 59). And as the "Great Vulture" begins to demand more human heads, Mike too becomes an automaton of the cult. He is turned into a killing machine and given a magical mirror in which to conjure the images of his victims, but, like Andy, Mike cannot escape the torment of his victims' ghosts.

While Mike's actions are despicable, he is, to some extent, seen as the victim of his wife's initial desire for more money, the fraudsters' dishonesty, and the Great Vulture's quest for human blood. The real scorn in the film seems to be reserved for Chief Collins, who cruises the town in his menacing Mercedes to look for people to dismember. In what is perhaps the pivotal moment of the film—and the one moment when the mobility and trafficking of the cultists is actually stopped in it tracks—Chief Collins's Benz is pulled over at a police roadblock. Collins is not in the car, but his cronies have the dead bodies of two young boys in the trunk, boys that in a previous scene had been tricked into the car by the promise of a small job. In a scene reminiscent of the opening of *Goodfellas,* the police open the trunk and discover the bodies. The henchman are captured and tortured and eventually confess to working for Collins. In the next scene, Mike looks into the mirror that he uses to conjure images of his future victims, but this time, rather than showing him the person he is about to kill, the mirror shatters and Mike's victim escapes. I read the juxtaposition of these two scenes as a comment on the way in which Collins's Mercedes, like Mike's paranormal mirror, again acts as a prosthetic extension of the self. But whereas Andy Okeke's Mercedes was a prosthetic that would allow him access to the pleasures of global modernity, Collins's Mercedes and Mike's mirror (a mirror that reflects his victims rather than his own image) become an extension or reflection of a vulgarized self. The car and the mirror are both "stopped" at the same moment because they are both objects that have morphed the human into the monstrous.

Today, as was the case in the colonial-era stories Luise White describes, the occult anxieties people have about cars are linked to the obscure and mysterious labor practices of their owners, which suggests why ritual murderers and criminals like Mike, Chief Collins, Chief Omego, and Andy are often identified by and coupled with their cars. (And in the Ghanaian movie *Girl at 18* a businessman who kills young women and sells their organs to European colleagues is even named "Black Jaguar," after his car.)[30] What Nollywood's occult melodramas do is force the enigmatic money-making activities, like organ trading, 419 fraud, and cult ritual, into a public space where it can be judged according to the audience's moral codes. Prying open the trunk of Collins's Mercedes and the shattering of Mike's mirror, then, are not just acts of exposing the truth, just like *Blood Money* is not merely an explanation of why some men and women seem to have no problem accumulating wealth. Rather, these moments are just as visceral and affective as they are symbolic. Here, the audience becomes virtual Owerri rioters who can take pleasure in the destruction of the monstrous prosthetic, the excessive parade of goods that comes at the cost of human life. But they can also take pleasure in the fact that, at long last, the criminals will be held accountable. As Moradewun Adejunmobi writes, "Nollywood's audiences are entranced by the spectacle of odious human behavior matched only by the certainty of commensurate judgment" (2010, 111). And in *Blood Money,* the characters who are judged are those very automobile, car-owning subjects who have impinged on the personal liberties and mobility of others by taking their lives, their organs, or their free will—they have, in fact, acted against the liberal ideals of automobility and the pursuit of personal freedom by denying this pursuit to others.

Inherent in the film, then, is a humanist critique of the object or prosthetic that enables the formation of subjects who have devalued human life. While celebrants of what Terranova calls "the automotive prosthetic" often exalt the posthuman body that can willfully re-create itself through technology, *Blood Money,* like other occult melodramas, is concerned with the proliferation of "disposable bodies" that become (immobilized) collateral damage in the quest of upward mobility. Moreover, in Collins's nefarious dealings—where bodies are being bought and sold and transported in tight spaces—there are strong echoes of the trans-Atlantic slave trade. For Gilroy, such echoes also exist in African American vernacular culture where cars are sometimes referred to as "whips," as is the case in *Get Rich or Die Tryin.* Gilroy argues that this term "suggests that deeply repressed and fragmentary acknowledgements of the painful slave past may be quietly active, undergirding the patterns of sometimes ostentatious and excessive market behaviour associated with black consumerism in general and the African American desire for automobiles in particular" (2010, 16). But in *Blood Money,* the traffic in human bodies, a traffic that leads to wealth for a select few, is neither repressed nor fragmentary: it is front and center; it is exposed and judged accordingly.

As Arjun Appadurai argues, the global trade in human body parts, as well as the trade of whole humans as laborers, is one of the forms of the flexibility of globalization. It represents for him the "new circulatory logics" of global finance and typifies a world no longer marked by the "social life of things" (as his earlier work suggests) but by the liquidity and malleability of humans in the marketplace. In *Blood Money,* the Vulture Men meet in a high-rise building, they live in mansions, dress in the latest global fashions, and trade on the international market. They are clearly no strangers to the world Appadurai describes, "in which cyborgs meet flexible citizens, clones meet split subjects, and organs for sale meet cyber sociality" (1999, 36). However, the objects that they use to define themselves and to participate in the global networks of trade indicate that the world of services or practices and the world of things are inseparable and mutually dependent. Furthermore, to relegate the world of objects to the margins is to miss the point that possessions, like Collins's Mercedes, represent a world of values gone awry where the human body is something that can be replaced by

Figure 24. Blood Money. *Chief Collins pulls up to the morgue and meets with one of his business partners in the back of his Mercedes.*

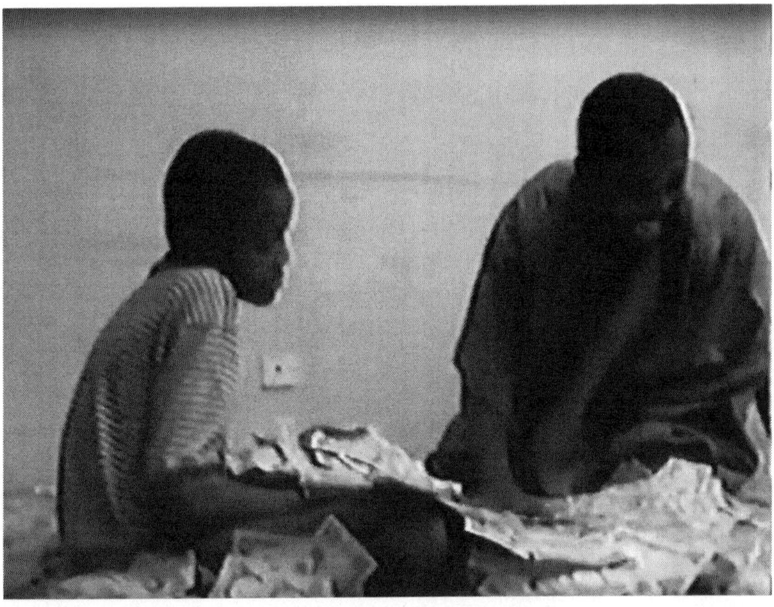

Figure 25. Blood Money. *A zombie boy spits out cash for Mike.*

material goods, where the Mercedes is tied both to vehicular traffic and the trafficking of bodies and organs. And it is this type of critique that is present in virtually all the occult melodramas that launched the Nollywood film industry in the 1990s and that carries over to the 419 film genre that, in the early 2000s, popularized stories about Internet scammers and what Nigerians call "advanced fee" fraud.

"First Thing Na Hummer": *Boys Cot*

Like the protagonists in *Living in Bondage* and *Blood Money,* the young men in Afam Okereke's 419 film *Boys Cot* are trying to figure out how to become financially successful subjects in an economy where wealth is often acquired in very opaque ways. But rather than turning to blood money cults, the protagonists of *Boys Cot* take advantage of increasingly available communication technology and enter into the world of Internet fraud. Beginning around 2005, particularly with the release of Andy Amenechi's highly popular 419 film *The Master* (2005), Internet and advance fee fraud have become the subject of many films that, like occult melodramas, attempt to demystify the often obscured workings of neoliberal capitalism. These films dramatize a variety of different scams where someone is tricked into sending money to a Nigerian bank account or asked to pay some sort of "advance fee" in order to secure a contract or to have funds released. For instance, a victim might be contacted to help a widow secure her husband's fortune that is stashed away in a Swiss bank and asked to pay certain fees up front with the promise of receiving millions later. Though the victim is often strung along, required to pay several fees, and eventually receives nothing for his efforts, his own willingness to circumvent the law and his eagerness to receive millions of dollars for doing nothing makes him somewhat complicit. And because the crimes the scammers commit are often not as heinous as those committed by the cultists, 419 films have a slightly more nuanced relationship to the luxury goods they exhibit.

In *Blood Money* Chief Collins and Mike Mouka represent the worst sort of criminals because their participation in the occult economy is motivated by sheer greed. Most audience members do not identify, nor can they sympathize, with rich men trying to get richer. When Collins is arrested and the ghosts of Mike's murder victims hunt him down and turn him back into a vulture, the audience feels vindicated. Yet, as Andrew Apter points out, in certain cases—especially when the crimes are nonviolent—there is a degree of Robinhood-esque righteousness attached to 419 scams. Because 419 scams often dupe corrupt businessmen and politicians or "First World" victims who have typically been the ones to benefit from the flows of global capital, 419 can be seen as a form of wealth redistribution. For instance, the chorus to "I Go Chop Your Dollar," the theme song to *The Master* that became independently popular, repeats the refrain, "419 no be thief. It's just a game. . . . I am the master. *You* are the *mugu*. . . . I am the winner. You are the loser." In *The Master,* a comedic 419 film, the main character, Dennis, joins a group of scammers after he is scammed by them himself. The film tracks the way Dennis transforms from ignorant country bumpkin to a skilled performer who is able to use dress, costumes, and fleets of automobiles in order to trick his victims into thinking he is a legitimate, wealthy businessman. Though some of Dennis's dupes are innocent, he seems to be engaging in 419 scams at first in order to recoup his original losses. And as he continues, it becomes clear that those he tricks are often the types of foreigners who come to Nigeria eager to take advantage of corrupt business practices. In many 419 films, the scams attempt to reverse the power dynamics that have long-since placed "Third World" subjects in positions where they are anything but "master." And since the 419 schemes—that is, when they do not involve murder and kidnapping—work with the somewhat willing participation of greedy victims *(mugus)* who believe that they too will profit from the scam, there is a sense that the 419ers, many of whom come from humble backgrounds, are simply using the tools of global modernity, such as the Internet, fax machines, cell phones, and international banking, to their own advantage. They are in essence fighting back against the unevenness of global capitalism with the very resources it has generated.

In *Boys Cot* the main characters—Kelvin, Philip, and Duran—have just finished their stints in the National Youth Service Corps and are excited about moving into the "real" world, making money, and starting families. However, four years after their graduation, Kelvin, who dreamt of becoming a big oil executive, is working for a small company but is not earning enough money to pay the rent on his three-bedroom apartment. He has also lied to his girlfriend, telling her that he works for Chevron, and is now expected to buy her new clothes and pay her school fees. Philip is unemployed and desperately trying to get a visa to the United States. He is constantly fighting with his father, a civil servant who doesn't have the money to send him abroad. After threatening to cut off his father's head, Philip screams, "I've been combing every nook and cranny. I want to work but there's no work. . . . I'm going mad." Duran, who is shown carousing in a Hummer, wearing designer clothes, and living in a mansion, is the only one able to live the lifestyle they all desire because he has become the assistant to a prosperous 419 man. Duran has all the outward signs of success and global citizenry that his friends lack.

Yet Duran feels that his boss, who has a bigger home and several Benzes at his disposal, should be paying him more. He decides to go out on his own, and he enlists the help of Kelvin, Philip, and Philip's girlfriend, Cleo. The group spends months stationed at Internet cafés looking for *mugus,* or fraud victims, until finally they find a wealthy and gullible Westerner willing to send them $500,000. (Because the successful "hit" occurs moments after Kelvin complains that they have spent time doing rituals for nothing, the film suggests that their luck has changed because of some occult practice. But unlike in the occult melodramas above, witchcraft is not shown, and is simply just a passing reference or explanation as to why the scamming suddenly works.) Once they have their initial seed money, they are able to reel in dubious Nigerian politicians looking to hide their illegitimate money as well as avaricious foreigners who are eager to make fast money.

It is only when they begin to target innocent victims that they lose audience sympathy and begin to attract the attention of the police. Kelvin, posing as a white American, meets a British woman on the Internet, becomes engaged to her, and then dupes her out of her entire life savings. Then, in a scheme that takes him months to execute, Kelvin sells Philip's sister to a Kuwaiti slave trafficker by convincing her that the Kuwaiti works for Steven Spielberg and will be helping her to make it big in Hollywood. Philip's father, who notices his son's new automobiles, assumes that Philip has killed his sister in a cult ritual. But unlike in *The Master,* which comically plays on the fact that scammers become "masters" rather than victims, Kelvin's actions, which again connect him to slave traffickers or "masters" of the past, are neither lighthearted nor justifiable.

As was the case with the occult melodramas, Kelvin, Philip, Duran, and Cleo epitomize both the ideals and excesses of automobility, which in this film, seem to be captured in the Hummers and SUVs that were popularized around the start of the Iraq War in 2003. As Terranova argues, the Hummer, modeled off the American High Mobility Multipurpose Wheeled Vehicle (HMMWV, or Humvee), served as an icon of normalized cultural militarism in the United States: "Obfuscating the brutality of the real war, the Hummer embodies a fantasy world of denial defined according to a myth not only of endless oil reserves, but of manifest destiny, homeland security, and American exceptionalism.... It promotes an ideology of radical self-governance which, similar to its drivers' oblivion of the war, can be fathomed without true recognition of the anarchy such statelessness brings" (2014, 192). Commenting on African Americans' participation in SUV culture in the early 2000s, Gilroy makes a similar remark and argues that embracing such individualized automobility emphasized the political disconnect between blacks in the "oil-seeking" United States and those in Nigeria protesting oil companies like Shell. Indeed, the Hummers and SUVs showcased in *Boys Cot,* and the majority of Nollywood films made around then, do indeed seem to reinforce the idea of "radical self-governance," and, in a sense, Gilroy's argument could be extended to apply to the Nigerian urban elite who are often just as politically distanced from the Nigerians suffering from environmental degradation in the Niger Delta as the African American elite.

But I see the SUVs and Hummers in Nollywood as occupying a more ambivalent position. To begin with, their popularity in Nigeria comes in the wake of military rule, which ended in 1999 with the election of Olusegun Obasanjo, and not, as is the case with the United States, in the midst of "preemptive" war. The presence of Hummers and SUVs in popular video films does not therefore repress "the violent realities of war" (Terranova 2014, 192), but rather brings to the fore the imbrication of violence and consumer culture that persists in a postmilitary period where, in the face of government corruption, lack of basic services, and rampant nepotism, "radical self-governance" continues to be one of the few paths to financial success given the lack of state support and formal employment opportunities. In *Boys Cot* the 419ers drive their Hummers and SUVs around the city to show that they can move about when and how they please. They cruise around and use their money to bribe government officials and purchase false documents that give them access to places and pools of information that are usually off limits. Cleo even buys herself a university degree. Like Georges-Marie Haardt and Louis Audouin-Dubreuil crossing the Sahara in Citroën half-tracks, they have used technology to conquer space, and although the Internet is the tool they have used to do so, their large automobiles remain the most recognizable signs of their success.

The film, in fact, opens with a scene in which Duran spends several minutes speeding through the city in his Hummer with a girl and a bottle of Hennessy at his side. Although the scene is never connected to the plot and, in fact, occurs temporally out of place, it serves as an invitation for the audience to join along in the consumption on display and to experience its delights. In the first shot of the film, we see Duran's black Hummer driving toward the camera at dusk. The streets are smoothly paved, there is almost no traffic, and there are no itinerant vendors, motorcycles, or buses. The segment, about a minute and a half long, alternates between two cameras. One is tracking the Hummer as it drives through this wealthy neighborhood. The other is in the backseat of the car, capturing Duran's shoulder and arm, the steering wheel, the girl's shoulder and arm (holding the bottle of Hennessy), and the view through the windshield. In this way, the viewer becomes a passenger, and the windshield (or windscreen) becomes another lens through which to view Lagos. Unlike African art films, there is no irony, no distancing: the viewer at this particular moment is supposed to feel connected to the pleasure being reproduced on the screen. It is also worth noting that the production values of this scene are quite professional, that the technology of Nollywood has gotten much better since the 1990s and can therefore more easily reproduce images of speeding cars, which requires high levels of coordination and, in the case of *Boys Cot's* opening sequence, either multiple cameras or multiple takes. Just as the proliferation of technologies allows for 419 scams (and 419 films), it also allows for more aesthetically appealing images of consumption.

As the Hummer zips through the city, Duran and his companion are singing along to Olu Maintain's hit "Yahoozee," a song that played constantly on the radio and in clubs the year *Boys Cot* was released and that was likely inspired by 50 Cent's anthem to auto and upward mobility, "Poor Lil Rich." The word "Yahoozee" comes from Yahoo, the email host used by most of the original Internet scammers, and refers to the actual fraudsters (also sometimes called Yahoo Boys), to the act of 419, or, in the case of Olu Maintain's song, to both a dance craze and to the upscale lifestyle of fraudsters. The lyrics to "Yahoozee" celebrate the high-flying standard of living that operates at what the song calls, in a made-up and slang term, a "kentro level," a level way above the rest. Olu Maintain (the stage name for artist Olumide Edwards) sings, "If I hammer, first thing na Hummer" ("once I hit the jackpot, first thing is the Hummer").[31] In the music video, which begins with a shot of a black Hummer almost identical to Duran's, Olu, sporting a belt buckle made of a stack of dollar bills, stands in front of a row of seven cars, each with a license plate embossed with a day of the week. As the camera pans the Audis, Mercedes-Benzes, and different colored Hummers, Olu sings, "Monday, Tuesday, Wednesday, Thursday, boys dey hustle. Friday, Saturday, Sunday, Gbogbo aiye. Champagne, Hennessy, Moet for everybody." (*Gbogbo aiye* can be translated to "we live it up.") In *Boys Cot* these are the words that Duran and his friend are singing along to as they drive through the city, and when Olu Maintain sings about Hennessy, Duran's friend raises their bottle of Hennessy so that it takes up a large portion of the screen. Okereke makes Duran's actions and lifestyle visibly and audibly match that of Olu Maintain's, capitalizing on the success of "Yahoozee" and making *Boys Cot* part of the popular discourse about 419 men and their cars. The singer himself admits that he made a similar move when he wrote "Yahoozee" and capitalized on an already popular dance of the same name (2013). Like the characters in the films, Nigerian artists use the images and cultural symbols of the marketplace for self-advancement.

Notably, "Yahoozee" also plays in a club scene when, in part 3 of the film, Duran and Cleo run into a government minister that Cleo has just duped out of a large sum of money after promising him that she would hide his illicit funds in a Swiss bank account. In this scene the minister spots Cleo on a packed dance floor where dancers are imitating the moves of the "Yahoozee" video by keeping their legs planted as their arms move in multiple directions. Jeremy Weate argues, "Standing firm as your arms slowly spin in circles with pointed fingers is the illusion of movement underpinned by the reality of stasis. Yahoozee is therefore the reflection of a listless youth, with no direction, no intention, no master plan, no resistance, no politics, no ideas. All the youth can do, while dancing Yahoozee, is to think idly about those who are living large out of fraud, and slowly consider the prospect for themselves" (2008). Indeed, as the partiers in *Boys Cot* dance the Yahoozee, Olu Maintain's lyrics match the (often unfulfilled) desire for global mobility: he sings about going to Tokyo, Jamaica, and even just spending a few days in Germany. And, as Weate seems to suggest, there might be a certain irony that those so often stuck in Nigeria and stuck at a certain economic level will move to and embrace this dance and the lyrics. But I also think that the song, with its catchy upbeat Afro hip-hop rhythm, and its celebration of Hummers, "Benjamins," and world travel provides a dreamscape that allows one not to be stuck in a rut of despair, despite pervasive unemployment. In fact, the next time "Yahoozee" plays in *Boys Cot,* Duran runs into a friend and ex-girlfriend who turned on him when he was broke. He hands each of them a stack of money and then asks them to move out of his way, saying, "This is a very expensive car. I don't want it to run over anything cheap." The "Yahoozee" soundtrack kicks in as the Hummer pulls out and the camera zooms in on their astonished faces. In this case, "Yahoozee" becomes more than just a reflection of the "listless youth." It becomes an anthem, a reminder that success is possible for those willing to play the system, that global technologies are there for the taking, and that objects can extend one's power and speed in society.

This extension of power also becomes evident in the case of Cleo, who, at the beginning of the film, has resorted to prostituting herself in order to help get money for Philip's American visa. After becoming a successful 419er, Cleo pulls up to her girlfriends' apartment in a new, red SUV. Her two friends immediately begin ogling the car, caressing it, and peering inside. But their initial assumption is that Cleo has gotten the car from a sugar daddy. Indeed, in many instances the women who drive fancy cars in Nollywood films are good-time girls, prostitutes, or the wives and mistresses of corrupt or philandering wealthy men. But Cleo surprises her friends when she says, "Girls, please, I run things these days, things don't run me. I make my money pure and simple. I just make money work for me, so I don't need to sleep with any rotten fool to get me one of these." Her friends nod in approval and respond, "That's power, girlfriend." Unlike prostitution, in which Cleo exchanges her body for money or gifts, here she has the control: she makes the money work for her and she flaunts her car as a sign of her independence and autonomy from men. Her friend's "that's power" comment suggests a sort of feminism through consumerism, an inverted Marxist feminism, where private property becomes the solution to rather than the cause of female dependence. While I discuss this more in the following chapter on women drivers, here I want simply to note that 419 enables Cleo's self-mobility, that it allows her to drive around the city as her own woman.

However, if automobility is about the liberal pursuit of personal freedom—about the ability to be able to do what one wants, when one wants—the characters in *Boys Cot* are clearly hemmed in by the limited economic opportunities available to them and forced to turn to crime in order to fulfill their fantasies of the good life. And unlike songs and music videos, 419 films, beholden to the melodramatic format, must eventually punish those individuals who have transgressed moral codes: in 419 films, just as in occult melodramas, the criminals are always caught and punished. Eventually, after the Kuwaiti smuggler who purchased Philip's sister is apprehended, the Nigerian Economic Financial Crime Commission (EFCC) is able to track down Cleo and the boys. Kelvin, Philip, and Cleo are all arrested, and Duran is shot by his former boss and then apprehended by the police. What I suggest here is that, despite the initial sympathy one might have originally had for these youngsters, given the high level of government corruption and the impunity of many 419ers, this ending too may be read as a dream of development. Regardless of the popularity of songs like "Yahoozee" and films like *Boys Cot,* Nigerians often express frustration that the government is too inefficient or corrupt to catch criminals. An example of this can be seen in the hashtag #ifitwereNigeria that surfaced on Twitter immediately after the culprits of the Boston Marathon bombings in 2013 were apprehended. Impressed by the swiftness and efficiency of law enforcement officials who put the entire city of Boston on lockdown for a day, Nigerians added the popular hashtag to satirical statements about how the Nigerian police force would have bungled the pursuit.

Likewise, those in the Nigerian business community express frustration that their reputation has been hurt because of the prominence of 419ers, and Nollywood filmmakers and musicians also often wish they could rely on the government to stymie the rampant piracy that makes it difficult to profit off of art. In the 419 film *Yahoo Millionaire* (2007), director Lancelot Imasuen actually appears in a cameo as the director of the EFCC who eventually catches the fraudster. And this is not surprising considering that Nollywood practitioners are also negatively affected by Nigeria's reputation for fraud. Veteran Nigerian filmmaker Tunde Kelani, for instance, describes trying to release a film online for the first time: "The hassle [our technical director] went through before he could get certified by Visa and Mastercard outside Nigeria was terrible. I see problems, too, because people are still very wary about using their cards online for Nigerian products" (Ryan 2014, 175). While some might fantasize about having a Hummer or Mercedes for every day of the week, dreams of development also come in more political versions, like the dream for more formal employment opportunities and a functional government that can reduce fraud. 419 films do in fact celebrate the possibilities of automobility that exist in the increasingly flexible global market, but they still critique the conditions that prevent Nigerian youth from obtaining it and they show that automobility in postcolonial Nigeria often masks and compensates for a lack of real autonomy. Furthermore, like the occult melodramas, 419 films provide a portrait, and in some cases even an explanation, for the present historical moment in which global capitalism has led to hitherto unimaginable amounts of

Figure 26. Boys Cot. *Images of the opening sequence. Duran driving in his Hummer, drinking Hennessy.*

Figure 27. Boys Cot. *Duran delights in showing his ex-girlfriend his Hummer and a briefcase of money.*

Figure 28. Boys Cot. *419 men meet at Duran's boss's mansion.*

Figure 29. Boys Cot. *Cleo's friends ogle her SUV.*

accumulation without creating enough jobs, where the usual roads to financial security and the good life have been corroded by an immoral economy that runs on dishonesty and trickery.

The Global Good Life

If the means by which wealth is obtained has led to mixed feelings about the characters who drive luxury cars, it is clear that in the world of Nollywood, to be a modern, financially successful auto-mobile subject is still exceedingly desirable; it is, in fact, what the video-makers themselves are hoping to, and even have, become. While some critics accuse video films of unabashedly portraying irrationalist and "backward" aspects of African culture, what strikes many Western viewers is the undeniable modernity of these films that show characters dining in fancy restaurants, talking about trade in Dubai, and playing Beyoncé and Wyclef Jean on the sound systems of their Hummers. Though Wendy Griswold has argued that the traffic jam (or "go-slow") is the single most common scene in Nigerian literature, and contemporary novels are replete with descriptions of chaotic and death-filled roads, in video films, cars typically drive through the city with very few obstacles.[32] As Garritano points out, Nollywood films gloss over these everyday scenes of underdevelopment—the camera only inadvertently captures potholes (2012b). Rarely do we see harried characters traveling by means of buses or *danfos* (collective vans or mini-buses) or even motorcycles that so many Nigerians use for transport. And the street hawkers, crowded markets and densely populated areas that are an inevitable part of daily life in African cities are also noticeably sidelined. For the most part, in fact, the camera avoids filming the less-flattering aspects of the city. When such scenes are depicted, they are brief and are most often used to contrast a character's life either before or after he is wealthy, as was the case at the end of *Living in Bondage*.

Even the way car accidents are portrayed in Nollywood films reveals the video-makers' reluctance to linger on the more hazardous aspects of daily life in urban Nigeria. Though early Nollywood films tended to avoid car accidents, they have become more common in the 2010s perhaps, as Noah Tsika argues, in the wake of megastar Stephanie Okereke's near-fatal accident on her way to the African Movie Awards.[33] But more often than not, accidents are used as melodramatic plot devices rather than, as was the case in Soyinka's play, commentaries on the danger of Nigerian roads or, as was the case in Francophone films, meditations on the types of movement available or unavailable to certain segments of the population. In their depictions of the good life, Nollywood films do not tend to highlight the infrastructural conditions that make driving on Nigerian roads particularly unsafe.

Moreover, what also remains noticeably absent in Nollywood films is the commodity of oil, a commodity that literally makes the Nigerian economy (as well as the automobiles) run. With a few exceptions—Ikenna Emma Aniekwe's *Liquid Black Gold* (2008) and Jeta Amata's *Black November* (2012) are perhaps the most notable—films tend to ignore the devastation of the Niger Delta and to leave out any mention of the extraction of oil, the buying and selling of crude, or the oil subsidies that became so controversial when on New Years Day of 2012 they were suddenly removed. For the most part we only hear of oil when one hopes to attain a job at an oil company, as was the case with Kelvin who graduated in the top of his class with a geology degree, or when oil contracts become fodder for 419 scams. We see the latter in *Boys Cot* when Duran is sending an email to a *mugu* that reads, "We just received confirmation and the honorable minister of petroleum will sign your concession immediately." Such scenes also occur in popular 419 films like *The Master* and *419 Dangerous Game* (2004). But by not depicting oil as an actual commodity, the Nollywood films act out the way that consumption rather than production has become, according to the Comaroffs, the "invisible hand" or "moving spirit" of the present age (1999, 17).

Although it goes without saying that consumption is utterly dependent on the production of goods, what the Comaroffs argue is that on a global level production and labor have become less salient in the creation of value, identity, and class consciousness. Or to put it differently, discourse about actual production seems to have given way to concerns about a more abstract "production of modes of existence" (Bayart 2007, 130) that is dependent on sites of consumption. In West African economies, this waning of the importance of labor and production on social life might have quite a bit to do with the fact that the consumption of goods actually seems more concrete or attainable than the production of goods. In Nigeria there are no infrastructures for the refinement of oil (crude is exported and then imported as petroleum) and hardly any factories for the production of automobiles or the manufacturing of other electronic goods that Nigerians use on a daily basis. Fantasies of the global good life, then, often attach to objects or things rather than to education or labor because only the former are available as modes of self-fashioning.

Though the Nollywood industry is constantly growing, diversifying, and generating new genres, the industry's focus on consumption and displays of wealth seem to be an enduring hallmark. In recent years, a handful of films, categorized under the rubric of "New Nollywood," have been produced with bigger budgets, higher standards of production, theatrical releases, and more affluent cosmopolitan audiences in mind.[34] Given the higher budget of these films, the cars and lives of the characters appear even more glamorous, and the images of the city are glitzy and fashionable. Biyi Bandele's glossy film *Fifty* (2015), for instance, features not only the iconic Mercedes-Benzes and SUVs of Nollywood but also shot after shot of the Lekki-Ikoyi Link Bridge, Nigeria's only cable-stayed bridge, which was commissioned in 2013 to connect the affluent neighborhoods of Lekki and Ikoyi. The film even ends with an image of the beautifully modern bridge sparkling and lit up at night in a rare cinematic display of postcolonial infrastructural pride. But in New Nollywood movies, the wealth and success of the characters seem ordinary rather than extraordinary, and because the characters' wealth is accumulated before the movie begins, it becomes neither the focal point of the films nor a source of moral anxiety (Adejunmobi 2015, 36–37). In the meantime, "old" or "mainstream" Nollywood continues to produce hundreds of lower-budget videos in which codes of morality come into intense conflict with the acquisition of material goods (42). And even as consumption becomes more highly stylized and less conflicted in some of these mainstream "old" Nollywood genres, the romantic disputes, family turmoil, and moral dilemmas show that the elite are still in a precarious position: cashing in on the global good life often leaves one in an unstable situation, and excess clearly remains at odds with normalized social life. But in both new and old Nollywood, the emotional investment in outward signs of success remains despite, or perhaps because of, the obvious infrastructural impediments faced by all Nigerians, including Nigerian video-makers.[35] Nollywood's continuing commitment to the visual pleasure economy of cars, clothes, and cash and the fantasies of smooth roads, regular electricity, and flawless buildings therefore prove that the shiny surfaces of global modernity are indeed very attractive, regardless of the complications inherent in Nigeria's moral economy.

· CHAPTER 5 ·

Women in Traffic: Toward a Feminist Automobility

If it is women who are being transacted, then it is the men who give and take them who are linked, the woman being a conduit of relationship rather than a partner to it.... The relations of such a system are such that women are in no position to realize the benefits of their own circulation. As long as the relations specify that men exchange women, it is the men who are the beneficiaries of the product of such exchanges—social organization.

—Gayle Rubin, "The Traffic in Women"

"Fatou, what do you have in tow?"
"You mean this? ... Top of the line caboose: not for public transportation."

—*Faat Kiné*

THROUGHOUT THIS BOOK I have discussed texts in which women have been exchanged for cars, displayed in cars, murdered for cars, and even magically transformed into men in cars. This chapter, which focuses on Ama Ata Aidoo's novel *Changes: A Love Story* (1991) and Ousmane Sembene's film *Faat Kiné* (2000), examines what happens when women instead of men become the owners, drivers, and accumulators of automobiles. Both texts work dialogically with earlier stories about male drivers and car owners, reframing the postcolonial subject's relation to commodity culture within a feminist context and highlighting the ambivalent way that financially independent women constitute their identities and access power in West African urban centers. In *Changes* and *Faat Kiné,* the automobile seems to give women a practical advantage: it enables them to engage in the daily activities of work, household errands, and socializing in a more convenient and pleasurable manner. But what I argue is that the car figures much less as a sign of upward mobility or the good life, as it did in the Nollywood films, and more as a constant practice of "maintenance," a term that suggests both the daily ins and outs of car ownership and the affective experiences of middle-class African women who are trying to maintain their standard of living and keep moving in a system that is often a drain on energy.

At the beginning of Aidoo's second novel, *Changes,* Esi Sekyi, a Ghanaian government data analyst in the Department of Urban Statistics, is driving her unreliable car through the streets of Accra to arrange the details for an upcoming business trip to Lusaka. Esi's car continues to stall as she makes her way to the travel agency, prompting crude remarks about women drivers from the taxi drivers whom she blocks. Immediately, however, the reader is made to understand that Esi's mobility is not only hindered by the failures of her car; it is also circumscribed within the male-dominated social system. On this particular occasion, Esi is driving to the travel agency because the office secretary has called in sick and Esi's male colleagues assume that it should be a woman's responsibility to complete her tasks. It does not matter that their positions are equal to Esi's or that they too are to take part in the upcoming trip.

Still, Esi's relatively high level of mobility and autonomy are contrasted with the even greater limits placed on her best friend, Opokuya. Esi is an independent working woman who divorces her husband, drives her own car, decides to have only one child (whom she lets her ex-mother-in-law raise), and does not need to rely on men for either money or day-to-day mobility. Opokuya, by contrast, shares a car with her husband, Kubi, who insists on keeping it parked outside his office all day for his colleagues to see. This makes it exceedingly challenging for Opokuya to commute to work and to do all of the errands necessary for maintaining the household, which, as a woman, remain her responsibility, despite the fact she works full time. Eventually, when Esi receives a new car, she gifts her old car to Opokuya, easing the burden of her friend's daily tasks.

The novel, a melodramatic tale of the difficulties of heterosexual romance, is largely about the decisions that these two women make as they negotiate their status as both consumers and commodities in an Accra that is in the midst of the IMF structural adjustment programs that ushered Ghana into the neoliberal economy in the late 1980s and early 1990s. But in *Changes* cars do not only set the novel in motion, they also become part of its meditation on the disillusionment with feminist fantasies of autonomy and hopes for (self-)development. The novel, therefore, presents an ambivalent portrait of women during a period when Ghana's Economic Recovery Program (ERP) was reversing the decline the economy had experienced in the late 1970s and early 1980s but, at the same time, increasing social inequalities and making the prices of food, health, clothing, transportation, and fuel beyond the reach of many citizens.[1]

In Ousmane Sembene's penultimate film, *Faat Kiné,* the protagonist, Faat Kiné Diop, is, like Esi Sekyi, an auto-mobile woman in a traditionally male job. Faat Kiné, born in the year of Senegalese independence, is presented as a figure of a new Senegal, a Senegal where a gender revolution is altering the dynamics of heterosexual romance, where women are becoming more prominent in the business community, and where a spirit of entrepreneurship is replacing some of the stale platitudes of a socialist, patriarchal government. The film, in fact, takes place on the cusp of Senegal's transition from forty years of socialist rule to the neoliberal government of Abdoulaye Wade.[2] Though *Faat Kiné* is set almost ten years after *Changes,* both texts reflect the various emotional, practical, and structural "adjustments" women make during their country's transition to neoliberalism. Faat Kiné not only drives about Dakar, dropping her children off at school, depositing money at the bank, going on dates, and meeting friends for ice cream, she also runs a Total petrol station where she honks a handheld horn to summon her subordinates. Unlike Esi, however, Kiné is not an educated woman. After having been impregnated by a high school professor, Kiné was expelled from school, disinherited by her father, and duped out of her savings by another lover. She began to work as an attendant at the Total station until she was promoted to a managerial position. At first glance, Kiné seems to be a paradigmatic feminist hero, succeeding as a pleasure-seeking, single, working mother in a world where the odds are so clearly stacked against her. She chooses her lovers, supports her family, and manipulates the mobility of those around her. But Kiné's vulgar language and sometimes cruel actions—her maid says that she has the heart of a man—constantly remind the viewer that life for a single mother in Dakar requires hard sacrifices.

Furthermore, despite the constant images of Kiné driving in Dakar, the film is punctured with tropes of immobility and impotence, which are reminiscent of Sembene's earlier films. Building on the work of John Mowitt, who suggests that *Faat Kiné* is an "inverted rearrangement" (2005, 119) of *Xala,* I suggest that *Faat Kiné* is a restructuring of the impasse at the end of

Xala, an impasse that in the earlier film is marked both by the betrayed masses and by bourgeois over-consumption. *Faat Kiné,* however, opens up a discussion of how, as Inderpal Grewal argues, neoliberal technologies produce forms of agency that cannot help but fracture the presumed coherence of neoliberal discourse (2005, 19). In other words, while *Xala* takes the postcolonial nation to task for failing to achieve true autonomy, *Faat Kiné* examines the possibilities still open within late global capitalism. And while the film makes it clear that corruption, neocolonialism, and sexism clearly continue to be a part of everyday life, Kiné has found ways of not being incapacitated by them. Both Kiné and Esi engage in a feminist politics of negotiation, or what Obioma Nnaemeka calls "nego-feminism."[3] And as they do so, they "cope with successfully/go around" African patriarchy (Nnaemeka 2004, 377) and find ways to successfully "go around" a neoliberal African society where automobility becomes a way to adjust and adapt to bumpy terrain.

Gendered Automobility

As Sarah S. Jain has argued, historically, the car has been a tool of masculinity, a space where men in the driver's seat could assert their role as head of the family and, at the same time, escape the family and domestic sphere when needed (2005, 195). Though Jain's focus is on Western forms of automobility, Jennifer Hart, referring specifically to West Africa, argues that driving in the region was also historically considered a male activity, and though women participated in long-distance trading, it was generally assumed that women were not suited for the physical demands of driving on poor roads (without power steering), dealing with breakdowns and rowdy customers, and loading and unloading vehicles (2016, 100). And while there have been, as Hart observes, records of a few female commercial drivers, in *Riding the Demon* (1999) Peter Chilson, who writes about his road travel in West Africa in the 1990s, claims to have found perhaps one of the only licensed female commercial drivers in the region at the time, driving for UNICEF in Niamey, Niger. Moreover, anthropological and historical accounts about African motor transport rarely mention women drivers. For instance, the collection *The Speed of Change: Motor Vehicles and People in Africa: 1890—2000,* one of the most comprehensive social histories of the motor vehicle in sub-Saharan Africa, fails to mention a single female driver. Likewise, *Les transports et la ville en Afrique au sud du Sahara,* the most wide-ranging and thorough Francophone collection of articles on transportation, contains just one brief chapter on gender and it is one that focuses on women's exclusion from the transportation sector.

Slowly, more and more women are beginning to join the ranks of professional drivers. In 2007, for instance, the Senegalese government began the Taxi Sister project and offered ten women the opportunity to rent or lease hatchbacks in order to become some of Dakar's first women taxi drivers. The government's goal was to put two thousand women Taxi Sisters on the street by 2015 (Hinshaw 2010), but setbacks due to harassment from male drivers and the cost of maintaining cars have impeded the program's growth, despite increasing interest in it. The fact remains, then, that when women drive in West Africa, they typically drive their own private vehicles rather than commercial vehicles. And while this once was an extraordinary and notable act—Fela Kuti's mother, Funmilayo, is often touted to be not only a key women's rights activist but the first woman in Nigeria to drive—women drivers are now common throughout West Africa.

What this chapter examines are the ways that both *Changes* and *Faat Kiné* can be read as feminist texts that depict the complex lives of these modern women drivers and car owners who re-gender automobility. I call these texts feminist while acknowledging that feminism has occupied a rather contentious position in postcolonial literary criticism and African gender studies. Critics like Chandra Talpade Mohanty and Gayatri Chakravorty Spivak have famously argued that Western feminism is neoimperialist and preoccupied with the white, educated Euro-American female subject who is often contrasted with the poor, subjugated "Third World" woman in need of rescue. Likewise, Oyèrónké Oyěwùmí maintains that feminism, like Marxism, structuralism, or poststructuralism, is only one of the latest Western theoretical fashions to be applied, one-size-fits-all, to African subjects (2005, 16). While these critiques often fail to account for the diversity of Western feminist theory, it is nevertheless true that "First World" feminists often fail to speak to the specific concerns and negotiations of African women. However, as Juliana Makuchi Nfah-Abbenyi has argued, "indigenous" African feminist theories can often be found in fictional works "embedded in the polysemous and polymorphous nature of the narratives themselves" (1997, 20). Moreover, Nfah-Abbenyi emphasizes that African women authors have used fiction and successfully "reconstituted and reconstructed the multiple, shifting, and sometimes contradictory identities and subjectivities of African women" (33–34). Extending

Nfah-Abbenyi's arguments to fictional film and to feminists in general, not just to women, I discuss how feminist texts can speak to the multiple subject positions women drivers choose to and are forced to occupy.[4]

Indeed both Sembene and Aidoo have been particularly adept at foregrounding the ways in which women maintain and exhibit economic power but are also, at the same time, limited and hemmed in by the patriarchal systems that posit them as objects of exchange. Both texts I examine in this chapter highlight the social challenges and emotional complications that middle-class women face when they assert their independence and earn money on their own, even though, as Aidoo emphasizes, African women throughout history have had their own financial income. What I discuss here are the dense social spheres that African women drivers occupy as they navigate the gender dynamics, less-than-optimal infrastructure, and postcolonial urban spaces that require constant negotiation and maneuvering.

"An Impossible Situation"

From its opening lines onward, *Changes* is a novel full of the minutiae of driving. Aidoo provides active descriptions of checking tires, opening car doors, situating oneself in front of the steering wheel, putting the keys in the ignition, parking, backing out, and locking the gate. What she emphasizes is the everyday use of the automobile as it transports characters from home to work to errand. Aidoo therefore breaks with an African male literary tradition in which the car, albeit as a satirical object, is quite literally a projection of the phallus. For instance, Nkem Nwankwo's aptly titled novel *My Mercedes Is Bigger Than Yours* (1975) begins with the following description of Onuma Okudo driving his new golden Jaguar:

> Once upon a time a young man was savouring the pleasures of a new car. . . . It was like when you have gone into a woman. Some of the time is taken up with clumsy flopping about; trying futilely to find the perfect position and rhythm. Then there are moments of complete synchronization of limbs which seem to come about without effort. (1)

In contrast to Nwankwo, whose sexual language is not unlike Sembene's in the novel version of *Xala,* Aidoo focuses on the taken-for-granted banalities of driving. Aidoo therefore ushers in a language of driving that ties the car's everydayness to the gendered personal and political lives of its drivers.

More broadly speaking, Aidoo is also writing back to an African male literary tradition that has underemphasized the economic independence of African women. In her introduction to the 1969 Macmillan edition of Ayi Kwei Armah's *The Beautyful Ones Are Not Yet Born,* Aidoo criticizes Armah's depiction of women, calling his portrayal of the greedy mother-in-law and the dependent wife atypical because most Ghanaian women would have some means of earning money on their own, either through occupying a stall in the market or running some other form of small business. Aidoo says that in Ghanaian society "women believe that only two types of their species suffer: the sterile—that is, those incapable of producing children—and the foolish. And by the foolish they refer to the type of woman who depends solely on their husband for subsistence" (x). Aidoo goes on to remark that "the only group of females in the country who may not be sure of themselves are the educated" (x). What Aidoo stresses is that it is not an inability to work that prevents women from achieving equality or satisfaction, nor does education allow women to bypass gender inequality. Rejecting an economic explanation for women's oppression, Aidoo focuses much of her writing on locating the social systems that perpetuate women's subjugation. And in *Changes* these critiques have a particular resonance as they are set against the backdrop of IMF development programs like the Program of Action to Mitigate the Social Cost of Adjustment (PAMSCAD), a quick-fix program that stressed job creation for women but failed to address broader social concerns or long-term solutions and rarely enabled women to benefit from their training.[5]

What *Changes* foregrounds, though, are not these types of development programs per se (they go unmentioned in the novel) but rather the particular dilemmas of the educated, middle-class woman as she tries to sustain an emotionally fulfilling life. The difficulty for such women, who clearly have an advantage in surviving the instabilities of postcolonial precariousness, is not primarily about financial self-sufficiency: it is that her social and romantic attachments are, as Lauren Berlant argues in a different context, "as brittle as the economic system that hails" her (2011, 171). In *Changes* women are part of a system of male transaction, there to benefit the men who exchange and possess them. But in West African feminist texts women drivers inhabit the automobile as a way out of circulation in this type of phallic economy, an economy where women, as Claude Lévi-Strauss argues, are the objects rather than the subjects of exchange. Therefore, when women take the steering wheel they do so not only to gain access to privileged forms of consumption but also to escape being consumed, to escape what Gayle Rubin (borrowing from Emma Goldman) calls "the traffic in women"—a social and economic situation in which women's value is directly related to their ability to gratify male needs, desires, and relationships. And while, as Ifi Amadiume argues, woman exchange was not necessarily foundational to precolonial African societies, Aidoo makes it clear that in contemporary Ghana women are often valued as commodities and exchange objects.[6]

In the novel, Esi's first husband, Oko, demonstrates his opinion of women when, moments before raping his wife, he complains that his friends are laughing at him for allowing Esi to put her career above her family. When Esi first meets Oko, he is attracted to her intelligence and air of independence and spends years courting her. But as time progresses Oko begins to resent Esi's success and scolds her for not spending enough time at home. After he forces himself into her one morning, parading around afterwards like an "arrogant king," Esi decides to leave him. She decides to keep the rape a secret because she knows that in Ghanaian society he has the right to have sex with her whenever he pleases. So she explains to her friend Opokuya, not being entirely dishonest, that Oko was simply too demanding of her time. Opokuya acknowledges that the few men who claim to be attracted to independent women "are also interested in having such women permanently in their beds and in their kitchens" (45). Therefore, Opokuya and Esi agree that intelligent women in Ghana are in "an impossible situation" (45). Even Esi's grandmother reminds her that women are pampered on their wedding day because the "whole ceremony was a funeral of the self that could have been" (110). After marriage women must focus their energies on satisfying the sexual and domestic needs of their husbands and not on their own aspirations or desires. All of Esi's friends and family think she is mad for leaving a man who desires her and actually wants to spend more time with her. However, when she makes it clear that the relationship is over, Oko's mother finds another young woman and deposits her at Oko's doorstep. Oko is surprised that there are still women who would agree to be carried off to marry a total stranger, but he is flattered at his mother's gesture and decides to keep the woman. Although he prefers Esi, he acknowledges that women are indeed transferable.

Esi also remarries, but she does so with the explicit knowledge that the man she loves, Ali Kondey, sees her as "occupied territory." Moreover, Esi has decided to marry a man who is already married, and while his status will be augmented, hers, as second wife, will diminish. What makes the situation an acceptable compromise to Esi is that, besides being enamored with Ali, she believes that being a second wife in a polygamous urban marriage will allow her time to devote to herself and to her job. Since Esi will stay in her own bungalow and Ali will spend most nights at home with his first wife and children, Esi will not be obligated to fill the role of homemaker. She will not be reduced to the role of mother. Indeed, Esi feels relieved that Ali is not making demands on her, and she enjoys being able to participate in meetings and conferences to the full extent that her male colleagues do. She even delights in her purchase of a personal computer that allows her to take work home. She takes pleasure in her own automobility in all its iterations.

However, the freedom that Esi cherishes also has its drawbacks and limitations. Because he and Esi have no obligations toward each other, Ali begins spending his time with his new secretary and the marriage becomes sour. It only dawns on Esi then that if a man can "occupy" two wives, he can certainly have three, or four. Esi becomes depressed and lonely but decides to stay in the marriage and avoid the embarrassment and hassle of ending it. Ali, then, despite his several degrees and his training in England, continues in the tradition of his male ancestors. Ali's father, Musa Musa, was a traveling salesman who amassed a great fortune and numerous young wives throughout West Africa. Ali's grandfather, likewise, had been a wealthy man: "He owned an impressive number of sons, cattle, horses, sheep, goats, wives, and daughters. All definitely in that order of value" (24). When Ali establishes his travel agency with offices in capital cities throughout West Africa, he becomes exactly like his father: constantly on the move and collecting commodities—clothing, electronics, foods, and, of course, women—from his travels.

It becomes apparent, then, that there is an element of irony in both the title and subtitle ("A Love Story") of the novel. Like the audience of *Quartier Mozart,* who realizes only at the end of the film that Bekolo surely must have been joking when he declares that nothing in the neighborhood will remain the same, the reader of Aidoo's novel does not immediately appreciate the sarcasm of the title. In fact, when Esi divorces her husband and allows her daughter to live with his family, it seems that she is breaking out of the mold of essentialized womanhood. By refusing to be both wife and mother, Esi is stepping out of the identities normally allotted to Ghanaian women. But as Ali begins bribing Esi with gifts only to maintain his exclusive right to occupy her, she realizes that the relationship is not nearly as equal as she thought. Ali is the giver; she is the receiver, not an equal partner. Similarly, Ali's first wife, Fusena (for whom Esi, incidentally, expresses very little sympathy), has little to say when Ali decides to take a second wife. When the patriarchs of Ali's family ask their women to speak with Fusena, she realizes that, like the women of previous generations, she must accept her role as one of Ali's possessions. Aidoo writes, "The older women felt bad. . . . It was a man's world. You only survived if you knew how to live in it as a woman. What shocked the older women though, was obviously how little had changed for their daughters—school and all!" (107). It seems, then, that the women have arrived at an impasse. Technology, education, and urban life do not instantiate any changes or improvements in emotional life. By and large, the women in *Changes* are circling in a "holding pattern."[7]

A Car of One's Own

In many ways, *Changes* might be read as the Anglophone sister text to Mariama Bâ's 1981 *So Long a Letter (Une si longue lettre),* an earlier story about the emotional emptiness and romantic failures of educated women in a patriarchal and postcolonial setting and a story in which the exchange of cars becomes a defining moment. Bâ's story, like *Changes,* works in dialogical relation to earlier male-authored texts, most notably, as Susan Andrade notes, Ousmane Sembene's *Xala. So Long a Letter,* which has become an ur-text of African feminism, is a letter written by Ramatoulaye to her friend Aissatou who works in the United States for the Senegalese embassy.[8] Ramatoulaye writes the letter, a tale of both friends' unhappy marriages, as she mourns the sudden death of her husband, Modou. While Aissatou chooses to divorce her husband after he takes a second wife, Ramatoulaye explains the complex emotional reasons why she could not bring herself to do the same after her husband took a teenaged wife twenty-five years into their marriage. In this way, *So Long a Letter* rewrites *Xala* from the wives' point of view and, as Andrade suggests, "promotes gender from a secondary to a primary category of analysis" (2011, 77).

However, a key difference between *So Long a Letter* and *Xala* is that in *So Long a Letter* both friends are educated, and, technically speaking, economically self-sufficient, unlike El Hadji's three wives. Having attended the prestigious Ponty-Ville school for girls, Ramatoulaye is able to support herself and her children with a teaching job when her husband spends all of his money on the new wife. But even with an income from teaching, Modou's excessive spending on his young bride, Binetou, puts Ramatoulaye and her children in an uncomfortable position. Ramatoulaye writes to her friend:

> I survived. I experienced the inadequacy of public transport. My children laughed at themselves in making this hard discovery. One day, I heard [my eldest daughter] advise them: "Above all, don't let mum know that it is stifling in those buses during the rush hours." . . . I shed tears of joy and sadness together: joy in being loved by my children, the sadness of a mother who does not have the means to change the course of events. I told you then, without any ulterior motive, of this painful aspect of our life, while Modou's car drove Lady Mother-in-Law to the four corners of town and while Binetou streaked along the roads in an Alfa Romeo, sometimes white, sometime red. (53)

Ramatoulaye says, "I survived." She's expressing her activity of making do, or getting by, despite the physical discomforts involved in riding in inadequately maintained and overcrowded public transportation and the shame she feels in being taken down a notch in life while her younger co-wife moves up and about. Aissatou responds to her friend's pain by buying her a new car.

Receiving the car becomes a singular moment in Ramatoulaye's otherwise glum life. She describes how her children gave "cries of joy" knowing that they would no longer have to suffer the hassle that many other students faced and that they could now look Binetou and her mother in the eye. She tells her friend, with pride and gratitude, how she obtained her driving license despite her fear, learning how to shift gears, brake and accelerate, and apply the correct amount of pressure. The car provides Ramatoulaye with a sense of ownership and self that was broken when she had to share her husband—she says, "The narrow space between the wheel and the seat was mine" (54)—and it also reminds her that the bonds of friendship are often more enduring than those of romantic love. But what are we to make of this almost euphoric moment in a text that is otherwise so despairing?

Ramatoulaye's crisis is not a crisis of the failed postcolonial state or the informal economy—though that's there too in the references to public transportation and in the mention of Modou's anti-union stance—but of domestic life, of "survival" in an emotional sense. Here, the ordinariness and extraordinariness of driving her own car becomes a disruption to Ramatoulaye's daily life of just surviving. Like the women in *Changes,* Ramatoulaye is an educated woman who believed in the possibilities of romantic love, but now finds herself at an impasse. In *Cruel Optimism* (2011), a book that examines the cruel nature of attachments to love, the good life, and stability, Berlant argues that the impasse marks a time from which one cannot move forward. According to Berlant, "An impasse is a holding station that doesn't hold securely but opens out into anxiety, that dogpaddling around a space whose contours remain obscure. . . . It marks a delay that demands an activity. . . . That delay enables us to develop gestures of composure, of mannerly transaction, of being-with in the world as well as of rejection, refusal, detachments, psychosis, and all kinds of radical negation" (199). In this sense, and following Berlant's logic, Ramatoulaye's driving is a gesture, a small opening, that allows her to reorient herself within the impasse, to adapt, and to find new attachments. Clearly, the car is not a solution to the crisis (national, domestic, economic, or otherwise), but it is an adjustment that makes the crisis more bearable. Likewise, cars in *Changes* act in a similar way: they clear space, make things possible, and they allow Esi and Opokuya and even Fusena to catch their breath, albeit always within the circuit of the impasse.

In this way, driving for the urban women in *Changes* constitutes what Michel de Certeau might describe as a tactical speech act, an act in which the Other—"the weak"—may poach the property of the dominant, or "the strong." For de Certeau, "many everyday practices (talking, reading, moving about, shopping, cooking, etc.) are tactical in character. And so are, more generally, many 'ways of operating'" (1984, xix). While driving is not among his list of everyday practices—perhaps because it is so often the speech act of the strong—in *Changes* it becomes one of the ways that women can react against their imposed silence. Esi, for instance, cannot utter the phrase "marital rape"—she points out that the concept does not exist in any African language—but because she has her own job and her own means of transport, she can leave the man who committed the act. Fusena, too, finds that she can only express anger at Ali through her driving. When she hears he will be taking another wife she utters just two questions: "She has a university degree?" (99) and "Is she also a Muslim?" (100). When the affirmative answer to the first question leaves her speechless and the negative answer to the latter only reinforces her shock, she can do nothing other than get behind the wheel of her "small two-door vehicle [that] she had come to love unreasonably and fiercely" (99) and "screech [it] into life" (99). She bangs her car door and backs out so violently that she almost sideswipes Ali's "elegant and capacious chariot" (99), which, described as such, evokes the "kinglike" arrogance of Oko after he rapes Esi. Other than the above questions, Fusena barely speaks throughout the novel. Moreover, when she does express her own desires to teach, or to continue her education, she is always met with a no. The extent of her rage, then, becomes expressed only in her driving, her small gesture of outrage.[9]

For Esi's friend Opokuya driving is also linked to language and to tactical gestures of adaptation. Opokuya's daily life is largely inscribed within the constant fight, or *wahala,* that she has each day with her husband Kubi over who should drive their shared car. Kubi believes that, like his other male colleagues in the civil service, he should drive the car to work and park it all day for his colleagues to admire. Opokuya insists, on the contrary, that "a car is to be used" (17), that parking it all day is a waste: she argues for use-value over exchange-value. Opokuya also knows that she is solely responsible for maintaining the household, even with her full-time job as a midwife, and she feels that having her own transportation is essential for performing the tasks involved in feeding and clothing a husband and four children. On the days that Kubi wins their *wahala* and parks the car at his office, Opokuya remains silent as he drives her to work and whistles. When Opokuya wins the car for the day, she hums all the way from his office to the hospital. Her humming, in contrast to Kubi's self-important whistling, signifies her muffled victory, a victory somewhat overshadowed by the lengthy list of errands she feels she must complete on her rare day with the car.[10] As is the case with Fusena, the subaltern may not speak, but she can drive.

However, at the end of the novel, a three-way exchange of cars complicates the small gestures of driving and imitates the almost-euphoric moment of friendship and independence in *So Long a Letter,* albeit with a key difference. Ali, who had been spending much time with his new secretary, shows up at Esi's house one morning with a brand new car, which, as Esi suggests, is a rarity at the time. The new car, like the many other gifts Ali heaps on Esi, is meant to be a bribe, a "substitute for his presence" (147). Esi accepts the gift but understands that the car is a final verdict on the impossibility of egalitarian romantic love as it places her within the very economy of exchange she sought to escape. But because Esi already has a car—one that her government job has enabled her to purchase—she, like Aissatou in *So Long a Letter,* is also in a position to give. She turns around and sells her car to Opokuya for next to nothing, accepting a small sum only to spare her friend's pride. Esi puts much time and effort into retrofitting the car with a host of spare parts handmade by her mechanics (she says the cost of new, imported spare parts is prohibitive), and she has the car repainted and thoroughly worked through before handing it over to her friend. Notably, the exchange between Esi and Opokuya is the first and only exchange in the novel that occurs beyond the scope of male needs and desires. And, even more importantly, it works to bolster Opokuya's self-reliance and reduce her dependence on Kubi, giving her the "freedom of movement" (56) she had always envied in her friend. In fact, driving Esi's old car gives Opokuya a renewed sense of power and "clarity of vision" (161)—her elation is much like Ramatoulaye's.

And yet in *Changes,* unlike in *So Long a Letter,* the gifting of cars between women indicates a fraying of relations rather than a solidifying of them. When Opokuya arrives at Esi's house to pick up her "new" car, Esi has just ended her relationship with Ali. Esi wishes to be alone, and Opokuya is too excited about the car to stay to console her friend. Then, when Opokuya does not return home, Kubi drives to Esi's in search of his wife. Finding her gone and Esi feeling vulnerable, Kubi immediately attempts to take advantage of the situation. At first, Esi does not resist his sexual advances and even considers it to be a good solution to her loneliness. After a moment, though, she remembers Opokuya's face and her grandmother's warning that "a man always gains in stature any way he chooses to associate with a woman—including adultery. . . . But, in her association with a man, a woman is always in danger of being diminished" (164). Esi pulls away from Kubi, realizing that she could not afford to lose Opokuya's friendship, as it was the one solid human bond that she still maintained. But Esi's near-betrayal indicates that Esi and Opokuya are not able to entirely escape the economy of exchange where women, as commodities, relate to each other as rivals.

An Individual Solution

In *So Long a Letter,* questions of development or "underdevelopment" linger in the background. Ramatoulaye's real shame is not necessarily in having to take public transportation but in having to do so while her teenaged co-wife drives several cars paid for from loans borrowed against Ramatoulaye's villa. But in *Changes* the crisis of public infrastructure and utilities is impossible to miss, and it becomes clear that while the new neoliberal economy might be working for some, the most economically vulnerable have not benefited from the "changes." For instance, as Esi is pulling into the significantly named Hotel Twentieth Century, which was "consuming enough electricity to light up the whole nearby fishing district" (43), she finds herself thinking about the villagers there who have no electricity. She wonders when the government will provide motorized boats and fishing nets to the Ghanaian fishermen who feed the country and when the Minister of Power will stop raising the price of kerosene. When Opokuya and her husband fight about who will drive the car each day, their situation is aggravated by the fact that the city buses are constantly breaking down and that the hospital vans Opokuya can take to and from work make it impossible for her to do after-work errands. Although it is curious that *tro-tros* and taxis are not mentioned as alternative modes of transport, especially given their ubiquity on the streets of Accra, it is still the case that the failure of public infrastructure mentioned throughout the novel makes it increasingly necessary for Ghanaians to find individual solutions to their problems even if these solutions are less than ideal.

But as Esi's second marriage is crumbling, she becomes well aware of the impossibilities of trying to solve problems as a sovereign individual. Aidoo writes, "[Esi] was going to be humble enough to admit that the answers . . . could not come from her, an individual. Hopefully a whole people would soon have answers for them. In the meantime she would listen to her grandmother. She would not pity herself" (115). In this way, the failures of public infrastructure mirror the failures of Esi's romantic life in a patriarchal society: both problems, given the social constraints, can only be met with individualized solutions, but, at the same time, these solutions, because they do not address the social, are always inadequate.

This emphasis on the individual is indeed what makes *Changes* part of the Anglophone novelist tradition. As Nancy Armstrong argues, the hallmark of a novel is that it thinks like an individual, an individual who is dissatisfied with and wishes to exceed his or her social world, but who, at the end of the day, is disciplined, contained, and sublimated. The novel is therefore very much like the ideology of automobility: both reproduce notions of sovereignty and personal development that obscure the system of dependent relations that is always at work. Discussing the rise of the

British novel, Armstrong argues that there is a certain homogeneity between the history of the modern subject and the modern novel. She writes,

> To produce an individual, novels had to think as if there already were one, that such an individual was not only the narrating subject and source of writing but also the object of narration and referent of writing. To produce an individual, it was also necessary to invalidate competing notions of the subject—often proposed by other novels—as idiosyncratic, less than fully human, fantastic, or dangerous. The result was a cultural category and a bundle of rhetorical figures that were extremely fragile and always on the defensive yet notably flexible and ever ready to adapt to new cultural-historical conditions. (2005, 3)

As Armstrong speculates, the adaptation of the global novel into a non-Western setting does not undo the main telos of the novel, which is to examine the struggles of the individual seeking fulfillment in his or her social setting. However, what I want to emphasize is that unlike many Western novels, *Changes* does not seek to defend or redeem the individual but instead foregrounds the limits of both personal and economic development.

While Joseph Slaughter argues that the novel has been complicit in shaping liberal humanist discourse and enabling the fictions of personal development, sovereignty, and self-determination,[11] Aidoo's novel, infused with popular forms, is openly skeptical of these types of narratives. Critics have in fact often pointed out that although *Changes* is a novel, it also takes the form of a modern-day Akan dilemma tale, or a performance where a series of dilemmas about everyday life are debated to no real conclusion (Simpson 2007, 158). The point of these tales, quite unlike the novel, is to pose social, moral, and political issues as riddles to an audience who then collectively debates them. As Waleska Saltori Simpson argues, the form of the dilemma tale, along with the poetic interludes, internal asides, and playscript dialogues throughout the novel, allow Aidoo, who comes out of the popular Ghanaian theater and performance tradition, to explore the complexities and multiplicities of female identity through different structuring devices. *Changes,* which incorporates various genres, therefore calls into question the autonomous, auto-mobile subject, and presents a heroine who is not undertaking a quest or assuring her future through wealth or marriage but rather treading water, holding ground, and maintaining until collective solutions can be found. In *Changes* there are no unscathed moments of individual euphoria, no dreams of development, not even any enduring romantic engagements: there is nothing in the novel to suggest that self-governance actually ever amounts to anything. Therefore, although Esi acts as if she can change her situation, the novel paints a picture of a society that is constantly pushing back against her individual pursuits.[12]

By the end of the novel Esi is at another impasse: neither work, nor remarriage, nor her new car have brought her the happiness she expects, despite the fact that they provide her with the autonomy or self-mobility she struggles so hard to hang on to. She cannot bring about new social forms on her own, and she cannot abide by the rules of the past. As *Changes* ends, Esi is depressed and has begun to take tranquilizers to help calm her nerves. Opokuya, the euphoric driver, has no idea that her loved ones came so close to betraying her. All the attachments in the novel—to people, ideals, automobiles—seem to be teetering on the verge of breakdown. And yet there is hope (as there is for Ramatoulaye at the end of *So Long a Letter*) as Esi recalls a highlife song with lyrics, "Yes, maybe one day," and the novel concludes with an ellipsis, an opening for something new to take place, something that, like music itself, moves beyond forms that think like individuals.

The Total Woman

Like *Changes,* Sembene's film *Faat Kiné* is a drama of negotiation and adjustment where the protagonist needs to figure out "how best to live on, considering" the conflicts she faces (Berlant 2011, 3). But while *Changes* chronicles the unraveling of Esi's attachments, *Faat Kiné,* perhaps because it takes place just before Wade comes to power and the failures of his neoliberal government manifest, has a somewhat utopian structure in which the main character's adjustments to hardship actually leads to a more successful life. Whereas Esi is stuck dithering in her impasse, Kiné is able to, in Berlant's words, "maintain [her] sea legs" and "co-ordinate the standard melodramatic crises" (4) that she faces. In other words, while Esi's form of maintenance often entails "dogpaddling" (199), a self-exhausting way of moving forward, Kiné adjusts to life's blows in a more economically and emotionally productive manner. Maintenance for her means maintaining the type of good life that she has acquired despite her setbacks and despite being hardened by the emotional failures of her loved ones. But even though

Faat Kiné seems to be more hopeful about the possibilities opened up for women in a neoliberal economy that is shedding its socialist past, the social changes that the film chronicles are still quite ambivalent. As Faat Kiné subverts traditional society, she is, as her mother suggests, part of a "generation of women that is affluent and conflicted." *Faat Kiné* therefore reads as a celebration—a decidedly hesitant one—of a financially independent woman who is dominated neither by the goods she consumes nor by the men who seek to consume her.

And yet it does seem odd that after having spent decades of his career critiquing bourgeois capitalism, Sembene would make an automobile-driving franchise capitalist the protagonist of his first film in a trilogy on everyday heroism.[13] However, as Sembene tells Mamadou Niang, defending his own willingness to accept foreign funding for his films: "In war, wherever you get the gun, what matters is that you know how to point it towards the enemy and shoot" (2008, 85). Thus, to Sembene, it matters very little to the plot of *Faat Kiné* that Kiné receives her paycheck from a French-owned company, or even that it is an oil company. What matters is that, like Sembene, she does what she wants. Of course, part of the dialectical gravitas of the film is that Kiné is by no means uncompromised. While Kiné is in many ways a modern-day heroine whose will to mobility has overcome innumerable blockages, Sembene has refrained from idealizing Kiné as a model African woman. Kiné smokes in public, attacks the wife of one of her lovers, spews out vulgarities to the men who have crossed her, snaps at her maid, and allows her son to call her by her first name. Her mobility has come at a cost.

As was the case with Esi in *Changes,* we first meet Fatou Kiné N'Daye Diop as she is behind the wheel of her car, a car that the camera often cuts to as Kiné is driving about the city, parking, or pulling into her garage. Kiné's car of choice is a royal blue Citroën Saxo hatchback—not the seamless magical Citroën D.S. (pronounced *déesse,* or goddess, in French) famously described by Roland Barthes in 1957, and not the slick white Mercedes of El Hadji. Just as Kiné is no object of worship, neither is her car. It is a practical car for a single working mother and it enables her to do her errands without having to hire taxis or ride crammed into unsafe *car rapides.* Through a series of flashbacks we learn that when Kiné was in high school she became pregnant with her philosophy professor's child and was expelled from school just two months before sitting for her baccalaureate, or bac, the exam that would have enabled her to continue her studies. Her hopes of becoming a judge or a lawyer were shattered and Professor Gaye took off to Gabon, assuming no responsibility for his new daughter, Aby. On the day the child was born, Kiné's father attempted to scald Kiné and the infant with a pot of boiling water, but Kiné's mother stepped in to shield them. Kiné is thrown out of her house and Mammy's back is forever scarred and stiff. Having to support herself, and without a high school degree, Kiné becomes a gas station attendant, or *pompiste*.

Evidence exists of female gas station attendants in Dakar since the early 1960s when the glossy *Bingo* magazine, the first of its kind to be aimed at Francophone African audiences, featured a celebratory story about Mame Binta, a twenty-six-year-old divorced single mother who was breaking barriers by becoming a *pompiste*.[14] But despite the fact that *Bingo* linked Mame Binta's job to a modernizing Africa, today female gas station attendants, like female professional drivers and female mechanics, are still not common in Senegal or in other West African countries. Therefore Kiné's job at the Total station, like Mame Binta's who began her job at BP around the time Kiné was born, is itself transgressive. It is also an instance of Kiné occupying male space in order to maintain self-sufficiency.

While working at the gas station, Kiné meets Boubacar Omar Payone, or BOP, a slick businessman who promises to build her a beautiful house full of imported furniture. But after Kiné becomes pregnant with his son, BOP tries to flee the country with false documents and Kiné's savings. He is caught by the police and imprisoned for most of his son's childhood. Kiné is left to raise and educate Aby and Djibril on her own, and she works her way up to become the manager of the Total station, determined to provide her children with the opportunities she was denied. Most of the film takes place in the days following the news that Aby and Djib have successfully passed their bac, completing the exam that their mother never had the chance to take. As Aby and Djib plot to find their mother a partner who will keep her company once they have gone off to university, Professor Gaye and BOP have heard news of their children's academic achievement and Kiné's financial success and are attempting to reenter their lives.

Kiné's will to mobility—her desire to enter traffic as a provider, commander, and consumer of mobility—must therefore be seen as a reaction to a society and system in which she has been trafficked for the benefit of others. Kiné, whose name suggests the kinesis of cinema—*ciné* in French, or *kino* in the Soviet Union, where Sembene did his training (Mowitt 2005, 125)—seems to define herself through a code of mobility. She not only drives herself and her children around the city and saves up for travel abroad but also distributes gas to the moving vehicles of Dakar. She purchases a wheelchair for a young handicapped man who visits her regularly, and she stations herself behind a spotless desk where she honks an oversized horn when she wants her assistant to come see her. But Kiné also takes pleasure in immobilizing others. She confiscates the keys of an arrogant and condescending woman who tries to pay for her gas in foreign (and, as it turns out, counterfeit) currency, and when the wife of one of her lovers threatens her, she attacks the woman with mace. And when Jean, one of Kiné's suitors, parks his car in front of hers and blocks her in for a half hour, Kiné becomes furious. Having spent her entire adult life overcoming the obstacles others have put in her way, she has lost all patience and sympathy for those who obstruct her path for their own purposes.

Kiné is also not interested in remarrying, for she knows that it would mean giving up her hard-won independence. She enjoys work and spends her free time with her other single friends, Amy and Mada, who are also successful businesswomen. The friends meet at the LGM, a local, upscale ice cream parlor, and discuss plans to travel abroad. The limits marriage places on mobility are underscored when Amy confesses to her friends that she cannot join them because she has bowed to parental pressures and (re)married the husband she had left fifteen years earlier. This time, she

Figure 30. Faat Kiné. *Kiné pulls into her garage after an afternoon with her friends.*

Figure 31. Faat Kiné. *Kiné sits at her desk with a hand-held horn to her side.*

Figure 32. Faat Kiné. *"Bitch!" Kiné expresses her anger at being parked into her spot.*

laments, she will be his third wife. So when Kiné needs sexual satisfaction she avoids becoming the exchange object and instead hires the services of a lover or seeks relationships in which she can maintain her power and autonomy. Kiné and her friends are acutely aware of the fact that their hard work and financial independence do not provide them with the social advantages that men have. Amy's new social status is a painful reminder that, as Esi's grandmother admonishes, while a woman will always add to the social status of men, her own status risks being diminished. Acknowledging the continuation of women's oppression, which persists despite their economic self-sufficiency, Kiné echoes Aidoo in her introduction to *The Beautyful Ones Are Not Yet Born* and remarks that "if it only took work to liberate women, women farmers would be liberated." Kiné and her friends therefore embrace a type of feminism that is not about work and production but rather about energetically, and sometimes desperately, consuming a code of self-mobility.

Kiné at the Pump

In the local lexicon of Dakar in the early 2000s, Faat Kiné, Amy, and Mada are the types of women often referred to as *diriyankes*. A *diriyanke* is typically a well-to-do businesswoman who dresses in fashionable traditional clothing, wears an abundance of jewelry and perfume, and attracts men with her seductive skills and financial flattery. She is often, although not always, a single mother or divorced woman who seeks pleasure and sexual satisfaction outside of the institution of marriage. Francis Nyamnjoh, in his brilliant discussion of sexual metaphors and the language of "commoditized sex" in Dakar, cites two possible explanations for the origin of the word *diriyanke*. One theory is that the word is a combination of the Wolof verb *direeku*, which means "to drag oneself," and the word "Yankee." According to this hypothesis, the word comes from the *diriyanke's* ability to drag, or carry herself, like a dignified and independent American woman who, consequently, can have her selection of African males. Another theory posits that the word is the combination of the Wolof *diri*, which means "to pull a load behind or keep on a leash," and the Pulaar suffix *yanke*, meaning "the person who." *Diriyanke* would therefore be the person who drags, or more specifically "the woman who keeps others on a leash" (Nyamnjoh 2005, 300). In either case, the emphasis is notably on the woman's ability to drag or pull. She is the active agent who chooses her men and moves around autonomously. I would also like to suggest that the *diriyanke,* as a person who drags, might also resonate with the French word *dragueur/draqueuse,* a man or woman who is particularly adept at luring the opposite sex. Furthermore, it is interesting to note that until Jean-Pierre Mocky's 1960 film *Les dragueurs,* the common meaning of the verb *draguer* was to fish with a dragnet. That fashionable men in Dakar are referred to as *thiofs,* an expensive type of fish, lends further credence to the overlapping of the word *diriyanke* with the French connotations of *draguer*. Yet, more importantly for the present discussion, it must be noted that the *diriyanke* resembles in many ways the figure of the Mama Benz (sometimes called Nana Benz) of Ivory Coast, Togo, Benin, and the Congo. The Mama Benz is also a successful businesswoman, usually in the cloth trade, whose trademark is a Mercedes-Benz.[15] Both the *diriyanke* and the Mama Benz are respected figures who embody the values of traditional, full-figured beauty and female self-reliance.

In Dakar, the female foil to the *diriyanke* is the *disquette,* a young, slender woman dressed in foreign fashions who uses wealthy men in order to participate in a consumer culture from which she would otherwise be excluded. A *disquette* is the French word for a portable floppy disk. Accordingly, these slim young women are known for their flexibility, for their ability to service different "hard drives," and for the ease with which they can be formatted and reformatted by different users (Nyamnjoh 2005, 311). *Disquettes* seek men who can provide them with one or more of the 4 Vs (*villa, voiture, voyage, virement bancaire*: house, car, travel, and bank transfers), although school-aged *disquettes* will often also settle for professors who can provide them with high marks (304, 306). In contrast to the *diriyankes* who control their men and keep them close, *disquettes* are portable and easily exchanged. (As Nyamnjoh notes, in Abidjan, these types of women are referred to as *portables* or *cellulaires*—both words for cell phones, which are smaller and more mobile, trendy, and flexible than phones fixed to a landline.) *Disquettes* are also compared to spare tires, which are nice to have but not necessary to keep, while *diriyankes* are likened to the (auto-mobile) wheels of a truck (304). In a similar metaphor, Faat Kiné refers to her own "caboose" as "top of the line, not for public transportation." Faat Kiné acknowledges the local euphemisms associated with the *diriyanke* and makes it clear that she will not transport just anybody—like any true *diriyanke* she can afford to be selective. The *diriyanke,* like the Mama Benz, is never dependent on another driver for her mobility.

At the Total station, Kiné is at the center of a male-dominated world, but, as a quintessential *diriyanke,* it is she who drags *(draguer)* and pulls the leash. In the sexually charged metaphoric language of Dakar, replete with its transportation euphemisms, it is significant that Kiné is "at the pump," distributing her gasoline to the various vehicles that come to fill at her station. She has the phallus both to give and to deny. It is at the gas station that the financially motivated Professor Gaye comes to see if Aby has passed her bac and is promptly ordered to leave Kiné's office. Kiné's command to "get out" is immediately echoed in a flashback where the school director shouts the same words, in the same harsh tone, to expel the young Kiné from school. Now, however, it is Kiné who has the power to command mobility. While Gaye is denied a seat in her office, Mossamba Wade, who has come to scold Kiné for cruelly pepper-spraying his wife, is told to sit off to the side. He is denied a seat on the opposite side of Kiné's desk where equals and customers sit. Then, a stunned Mossamba is "fired" and told that his previous sexual services will be compensated but that he will no longer be needed. Only Jean, who seems to want nothing from Kiné other than love and companionship, is treated with kindness. He passes several other stations on his way to "fill" at Kiné's, and, in the end, it is Jean that Kiné chooses as a romantic partner.

Jean is a significant choice because he is the partner that Aby and Djib have deemed the most suitable for their mother, and also the partner that Kiné's mother has declared entirely unsuitable. Mammy objects to Jean first because he is a Christian and second because he is a widower who may bring "bad luck" for his wives. But Aby and Djib do not believe in superstition and find that Jean, an honest businessman and a single father, has much in common with their mother. The relationship between Jean and Kiné promises to be one of equals, a point that is underscored when Aby berates Djib for talking to Jean about their mother as if she were an object of exchange. Here, the daughter objects to her brother's efforts to reinscribe their mother into an economy of exchange. And yet, while her children seem obsessed with finding Kiné a husband, Kiné never mentions actually marrying Jean and certainly does not intend to relinquish her autonomy. When she speaks about sleeping with Jean, she describes herself as active, never passive. In keeping with transportation metaphors, she tells her friends that she has already "driven him" and done it *bu baxx,* quite well, with gusto even.[16] In the final scene of the film Faat Kiné sits in a chair exposing her *petit pagne* (or small sarong), a seductive Senegalese undergarment, and

Figure 33. Faat Kiné. *"Top of the line caboose: not for public transportation." Kiné responds to flirtations with her own euphemism.*

beckons Jean to come and pleasure her. The last shot of the film is a close-up of Kiné's large toe wriggling in delight.

From *Xala* to Hatchback

Despite the fact that Kiné often flaunts her power over movement in typically masculine ways, in some instances causing physical harm to others and lashing out at the wrong people, *Faat Kiné* proffers a new and different type of relationship between pleasure and power. Whereas in both *Xala* and *Changes* sexuality was placed within the political economy of exchange and used to control women, in *Faat Kiné* it becomes an egalitarian, heterosexual exchange of pleasure. What I would like to suggest, then, is that *Faat Kiné* reconstitutes the phallocratic model of exchange and mobility in *Xala* by exploring the possibility for a new type of feminist automobility. As John Mowitt argues, the enunciative tropes of *Faat Kiné* might be productively read as an "inverted rearrangement" (2005, 119) of *Xala*. My argument is that in *Faat Kiné* Sembene has decided to explore what would happen if he were to take seriously the claims of autonomy mouthed by the businessmen who take over the Chamber of Commerce in *Xala*. In the opening scene of *Xala,* the narrator, speaking as if he were one of the new elites, declares: "We must control industry, our commerce, our culture, take in hand our destiny." But, of course, the actions on screen—the Frenchmen handing the new Senegalese leaders briefcases filled with money—contradict this spirit of independence and set the tone for a satirical fable of impotence and greed. In *Faat Kiné,* however, Sembene has created a protagonist who has no choice but to take her destiny into her own hands. This is not to say that *Faat Kiné* is not full of mockery, contradiction, or banter, but here Sembene creates a hero who, unlike the businessmen in *Xala,* succeeds at economic self-sufficiency. That this protagonist is a woman, and is joined by a small cadre of equally successful female friends, is crucial to the way in which *Faat Kiné* reorganizes some of the central tropes of *Xala* via a new politics of gender and automobility.

To begin with, the opening images of *Faat Kiné* are all taken from the playbook of *Xala*—automobiles of various makes and functions circling Dakar's central Place de l'Indépendance, striking panoramas of a city in motion, and women carrying plastic buckets of water on their heads. The first shot of the film captures these women crossing the Place de l'Indépendance where N'Gone had circled with her wedding car in tow, and as the camera pans out we see the Chamber of Commerce marginalized in the left hand corner of the frame. After the women make their way across the square, the camera returns to a medium shot of them walking single file with their buckets. In the next shot, Faat Kiné is dropping off her two children to find out the results of their bac. In *Xala* women carrying buckets of dirty water are a nuisance to El Hadji and his secretary Madame Diouf. They dump their water in the open sewer right outside the office, creating an unpleasant smell, and they would certainly be placed in the category of *déchets humains* (human rubbish) that El Hadji sought to remove from his environs. In *Faat Kiné,* however, these women walk deliberately and nobly across the screen, while the Chamber of Commerce, so central to the opening of *Xala,* remains in the background. *Faat Kiné* is a tale of everyday people *moving about* the city in cars, on foot, and in *car rapides,* not the elite "moving up" (like El Hadji or the businessman in *Borom Sarret*) at the expense of others. The juxtaposition of the sequence of the women crossing the Place de l'Indépendance with the shots of Kiné behind the wheel links the plight of the bourgeois protagonist to these less privileged city women. After Kiné's children exit the car, the women cross the street in front of the car and she must pause for them. Despite the fact that she is rushing off to work, she shares the city with them and even yields to them. Later in the film when another single-file line of people crosses her path—this time a group of blind children—Kiné steps out of her office to hand each one of them alms. For Kiné, unlike El Hadji, personal mobility and social responsibility are not mutually exclusive.

Similarly, as Mowitt points out, *Faat Kiné* dramatically restages the wedding celebration scene of *Xala* with its own lengthy celebration. In *Xala* the wedding of El Hadji and N'Gone occurs toward the beginning of the film and reaches its anticlimactic conclusion with the revelation that El Hadji has been stricken with the curse of impotence. As I argue in chapter 3, from this point on, the film becomes riddled with tropes of stasis and regression. El Hadji's movements become less and less aligned with his Mercedes until eventually the car is removed from the film. In *Faat Kiné* the celebration is in honor of Aby and Djib's successful completion of the bac, and it is organized by the Club of Utopia and Prospectives, a group of young men that wants Djib to be the future president of the federation of West African states. The celebration here occurs at the end of the film and finishes with the successful coupling of Jean and Kiné.[17] Central to both celebrations is a mockery of irresponsible male power. At his wedding, El Hadji is offered both traditional and Western sexual aids, but he refuses to use them. He learns only when it is too late that he should not have been so sure of his potency. At Kiné's party Amy recounts what happened when she asked her jet-setting husband to wear a condom to protect against HIV/AIDS: "His flag dropped from 12:00 to 6:30." But now that her husband wants nothing to do with her, Amy tells her friends that she is free to travel abroad with them. In *Xala* the loss of the erection is a tragic symbol of the failed leadership of the country. In *Faat Kiné* it is not only comedic, it is liberating. Without denying the possibility for heterosexual romantic love and pleasure, the women are successful at getting male power to lose its erection, to lose its ability to penetrate and dominate women's lives.

However, the most sustained critique of patriarchy comes not from the women, but from future president Djib—the figure of a new type of masculinity and leadership—who rallies the young party guests as he defends his mother and tells Gaye and BOP that "the rights of paternity imply responsibility." Although the feminist politics of the film are somewhat undercut by the fact that it is Djib and not Aby who represents the future of the country—which is part of the reason that I find the film to be an ambiguous celebration of female agency—the party scene nevertheless offers a rearrangement of the gender expectations that typically see women as immobile objects of exchange and men as mobile subjects.[18] While El Hadji's wedding launches a film that revolves around female subordination, religious and commodity fetishes, and male impotency, *Faat Kiné* ends in a celebration of youth leadership, female mobility, and a foot flexed in satisfaction. While one party is marked by stalled progress and the failure of the penis, the other is marked by deferred progress and the polymorphous sexual satisfaction that is implied by the final close-up of Kiné's erect toe.

Furthermore, in *Xala* El Hadji is defined in large part by his white Mercedes-Benz. His identity as a prosperous businessman, his facade of autonomy, and the range of his daily movements are dependent on it. By contrast, in *Faat Kiné* the Citroën hatchback is a minor figure whose main role is to allow Kiné to complete her daily errands. Moreover, rather than literally parading the car on a pedestal, as he does with N'Gone's car in *Xala,* Sembene allows the automobility of the Saxo to become one type of mobility among many. In other words, the Saxo helps Kiné maneuver the city in a privileged way, but it does not define her, nor does it mark her as in any way superior to the women walking with buckets on their heads, the disabled man in a wheelchair who works as a messenger, or even those passengers riding in the rickety *car rapides.* The hatchback helps Faat Kiné keep the rhythm of Dakar's polymorphic movements.

Likewise, the multiplicity of forms of mobility in *Faat Kiné* is underscored by the range of activities that occur at the Total petrol station, which is situated at a major intersection in Point E, a middle-class neighborhood in Dakar that evokes neither the elitism of the Plateau in *Xala* nor the poverty of the Medina in *Borom Sarret.* At the Total Point E the audience sees private automobiles as well as aging Toyota taxis and *car rapides* coughing black smoke, men on motorcycles, hobbling beggars, ambulant flower vendors, and Muslim motorists seeking a spot to pray. Thus, while the Total station may be a hub of transnational capitalism, it is also a place that, in Sembene's words, "symbolizes the energy of life" (Klawans 2001). What is not shown, however, are the broken-down cars that often rest and await maintenance in the median of the boulevard—which those familiar with Dakar know has ironically been dubbed the Champs-Élysées—where the Total Point E is situated. An observant viewer may catch a glimpse of these cars in the background of a few shots, but the camera does not pay them any attention. As he strives to portray a side of Dakar in which things work,

Figure 34. Faat Kiné. *Kiné's Saxo waits for women carrying buckets to cross the street in the film's opening sequence.*

Figure 35. Faat Kiné. *A* car rapide *pulls into Kiné's Total station. Dakar's "Champs-Élysées" can just barely be seen in the background.*

Sembene turns a cinematic blind eye to these broken-down automobiles, just as Aidoo fails to mention *tro-tros* as a potential option for Opokuya. *Faat Kiné* is, after all, a film about a woman who fuels Dakar's vehicles and whose name evokes the *ciné* itself: it is a film in which things are constantly in motion.

Faat Kiné depicts, for better and for worse, Sembene's vision of a changing and dynamic Dakar. It is a film about women with business acumen seeking to produce, consume, and exchange outside the phallic economy. It is about women who at times defy and at other times embody the dissolution of human relations that define capitalist society. Although Faat Kiné works hard to support and educate her family, life has hardened her. In *Faat Kiné* the *déesse* is certainly dead: she's been replaced by the gas-station manager and integrated into the world of hatchbacks, condoms, and cigarettes. The mother that Sembene holds out as his everyday hero is hardly perfect, and just as the consumer society she inhabits is not likely to rescue most Senegalese from their condition of chronic poverty, the automobility she has been able to obtain for herself will certainly not be available to all who seek it. But Faat Kiné, along with Amy and Mada, have been able to effect "mobile and transitory points of resistance" (1978, 96), as Foucault says, that help to produce cleavages and new types of power in a shifting society. And what is clear is that these points of resistance are manifesting within the sphere of global capitalism and not against it.

Violent Transmissions

I want to conclude by underscoring the fact that feminist automobility is often a reaction to patriarchal power that is not simply hierarchical and unfair but sometimes violent and brutal. In *Faat Kiné* and *Changes* Esi and Kiné are emotionally and physically abused by the men in their lives. In Jean-Pierre Bekolo's *Les Saignantes,* another decidedly feminist film, the relationship between violence and automobility is even more explicit. Here, two women, Majolie and Chouchou, traverse a futuristic Yaoundé in order to dispose of the body of a government official, the Secrétaire Général du Comité Central (SGCC), who had died in bed with Majolie. Upon discovering the SGCC's death, Majolie phones Chouchou to come to her rescue. Chouchou takes a taxi to Majolie, but in the dark of the night the male taxi driver threatens to rape her. In a later scene a government minister starts to rape a female acquaintance of Majolie and Chouchou in his car but is stopped by the two protagonists. The threatened rape and the actual rape, both occurring in cars, illustrate what might happen to women who are not privileged enough to have their own means of transport. These types of gendered power relations are made painstakingly clear when the minister, in a bold expression of biopower, says to his victim, "You don't have any idea of who I am. I have the power of life and death over people like you." But Bekolo's science-fiction film also presents ways in which the women can creatively insert themselves into the world of male automobility. When Majolie and Chouchou take the dead SGCC's voice-activated car, the girls must literally imitate his voice. Even though *Les Saignantes,* like *Faat Kiné* and *Changes,* underscores some of the impossibilities of feminist automobility, the car still becomes a machine that they can then use for their own purposes. It is a tool of survival.

Donna Haraway—who "would rather be a cyborg than a goddess" (1991, 181)—reminds us: "The machine is not an *it* to be animated, worshipped, and dominated. The machine is us, *our* process, an aspect of our embodiment. We can be responsible for machines; *they* do not dominate or threaten us" (180). The feminist texts discussed in this chapter seem to argue that in a society where women's autonomy is constrained and limited by patriarchal regimes, the car is a machine that can, in certain cases, instantiate new sources of power and pleasure, as Haraway suggests. Cars—like other technologies—allow women to recode themselves as "disassembled and reassembled" subjects (163) in order to evade both sacralization and other more violent forms of control. *Changes* and *Faat Kiné* therefore put forth feminist counternarratives where the car becomes a potentially transgressive tool. Like bell hooks, who, in her autobiography, *Wounds of Passion,* relishes the car with its "leather seats, the real wood on the dashboard, [and] the shiny metal" (1997, 47) as a way to escape the segregated buses and racism of the Jim Crow South, the female drivers of *Changes* and *Faat Kiné* use the car as a way to experience the freedom of automobility while, at the same time, evading at least some of the patriarchal structures that limit these experiences.

And yet while automobiles enable their drivers a temporary transgression of physical and social barriers that might otherwise prove difficult to surmount, they do not, in either text, enable women drivers to become the autonomously mobile figures of an ideally imagined automobility. In both texts automobility is determined, bound, and limited both by the economic disequilibrium that defines African city-spaces and by postcolonial gender relations. Esi Sekyi realizes that there are no individual answers to the problems that she faces. She sees her new car from Ali as a way to immediately improve her own day-to-day mobility, but she knows that the problems of government neglect, uneven capitalism, and highly stratified gender division will in no way be addressed by her new possession. Thus, as the novel closes, she clearly fails to embody the free, autonomous ideals that one typically associates with automobility. Although *Faat Kiné* also depicts the many constraints placed on African women, Kiné is, compared to Esi, more successful at becoming an auto-mobile woman. And yet, it is important to note that she does so in a film where the dominance of the car is mitigated by the multiplicity of other forms of equally valid mobility. What saves *Faat Kiné* from becoming a simplified celebration of women's automobility is that the automobile for Faat Kiné does not become a *means* of self-expression or freedom but rather, a part of a larger will to mobility, a will that she shares with all the Dakarois who are trying to navigate the neoliberal city. Thus, neither *Changes* nor *Faat Kiné* makes driving or consumer culture more broadly the solution to social or economic problems. But compared to texts that focus on male car owners and consumers, the private car in feminist texts is significantly less maligned, less mocked, and less implicit in forms of neocolonial inequality.

Global (Be)Longings

You have crossed that awkward, deeply uncomfortable, sometimes shameful social state of being without a car. I mean in some countries where the public transport system works, not having a car is no big deal. But you are in Nigeria, where public transport is living hell, and owning a car can be the difference between life and social death.

You had suffered the humiliation and attendant frustrations. You swore to yourself, after the girl you came to a party with left in an air conditioned car, that things must change. The Nigerian god felt your pain, heard your cries of affliction and consequently, after much tithing and prayers, blessed your hustle. Enough to buy your own car. I rejoice with you.

You have taken the car to the man of God and they have spent over an hour with the bonnet open, anointing your car and protecting it against the spirit of accidents that those jealous neighbours and village enemies are sure to send your way. That is fine. But you also need my advice.

—Elnathan John, "How to Behave as a Car Owner in Nigeria"

IN THE ABOVE EXCERPT from "How to Behave as a Car Owner in Nigeria" (2012), the former lawyer turned writer Elnathan John skewers the Nigerian car-owning elite in a satirical blog post that is part of a popular "How To" series published in the *Daily Times* and on John's website, The Dark Corner. John provides his readers with a host of important advice for Nigerian car owners. For instance, he tells his readers, "Now that you are a car owner, you need to realise that your status has changed. You need to treat pedestrians with the disdain they deserve. . . . You must never think like a pedestrian and do silly things like observing Zebra crossings. Those white lines are there to beautify the road. Speed across them and curse anyone who tries to get in your way." The car owner may be a self-made man or woman whose hard work has paid off (or whose "hustle" has been blessed), but what John suggests here is that this success means very little unless others can see the evidence of it. And, as John jests, these outward displays of auto-mobile triumph include gratuitously using the horn whether you are happy, sad, or angry, stopping your car in the middle of the road to say hello to friends, double parking, and "warming" the car every morning at 6:00 a.m. by revving the engine as loudly as possible. Moreover, John's post mocks the excessive performance of car owners who not only behave as if it is a sort of "social death" to be without a car but who also create a chaotic and violent atmosphere for pedestrians, taxi drivers, and more respectful car owners. Underlying John's satire is also the notion that, in light of the Nigerian government's failure to provide adequate public transportation and safe infrastructure, the individual must take matters into his own hands. John tells the car owners, "At night, it is important that you see the road clearly. Nigerian roads are dark and dangerous, so you must use your full lights at all times. It doesn't matter if you are blinding oncoming vehicles. Is it your fault that the government is not doing their job?"

But just as the blog, written in the style of the self-help manuals or how-to guides that are popularly consumed in West Africa, argues for self-reliance, it also seems to mock the very idea of the self. As Mohsin Hamid writes in the first paragraph of his novel *How to Get Filthy Rich in Rising Asia,* "A self-help book is an oxymoron. You read a self-help book so someone who isn't yourself can help you, that someone being the author" (2013, 3). According to Hamid, this does not mean that the self-help book is useless, though "it does mean that the idea of the self in the land of self-help is a slippery one" (3–4). In "How to Behave as a Car Owner in Nigeria," John "helps" his readers to perform a certain type of self, a self constituted on images made possible by the very slipperiness Hamid describes. So he advises, among other things, adorning your car with stickers to announce the self you have created:

> Get [a sticker] from your church or fellowship that declares this year to be your "year of anointing," or your "year of unsurpassed success." If your wife or husband goes to a different church, get one from hers too. You can never get too many. Get one sticker that declares your child to be a Star Student. Let those with dull children see it and regret that their wives didn't take enough vitamins during pregnancy. Because of Police on the road, get either an NBA [Nigerian Bar Association] sticker or an ARMY

> sticker. You don't have to be a lawyer or soldier to get them. Especially the NBA one—you can find that one in any court premises for one or two hundred naira.

In other words, the point is not who you are, but who you can pretend to be, or who you can make others believe you are. The car, as I have suggested throughout this book, acts as an extension of this self: the body of the automobile, here covered in bumper stickers, both protects the car owner from the physical violence of the road (a form of protection not available to the pedestrian) and extends the self, both literally and metaphorically, into the larger world.

John's emphasis on the performativity of the car owner also allows one to see how the automobile is part of what Sasha Newell calls "the modernity bluff." Building on the Comaroffs' suggestion that postcolonial identity is always associated with a "counterfeit modernity," Newell argues that the mimesis of modernity is key to understanding the way that new global relations and postcolonial subjectivities are produced in Africa. Focusing specifically on Ivory Coast and the figure of the fashionable *bluffeur,* Newell discusses the way in which the imitation, or the bluff, of modernity is tied to a sense of prestige. He writes, "A combination of dress, attitude, physical comportment, and spendthrift practices, the bluff is not only a performance of success beyond the financial means of the actor in question but also a demonstration of the superior person one would embody all the time if one had the money for it, a display of potential" (2012, 1). But in the case of the *bluffeur,* the performance is not supposed to be a deception—in other words, unlike the bluffing in 419 scams, no one is meant be fooled. Rather, the point is to call attention to the stylish performativity of the bluff. In the "How To" post, the excessive stickers, the revving of the car at 6:00 a.m., and the superfluous honking act in a similar way: the point of owning a car, John suggests, is to demonstrate your superiority, to highlight and perform it, and not to simply participate in banal driving practices.

Furthermore, Newell argues that inauthenticity is precisely what makes the *bluffeurs,* who are supposedly "counterfeiting" modernity, actually quite modern: they participate in the very modern act of privileging performance over authenticity, of conflating the copy with the original. The *bluffeurs* who successfully imitate Euro-American modernity, and in particular mainstream African American hip-hop culture and consumerism, are said to have "truly arrived" (11). In other words, if "to be fake is to not belong" (253), *bluffeurs* are not considered fake: they belong because they perform and are a part of modernity. And this, too, is the case with car owners. Though, automobility is never truly autonomous and mobility is always coupled with stasis, the car nevertheless provides its owners and drivers with concrete and indisputable social advantages. And, most importantly, it makes them de facto global subjects, subjects who are cosmopolitan and defined by their "first-class" status (Ferguson 2006, 187) rather than by a condition of poverty. Cars are important belongings, then, precisely because they allow one to belong.

Africa Driving, Africa Rising

Throughout this book my intent has been to use West Africans' complex and overdetermined relationship to automobiles and automobility to go beyond the totalizing narratives of teleological progress or failure and underdevelopment. The need for this type of approach is underscored not only by the continued presence of Orientalist narratives that see Africa as a place where technology and modernity have failed to reach but also by the recent popularity of the Africa Rising slogan used by media sources who have, almost overnight, reversed their stories about "hopeless" Africa.[1] As Porsche dealerships are opening up in Lagos, high rises are sprouting up in cities like Dakar, Yaoundé, and Accra, and Chinese, Indian, and Korean carmakers are making new cars affordable to middle-class Africans, reports of underdevelopment have been replaced by panegyrics of African economic success. The Africa Rising trope has become so common that Sean Jacobs, founder of the popular blog *Africa Is a Country,* has called it a meme.

What makes the Africa Rising discussion relevant here is that it seems to be another iteration of Walt Rostow's argument, articulated almost sixty years ago, regarding the stages of economic development. Rostow believed that all societies would eventually "take off," become "mature," and conclude their development in an "age of high mass consumption," an age where automobile ownership was the prime indicator of the advancement of lifestyle patterns. And while Africa Rising stories feature a range of mobile technologies—almost all articles cite statistics about the rise of the cell phone or laptop as indicators of Africa's new economic progress—it is still often the car that stands in as the most powerful visual symbol of development. Take, for instance, the photo that headed Mohamed A. El-Erian's

Figure 36. African children ogling a Mercedes. Photograph credit Sean Gallup/Getty Image News/Getty Images.

article "Into Africa," published online by the magazine *Foreign Policy* (see figure 36). The photo, placed right below the headline "Believe the Hype. Africa's Rise Is Real," seems to suggest that the much-admired Mercedes is a perfect example of a "booming" Africa, an Africa with a growing business class and a rising stock market poised for what El-Erian, sounding much like Rostow, calls "a breakout phase that would lift millions out of utter poverty and great misery." The implication seems to be that the children photographed in this unidentified African country, wearing a telling balance of modern and traditional clothing, are looking at, even touching, their own future, that the Mercedes they stroke will soon be within reach.

On April 29, 2013, Jacques Enaudeau (Twitter handle: @jacksometer) tweeted a link to the photograph preceded by the following text: "This is what #AfricaRising looks like for @ForeignPolicy. Bc *[sic]* nothing says empowerment like kids 'petting' a Mercedes." Whereas Africa Rising boosters see the image of the Mercedes as a sign of success, hope, and teleological development that is embodied in the child who, like Africa, may one day grow up to become prosperous, Enaudeau sees it as an absurdity, an example of consumer culture being overidealized and underanalyzed. While it is indeed refreshing to see Western media pushing past depictions of continual crisis and moving beyond paternalistic narratives about uplift, exuberance about Africa finally "catching up" to the West (or at least to India and East Asia) is neither new nor complex enough. Nor does it come anywhere close to the multilayered and richly entangled stories that Africans, in times of hope and crisis, craft about the selves they construct and the objects they consume and covet. Current development narratives, in whatever iteration they come, are still far from being able to capture the impact of technological breakdown on the psyche as Soyinka does in *The Road,* the inventive critiques and playful reimaginings in African art films, or the feelings of ambivalence in Nollywood films and feminist stories about women drivers. As I have shown throughout this book, encounters between subjects and technological objects are never straightforward, and narratives of Africa that take the car, or even the mobile phone or laptop, as unproblematic icons of success and development are inherently themselves problematic.

Although it is true that many positive things might come from the fact that African émigrés are returning back home to start businesses and that foreign investment, especially from China, is on the increase, what the Africa Rising meme so often ignores is that "global" success is almost always quite uneven and never truly global. As Jacobs writes, "Of course it is easier to write yet another new beginning for the continent (or rebrand it, if you prefer), than to offer substantial engagement with the current situation."[2] Poverty has not been erased, or even significantly reduced for most, corruption is still rampant, and infrastructure is still consistently inconsistent. Moreover, as has been the case in the past, development projects can often serve as justification for policies that adversely affect the poor. In Lagos, for example, former governor Babatunde Fashola earned international praise for building upscale shopping centers and housing developments (high profile enough to have been inaugurated by Bill Clinton) and investing in public transportation like the Bus Rapid Transit system that opened in 2008 and the light-rail that was scheduled to open at the end of 2016. But in order to make room for these projects, Fashola also cleared out popular slums and rendered tens of thousands of Lagos's poorest residents homeless (Nossiter 2013).

Likewise, other signs of development or improvement in automobility and infrastructure tend to look less rosy when more closely considered. For instance, several countries like Senegal in 2003 and Guinea in 2011 have implemented policies banning the importation of cars older than five years.

In Nigeria vehicles over fifteen years old are now prohibited from being imported, and in Ghana and Ivory Coast cars older than ten years incur a penalty fee (Martin 2015). While these laws, when they are not made irrelevant by smugglers, can certainly improve the quality of vehicles on the road and cut back on pollution and excessive breakdowns, they also make automobiles prohibitively expensive for many, and they do not seem to have been accompanied by any drop in serious accidents and road fatalities.[3]

Additionally, many are optimistic that a few West African countries are producing their own cars, albeit on a very small scale. In the summer of 2014, Peugeot Automobile Nigeria (PAN) and Hyundai Motors Nigeria Limited rolled out made-in-Nigeria cars designed to be more affordable to the middle class. A few months earlier the Stallion Group did the same thing with locally made Nissan vehicles.[4] And, in Ghana, Apostle Dr. Kwadwo Safo Kantanka, founder of the Kristo Asafo (Christ Reformed Church), has been locally handmaking several of his own electric Kantanka cars. While it is still unclear whether these developments will significantly change car consumption in Nigeria or Ghana, it is quite unlikely that these cars will be affordable to the majority of citizens or that they will help to improve infrastructure, public transportation, or accident rates.

Automobility from the South

What I find so limiting and inadequate about the Africa Rising trope is that, like older development narratives, it not only fails to account for the vast inequalities still present but also that it lacks the ability to explain what it *feels* like to drive a luxury car in posh African neighborhoods, or to bump along potholed roads, or to be crammed into collective buses "shuffering and shmiling" as Fela Kuti sings. John's "How to Behave as a Car Owner in Nigeria" provides one version of what it feels like to drive in West Africa: it feels quite good; it feels like you have finally "made it." In Adaobi Tricia Nwaubani's novel *I Do Not Come to You by Chance* (2009), the protagonist Kingsley expresses similar feelings as he moves from being a well-educated but unemployed college graduate to a well-dressed, cell-phone-toting, car-owning 419 man: "Heads turned as my Lexus sped through the streets. Eyes followed in wonder and admiration. Without braking, I honked at some pedestrians occupying the better part of a pothole-riddled road. The three men jumped away in fright. My windows were up and the air-conditioning was on full blast, so I could barely make out their invectives" (186). For

Kingsley the infrastructural deficiencies, like the crowded potholed roads that seemed to bother him when he took buses or motorcycle taxis, now become much less of a nuisance; they, in fact, make the leap to becoming a car owner even more pleasurable. In John's blog and in *I Do Not Come to You by Chance,* as was the case with many of the texts discussed earlier, cars help the precarious subject feel as if he or she belongs to the global order, that he or she circulates within rather than outside of its flows.

But at the same time, driving can also be a frustrating and alienating experience, and it can produce just as much longing as it does belonging. We see this longing, for instance, in Soyinka's Samson, who wants to take to the road but is held back by the traumatized driver Kotonu. Or in *Quartier Mozart's* Queen of the Hood, who longs for the mobility of the neighborhood boys and uses the site of the car to transform herself into one of them. Or in Nollywood characters like Andy, Mike, Kelvin, Duran, and Philip, who long for wealth and automobiles and are willing to go to extreme means to acquire them. Or even in the character of Opokuya in *Changes,* who longs for the freedom and automobility of her friend Esi. What becomes evident, then, is that cars shape the West African subject as much in their presence as in their absence.

Because the particular infrastructures of feeling produced by cars in West Africa are so entangled with the unique patterns of consumption in the region, I have focused much of my attention on the historical and cultural specificity of West Africa automobility. However, at the same time, I also wish to follow Jean and John Comaroff who, in *Theory from the South* (2012), suggest that one should turn to the Global South in order to understand the workings of the contemporary world at large. The Comaroffs advocate a type of analysis that pushes past the North–South division by looking at the way the Global South, or places previously considered "peripheral," might be central to discerning how neoliberalism produces certain types of encounters with everyday life. They argue that "as labor markets contract and employment is casualized, as manufacture moves away without warning, as big business seeks to coerce states to unmake ecolaws, to drop minimum wages," subjects in the North experience the "insecurities, instabilities, even forced mobility and disposability characteristic of life in much of the non-West" (14). It is difficult to say how precisely the instabilities of neoliberalism might shift the affective experiences of automobility in the West (though in the United States the prevalence of ride-sharing services, the increasing failure of infrastructure, and the increase in bike culture might be some indication). But what I want to remind readers of here is that the contradictions of African automobility are present in different forms and degrees in the West, where cars break down as well, poor people have significantly more obstacles to mobility, and the fantasies of individualized mobility are disrupted by the realities of traffic, accidents, oil availability, and racial profiling. No matter where they are, cars, like all material objects, are "intrinsically contradictory" (Miller 2010, 62). Though my focus has been on West Africa and the particular contradictions of automobility experienced there, it is my hope that theorizing how automobility is lived and felt "from the South" might put some of these larger issues into relief.

Throughout this book I have aimed to position the car as part of a global modernity that is less about temporality (modern versus backwards) or geography (central versus periphery) and more about feelings of participation and lived experiences of belonging or unbelonging that have often played out in messy and surprising ways. In the colonial moment, for instance, it was often Africans who wanted cars and who took the initiative to import them while colonial officers often remained ambivalent and in some cases hostile to the idea of modernizing and motorizing Africa. In the immediate post-independence and recent neoliberal periods, cars have been potent symbols of freedom, individualism, modernity, and capitalist success, even as those key values are often simultaneously critiqued or subverted. Cars, then, are productive objects of inquiry precisely because they are inseparable from the paradoxical ethos of mobility, autonomy, and status that make up global modernity and because they so often embody and set in motion the aspirations and anxieties of their particular users. As the texts I have analyzed demonstrate, automobiles and subjects' relationship to them can make palpable the complex ways that belonging to modernity has simultaneously been a struggle and a given.

Notes

Introduction

1. See, for instance, Henri Lefebvre's statement (quoted in the epigraph) that cars are the epitome of objects or Guy Debord, who referred to the automobile as "the sovereign good of alienated life and the essential product of the capitalist market" (1981,69). Likewise, Kristin Ross calls the automobile "the central vehicle of all twentieth-century modernization" (1995, 19), and, even more recently, Paul Gilroy, in *Darker Than Blue: On the Moral Economies of Black Atlantic Culture* (2010), assigns the car the status of the ur-commodity of industrial capitalism.

2. Though Sembene's name is sometimes spelled with an accent over the second "e" (Sembène), I follow David Murphy by leaving off the accent. As Murphy writes in *Sembene: Imagining Alternatives in Film and Fiction,* Sembene himself expressed the desire for the spelling without an accent (2001, 1).

3. According to the World Bank, West African countries have some of the lowest motorization rates in the world in the twenty-first century. While in 2011 the United States had 786 motor vehicles per 1,000 people, Burkina Faso had 10 and Niger had 8. Statistics available for 2009 show that Cameroon had 19 vehicles per 1,000 people, Ghana had 30, and Mali had 12. In 2008 Senegal had 22, and statistics for 2007 show Nigeria at 31, Ivory Coast at 20, and Togo, the least motorized in the world, at 2. The World Bank data do not distinguish between commercial vehicles and private vehicles.

4. In Levine's discussion of how literary and sociopolitical forms operate together as complex "organizing principles" (2015, 7), she argues that narratives are particularly valuable heuristic forms "because they can set in motion multiple social forms and track them as they cooperate, come into conflict, and overlap, without positing an ultimate cause" (19). She defends the value of aesthetic forms by citing Bruno Latour, who "mentions in passing that fiction writers often do better than sociologists at capturing social relations because they are free to experiment" (19).

5. As Charles Piot writes of West Africa, "There are fundamental features of the period after the end of the Cold War that are shared across the entire region—the pullback of the state and the advent of neoliberal reform, the transfer of the biopolitical to the NGOs and the human rights organizations, the rapid spread of

charismatic Christianity, the retreat of tradition in the villages, the rise of cultures of deception of identity fabrication, the desire for exile" (2010, 17).

6. See Peter R. Gould's *The Development of the Transportation Pattern in Ghana* for a discussion on the history of the mammy wagon and the origin of the term (1960, 79).

7. According to a 2013 World Health Organization report, "The African Region remains the least motorized of the six world regions, but suffers the highest rates of road traffic fatalities, with 37 of 44 surveyed countries having death rates well above the global average of 18.0 deaths per 100,000 population. . . . While the African Region possesses only 2% of the world's vehicles it contributes 16% to the global deaths. . . . More than one in four deaths in the African Region occur on Nigeria's roads."

8. See Quayson's *Oxford Street, Accra: City Life and the Itineraries of Transnationalism.*

9. The *Oxford English Dictionary* defines automobility simply as "the use of automobiles or motor vehicles as a mode of locomotion or travel" or "mobility by means of an automobile or motor vehicle" and dates its usage back as early as 1903.

10. Discussing the massive federal expenditure and highway expansions of the 1950s, Seiler argues that this new level of automobility was, in part, a response to the Cold War ideologies that pitted capitalism and communism against each other. Driving and automobility reaffirmed the capitalist ideal of the free, self-reliant, modern individual and, according to Seiler, justified U.S. foreign policy and quest for supremacy over alternative regimes (2008, 7).

11. As Tim Cresswell argues, while mobility is often considered a right, there are always "unspoken Others" who are "differently mobile." He writes, "Think of the Arab-Americans stopped at airport immigration, Hispanic-Americans in the fields of American agri-business or African-Americans 'driving while black'" (2006, 161).

12. The fantasy of unfettered automobility is also linked to what Imre Szeman calls the "fiction of surplus," the belief that there will always be enough fuel and that daily life will never be hindered by a crisis of energy (2011, 324).

13. Antonio Gramsci, writing in Italy not more than two decades after the first Model T rolled off the lines in 1914, was already pondering whether Fordism and Americanism would constitute an entirely new worldwide historical epoch. He saw Fordism as a comprehensive yet contradictory set of forces that were not limited to the production of automobiles but extended to questions about mass consumption, sexuality, urban and rural space, and new types of social discipline.

14. Jennifer Hart's book *Ghana on the Go* provides an excellent history of automobility in Ghana; however, her focus is more on the drivers themselves rather than the social and symbolic object of the car.

15. Jean Rouch's 1967 film *Jaguar* chronicles the stories of three young men from Niger who travel to Ghana and attempt to emulate the style and fashions of the Jaguars there.

16. Other posts of photos of old automobiles like Daimlers, Mercedes, and Austins also seem to be key in remembering the long-gone "good old days," as many members say. A post added on June 1, 2013, by Bunmi Okeowo of his grandfather Chief A. T. Okeowo dressed in fine robes and leaning against an Austin automobile in the 1950s garnered much attention from members of the group who remarked on the classiness of the car or the chief's "panache" and elegance that seem to be absent in the "big men" who now run Nigeria.

17. Timothy Brennan in "Postcolonial Studies and Globalization Theory" and Simon Gikandi in "Globalization and the Claims of Postcoloniality" both make similar claims about the way in which globalization theory borrows from the playbook of a poststructuralist postcolonial theory that argues for the ontological superiority of indeterminacy and "in-betweenness."

18. For a critique of the former privileging of depth over surface in discussions of African cultural production and a plea to go beyond this binary, see Kenneth Harrow's *Postcolonial African Cinema: From Political Engagement to Postmodernism.*

19. White discusses, for instance, a blood drive for overseas soldiers during World War II that failed in Tanganyika because people assumed that the blood was to be flown overseas and drunk by Europeans. A fire engine parked at the airstrip seemed to confirm this fear because firemen and their vehicles at the time were widely associated with vampires—firemen who were thought to be vampires even had their own Swahili name, *wazimamoto* (2000, 128). White argues that the stories about vampires in motorcars described the peculiarities of new and highly obscured labor practices and expressed the feelings of powerlessness that Africans experienced as a result of the colonial economy.

1. The Hum of Progress

1. Of course, road building in Europe and America was also at times controversial. In the United States and Britain, property owners initially opposed the widening and paving of roads because they wanted to keep high-speed vehicles (including bicycles and horsecars) off of residential streets. However, by the time the internal combustion automobile came to replace both the steam automobile, which had been prone to explosions, and the horse, whose manure and carcasses caused tremendous pollution and public health concerns, the motorcar was often enthusiastically welcomed. Automobiles were critiqued as status symbols of the elite, but they faced minimal regulation and public opposition except to address basic safety concerns. See Clay McShane's *Down the Asphalt Path: The Automobile and the American City.*

2. See David Scott (1999), who argues that colonial governmentality, as a form of modern power, aimed to create conditions under which colonial subjects would transform their conduct and behave, without coercion, as modern, "enlightened" subjects.

3. For instance, Harold Smith, a colonial officer in Nigeria during the decade of decolonization, discusses how he was instructed to use the vehicles of the Ministry of Labor in order to campaign on behalf of the political party that the British had selected to succeed them. Smith states, "To have cars and trucks in the bush at all gave you tremendous prestige... If a fleet of vehicles with maybe thirty or forty staff of clerks and administrators suddenly descended they would have made a very big impact as this was official, this was the government" (Thompson 2008, 54).

4. Mamdani argues, in fact, that British indirect rule, South African apartheid, and the French policy of "association" were all variations of "decentralized despotism" (1996, 8) rather than unique forms of rule. For a similar argument about the overlaps between French and British rule, see also M. Semakula Kiwanuka's "Colonial Policies and Administrations in Africa: The Myths of the Contrasts."

5. This was also the case in the Dutch Indies. See Mrázek (2002).

6. See Saint-Martin (1973) and Drummond-Thompson (1992).

7. For instance, William Schneider discusses the procolonial stance taken by editors and publishers in the French mass newspapers of the late nineteenth century. He discusses the ways the editorial content of the newspapers made the case for colonialism at a time when the merits of colonial expansion were being debated in popular discourse. The editorials linked the acquisition of colonies to the mitigation of the effects of the depression of the 1880s. Schneider also argues that ethnographic exhibitions provided an important way to mark Africans as savages in need of French civilization.

8. Adolphe Kégresse, the inventor of the caterpillar cars, originally designed them for the czar of Russia, who wished to have a motorcar that he could drive on the snow.

9. Although both the film and the book of the trans-African trek have the same French title—*La croisière noire*—the film is typically translated as *The Black Cruise*, whereas the English translators of the book chose the title *The Black Journey*.

10. After "conquering Africa," Citroën also organized *La croisière jaune* (the Yellow Cruise) through Asia and *La croisière blanche* (the White Cruise) through sub-Arctic Canada. A book was written on the "Yellow Cruise" and films were made of both expeditions.

11. See Berliner (2002) for further details on the cultural significance of what he refers to as France's first multimedia extravaganza.

12. Indeed, the films were even able to associate themselves with the popularity of Josephine Baker, who, after receiving a free Citroën, styled her hair in the large aureole style of a Mangbetu woman from the Congo who was featured on the promotional posters for the film (Bloom 2008, 93).

13. As Jan-Bart Gewald states in a discussion of the early motorcars in Namibia, "Motorized vehicles... were seen by the colonists as a material manifestation of

their technological superiority and hence by extension their natural moral superiority, which in turn legitimated their right to rule" (2002, 257).

14. Citroën received much political support from proponents of the highly contentious railway, but, ironically, the advent of airplane and motorcar transport made the railway redundant.

15. On the advertisements Citroën placed in official colonial journals in Guinea, see Odile Goerg, "Publicité et transports routiers en Guinée dans l'entre-deux-guerres."

16. For a discussion of the history of CITRACIT (Compagnie transafricaine Citroën), Citroën's failed attempt to launch regular tourist expeditions to North Africa, see Murray, "Le tourisme Citroën au Sahara (1924–1925)."

17. See Murray (2000).

18. In preparation for the expedition, extensive amounts of road had to be cleared, especially in the Belgian Congo. Haardt and Audouin-Dubreuil write that the Belgians used forty thousand natives to clear a stretch of seven hundred kilometers in just a few months. Impressed by the ability of the Belgians to exploit African labor, they write, "When we consider how difficult it is to get even one of them to work, we can but admire a result all the more exceptional because the black man does not carry out willingly any work of which he cannot clearly see the utility" (1927, 153). In fact, throughout colonial Africa, much of the road building was accomplished through forced or coerced labor. In *Voyage Au Congo* (1927), about his travels in 1925 throughout the Congo, André Gide describes seeing women with children on their backs repairing roads with their bare hands.

19. Although no other expedition reached the fame of the Citroën trans-Saharan and trans-African raids, the interwar years saw a series of expeditions sponsored by carmakers and undertaken by independent travelers. On their way to Cape Town, the Citroën expedition passed two British Crossley motorcars independently pursuing an all-British overland route to Cairo (Wolf 1991, 116). During the 1930s, Wilfred D. Hambly, collecting artifacts for the Field Museum of Chicago, drove a Ford truck through Angola and Nigeria and recorded his journey in a book titled *With a Motor Truck in West Africa* (1931). Likewise, Renault sponsored several African expeditions that culminated in the Mission Gradis and a film entitled *La première traversée rapide du desert (329 heures) (The First Rapid Crossing of the Sahara [329 hours])*. A Peugeot-sponsored Saharan expedition traced part of the route that eventually became the Paris-Dakar auto rally. The accumulative effect of these various travelogues was to open up Africa as a playground and racetrack for a new brand of tourist who wanted access to an exotic and disappearing landscape.

20. See, for instance, the historical accounts by Jennifer Hart, Philip Drummond-Thompson, A. M. Hay, and E. K. Hawkins, as well as the broad discussions of urban transport in sub-Saharan Africa by Xavier Godard and Pierre Teurnier.

21. Ford, in his autobiography, takes pride in the practicality of creating lightweight vehicles. He writes, "There is no more sense in having extra weight in an article than there is in the cockade on a coachman's hat. In fact, there is not as much. For the cockade may help the coachman to identify his hat while the extra weight means only a waste of strength" (2008, 15).

22. On the competition between Ford and Citroën, see Goerg (1992).

23. In Senegal in 1954, 90 percent of transport businesses employed less than ten people and less than 2 percent had more than twenty-five people (Hazemann 1992, 214).

24. For a discussion of the way that *The Boy Kumasenu* tells the story of a "journey to modernity" (24), see Carmela Garritano's *African Video Movies and Global Desires.*

25. Indigenous transporters were also not the object of documentation, which means there is very little archival or recorded information on French West African indigenous transporters in the colonial period (Hazemann 1992, 213).

26. See Ralph Austen's *African Economic History: Internal Development and External Dependency* as well as Frederick Cooper's *Decolonization and African Society: The Labor Question in French and British Africa.*

27. As Daniel Headrick notes, the history of technical training in West Africa is complex. For both the French and the British, education in the early stages of colonialism centered around training clerks and craftsman rather than engineers or technicians, and vocational schools were small and scattered (1988, 313). After World War I more technical schools began to open, with Ghana (then the Gold Coast) leading the way in "trade schools for road foremen, carpenters, locomotive drivers, masons, postmasters, and others" (315). However, because technical work was not often paid well, many West Africans preferred to be trained for higher paying clerical jobs.

28. Delgado's film further emphasizes the difficulty of transport by showing the problems the family must initially face in reaching the city hospital.

29. On noise as a function of mediation, see Larkin (2008).

30. At a conference at the University of Ghana in 2007, a music professor delivered a very well-received paper on potential solutions to the problem of loud music in *tro-tros,* collective minivans commonly used for travel. The decibel level and poor quality of the music seemed to be something that many audience members felt made for an extremely unpleasant experience during their daily commutes.

2. "No Danger No Delay"

1. See James Gibbs's "The Writer and the Road: Wole Soyinka and Those Who Cause Death by Dangerous Driving," which chronicles Soyinka's entire career with both the Oyo State Road Safety Corps and the Federal Road Safety Corps.

2. Enoch Okpara writes, "Touts can be defined as free-lance workers at railway stations, airports, ferry points, and especially motor-parks, who undertake the self-imposed responsibility of recruiting and organizing passengers who wish to travel by road, and for this work they receive a fee, or more appropriately, a 'commission,' that is generally paid by the drivers of the vehicles just before their departure" (1988, 327). Motor-parks—which serve as transportation hubs across Africa—are most often built and owned by local governments. However, the government does not participate in running them. Touts therefore essentially run the motor-park, procuring passengers and collecting fees for their drivers.

3. Brian Larkin has a similar critique of theories of media, which, he claims, assume that media systems and their infrastructure are "smoothly efficient," rather than "messy, discontinuous, and poor," as is the case in Nigeria (2008, 220).

4. Notable exceptions include Brian Larkin's *Signal and Noise*, Achille Mbembe and Janet Roitman's "Figures of the Subject in Times of Crisis," and Jojada Verrips and Birgit Meyer's "Kwaku's Car: The Struggles and Stories of a Ghanaian Long-Distance Taxi-Driver."

5. Virilio posits that these localized accidents, like car wrecks and train accidents, will eventually give way to more generalized accidents, such as nuclear spills or even global stock market crashes. He technically reserves the term "integral accident" to refer to these globalized accidents, but it is clear from his logic that the local accident is also integral, albeit on a smaller scale.

6. According to Freud, the body needs a protective shield, a layer of consciousness, to help defend the nervous system against the excessive stimuli of the outer world. For Schivelbusch it is important that Freud's text, which discusses the types of neurosis brought about by exposure to violent outside events, was written in the immediate wake of World War I. Schivelbusch argues that the theory of shell shock or war neurosis is very similar to the theory of railroad shock that was developed in the nineteenth century. In both instances, the victim is traumatized by violent activity without being physically harmed, and in both cases, the more the subject has been prepared, the better he or she parries these shocks.

7. See Jeffrey Schnapp's "Crash (Speed as Engine of Individuation)" for a further discussion of the history of the Euro-American romance with the car crash, which he traces back to "The Futurist Manifesto" of 1909. In *Blood on the Nash Ambassador*, Eric Mottram makes similar arguments, but he traces Americans' appetite for a constant state of emergency to the stock market crash of 1929 and its subsequent recovery.

8. According to Ola Orekunrin, "The World Bank predicts that in the next two years, road accidents could be the biggest killer of African children between 5 and 15. By 2030, according to the Global Burden of Disease study, road accidents will be the fifth leading cause of death in the developing world, ahead of malaria, tuberculosis and H.I.V." (2013).

9. For a history of the *bolekaja,* see "Transportation in Lagos (Part 4) Commercial Bus Services."

10. Though the *molue* buses might have been an improvement over the *bolekaja,* they were still seen to be an uncomfortable way of traveling. Fela Kuti famously sings about people packed like sardines into the *molue* in his song "Shuffering and Shmiling."

11. *Bolekajas* were also featured in a number of other fictional works such as Chinua Achebe's *Chike and River* and *A Man of the People.*

12. *Bolekaja* also refers to a type of literary criticism, originally intended by Chinweizu et al. (1983) to be a productive but outraged provocation to African literature to "cure itself of its colonial hangover" (xi). Soyinka, however, finds this type of criticism to be one that is hostile and stifling. He therefore reverses the positive connotation of the term by pointing out the aggressive and unpleasant aspects of *bolekaja* travel.

13. By way of contrast, Jeremy Packer points to the ways that in America a number of different discourses overlap to expel "mayhem" from automobility. He posits that "mobility without mayhem" has become the guiding principle on which we organize and regulate how different sectors of the population (women, African Americans, truckers) can access and utilize automobile-related mobility. Examining drivers education programs and popular media, he demonstrates that in America the accident has been smoothly integrated into a system of automobility that attempts to yield disciplined citizens. In Africa, of course, the accident is integrated into the system of automobility *with* its mayhem.

14. Robert Fraser writes, "The poet's reaction to this reminder is torn between a chastened recognition of man's limitations and a haughty dismissal of all that these imply. It is noticeable, for instance, that Soyinka supplies no answer to the rhetorical question with which the poem ends. Most commentators have assumed that the implied answer is 'Yes' and that the poet therefore fully identifies with the dead driver" (1986, 236).

15. See Gibbs (1995).

16. As Robert Fraser notes, many different versions of the Ogun story exist. Soyinka takes the Ogun myth and makes it his own, using it to suit his poetic purposes. Similarly, Biodun Jeyifo writes that Soyinka's appropriation of Ogun tends to be idiosyncratic and involves an "over-semiotization" of the god.

17. There are parallels here to Nietzsche's concept of the Übermensch as well as to his discussion of Greek tragedy in *The Birth of Tragedy*. But Soyinka warns against conflating his views with Nietzsche's. For him, Ogun is a combination of Dionysian, Apollonian, and Promethean virtues, but he also goes beyond them. Furthermore, Soyinka notes that while Greek tragedy built a fictive chthonic realm on which they established the principle of illusion, Yoruba tragedy plunges directly

into the chthonic realm, requiring no "copying of actuality." See Soyinka's "The Fourth Stage" in *Myth, Literature and the African World.*

18. Likewise, Lawuyi observes that almost all drivers use juju—fetish objects like feathers or a special comb—hidden behind dashboards or under seats. Juju, like the slogans, reminds drivers that they have enough power to survive danger and increase their wealth.

19. They are, in this sense, very much like Walter Benjamin's Baudelairian hero, who can expose the brokenness and ruptures of modern life under capitalism by revealing his own susceptibility to shock, whose plunge into chaos not only enables poetry but also trains or readies the human sensorium for the various jolts and ruptures of modernity. See Benjamin's "On Some Motifs in Baudelaire."

20. Mark Auslander, discussing roads in postcolonial Africa, writes, "The romance of the national highways—celebrated in conversation, oral narratives, and song—offers symbolic commentary on the complex urban-rural networks that emerged. . . . As the virtually bankrupt state ceases to be the supreme source of wealth and power, popular mythology has increasingly come to portray the tarmac and the world through which it courses as a nearly magical pathway to wealth" (1993, 182).

3. Moving Pictures, Mired Cars

1. My reading of this scene in *Heremakono* and my thoughts on issues of locomotion in West African Francophone cinema are indebted to Charles Sugnet.

2. See, for instance, Kenneth Harrow's *Postcolonial African Cinema: From Political Engagement to Postmodernism,* Akin Adesokan's *Postcolonial Artists and Global Aesthetics,* Jonathan Haynes's "African Filmmaking and the Postcolonial Predicament," and Bekolo's interview with N. Frank Ukadike.

3. The novel version of *Xala* is in fact one of the texts that Fredric Jameson uses to argue that all third world literature is national allegory in his famous essay "Third-World Literature in the Era of Multinational Capitalism."

4. See Paulin S. Vieyra's *Le cinéma au Sénégal.*

5. See Yves J. Saint-Martin's "Le premières automobiles sur les bords du Niger: Félix Dubois et la Compagnie des transports par automobiles du Soudan français, 1898–1913."

6. Ukadike further notes that the very earliest turn-of-the century films by the Lumière brothers and George Méliès, which were widely exhibited in Africa, already began to stigmatize and mock Africans. The image of the exotic and uncivilized African continued in later fictional and ethnographic representations of black Africa.

7. Even then it was generally agreed that the illiterate African audiences would be unable to understand most modern cinematic conventions. The Colonial Film

Unit avoided films that used montages or wipes—for fear that the natives would think that the machinery was broken—as well as panning shots, unconventional angles, or any device that would interrupt the visual continuity from one scene to the next (Pearson 1948, 25). They opted for longer scenes—"the native mind needs longer time to absorb the picture content" (25)—as well as transitions in which a moving person or object in one scene leads the audience to the next scene.

8. This did not, however, preclude Africans from watching foreign films and fashioning their own subversive meanings from them.

9. Perhaps the contemporary equivalent of the horse-cart ban is the banning of motorcycles in cities like Abuja in order to make the city appear more modern.

10. For discussions of *Xala's* "double fetishism," see Harriet Lyons's "The Use of Ritual in Sembene's *Xala*," Laura Mulvey's "*Xala*, Ousmane Sembene 1976: The Carapace That Failed," and Akin Adesokan's *Postcolonial Artists and Global Aesthetics.*

11. See, for instance, Karen Beckman, John Mowitt, Akin Adesokan, and Charles Sugnet.

12. As David Murphy notes, *Xala* was one of the first films to be coproduced with the *Société National du Cinéma* (SNC), the Senegalese government-backed production company founded in 1974 (2001, 99).

13. As Beckman argues, feminist scholarship has noted the multiple ways in which metaphors of mobility are frequently cast as masculine, while stasis is considered to be feminine (2010, 18).

14. This is made more explicit in the novel, where Sembene also explains that N'Gone's mother is concerned that this condition may not be met since prior to her engagement N'Gone had been spending time with disreputable men.

15. See Dick Hebdige's foundational *Hiding in the Light* for an argument about the oppositional value of Italian motorbikes and motor scooters.

16. However, films made in West African countries where the moped is the dominant form of transportation—Idrissa Ouedraogo's short *Ouagadougou, Ouaga Deux Roues* (1985) about the bicycles and scooters of Burkina Faso's capital is a perfect example—do not set up such a contrast between the car and scooter.

17. These observations have also been made by Charles Sugnet in his regularly taught African Cinema class at the University of Minnesota.

18. For a skillful rebuttal of Harrow's arguments, see Adesokan, who critiques Harrow for overlooking the fact that while early African film criticism might have privileged the didactic, "the films were themselves always more reflexive, open, and often contradictory" (2011, 75).

19. Mulvey builds on Teshome Gabriel's notion that *Xala* follows the African poetic form known as "wax and gold," where "wax" refers to the outward obvious meaning of a poem (the casting), and "gold," the valued object beneath, refers to the "true" but often inaccessible meaning.

20. Hebdige makes a similar point when he argues that the critic should not simply "demystify" the commodity but also track the object as it "passes through a maze of interlocking frames" (1988, 81).

21. According to Xavier Godard and Pierre Teurnier, in the 1990s old and substandard used cars in Cameroon came to be called *congelés,* a name also given to the frozen imported chickens forced on Cameroonians as part of structural adjustment programs.

22. The Ghost Town Movement in Cameroon eventually came to an end after promises by Biya's party to reform democracy and allow fair elections. However, after making a few superficial reforms, nothing changed within the Biya dictatorship. In 2004 Biya won the national election with 99.9 percent of the vote while, according to the global watchdog group Transparency International, Cameroon was ranked the fourth most corrupt nation in the world.

23. For a discussion of the queered time and space of *Quartier Mozart,* see Lindsey Green-Simms, "'Just to See': Fanon, National Consciousness, and the Indiscreet Look."

24. As Beckman argues, building on the work of George Baker, the encounter of cinema and photography, or the moments when the moving image and the still image share a single space, "can potentially enable old tired mediums to reinvent or reanimate themselves" and can call attention to the "complex engagement with the limits of film" (2010, 185).

25. The "preconditions for take-off" is modernization theorist Walt Rostow's second stage in the five stages of economic development that he believes all societies must go through. It follows "the traditional society" and comes just before "the take-off."

4. The Return of the Mercedes

1. Gilroy borrows the term "moral economy" from E.P. Thompson. I follow Gilroy in emphasizing that focusing on the moral economy is not to "downplay the fundamental significance or scope of political economy, but to contest the limited place provided in that paradigm for questions of morality and political culture" (2010, 7).

2. Though extremely popular in the diaspora, online streaming is still not widely available in Nigeria because of slower Internet connections. As Connor Ryan notes, in Nigeria, many producers prefer DVDs over VCDs because they are harder to pirate and decode. However, VCDs are still commonly used because they are much cheaper to produce (2014, 184).

3. See Noah Tsika's *Nollywood Stars: Media and Migration in West Africa and the Diaspora.*

4. Oftentimes the Hausa- or Yoruba-language films produced in Nigeria get lumped under the Nollywood rubric. However, these are separate industries with similar production models but different audiences, themes, and aesthetic codes.

5. For instance, for a brief period of time in the early 2000s the Ghanaian industry struggled to survive as it competed against the influx of cheaper, often pirated and typically more stylized, Nollywood films. And while co-productions and collaborations between the two countries invigorated the Ghanaian industry and expanded the legal markets in both countries, the Ghanaian film industry continues to face slumps and hurdles that the Nollywood industry does not (Garritano 2013, 167).

6. See, for instance, Paul Willemen, who argues that "melodrama is the drama of capitalist modernization, framed in such a way as to exclude the very possibility of change in a socialist direction" (1993, 188). In his analysis of *Andaz,* a popular Indian melodrama from the 1950s, Willemen claims that although the melodrama is able to capture the tensions involved in trying to adapt Indian precapitalist social relations to the present capitalist milieu, it does so by "forgetting that the Indian bourgeoisie is itself a colonial legacy" (186).

7. And it is also the case that many Francophone films are becoming more concerned with entertainment.

8. It is, of course, difficult to measure something like popularity in the absence of box-office and sales statistics, but I am, in any case, more interested in "popularity" as an indicator of the way in which a film resonates with audiences.

9. My use of the term echoes Lauren Berlant, who refers to the good life as one with viable fantasies of "upward mobility, job security, political and social equality, and lively, durable intimacy" (2011, 3).

10. For a more comprehensive history of Nigerian media, see Brian Larkin's *Signal and Noise: Media, Infrastructure, and Urban Culture in Nigeria*. Larkin explains that both the mobile cinema units used by the Colonial Film Unit and the state-produced media of the postcolonial government addressed the audience as political subjects in need of uplift and progress. According to Larkin, the video film industry is the first time Nigerian visual media has been able to exist outside of this type of framework, without government backing. Birgit Meyer, in "Ghanaian Popular Cinema and the Magic in and of Film," makes a similar claim about the trajectory of Ghanaian cinema. Of course, it is important to recognize that there have been many forms of popular culture, such as theater, concert parties, market literature, and music, that have also existed without state or foreign funding. The arguments that Meyer and Larkin make apply primarily to film.

11. See my "Occult Melodramas: Spectral Affect and West African Video-Film."

12. Both John McCall and Birgit Meyer have written on the popularity of the film in Nigeria and Ghana, respectively, and have noted the profound ways in which its warnings against the bloody nature of greed resonated with the local audiences

they studied. See McCall's "Madness, Money, and Movies: Watching a Nigerian Popular Video with the Guidance of a Native Doctor" and Meyer's "Prayers, Guns and Ritual Murder."

13. Though as Garritano notes, in Ghana the period between 1992 and 2000 was a time when some video-makers were making a conscious effort to "professionalize" and avoid films on blood money and witchcraft (2013, 92).

14. Other 419 films include Andy Amenechi's *The Master* (2004), Lancelot Oduwa Imasuen's *Yahoo Millionaire* (2007), Don Okolo's *The Stalk Exchange 419* (1997), Bolorunduro Michael's *ATM Masters* (2011), and Ghanaian films like Uriel Adjin-Tetty's *Café Guys* (2002) and Socrate Safo's *Sakawa Boys* (2009).

15. According to Andrew Apter, 419 scams may be Nigeria's second largest source of foreign money after oil.

16. The *Boys Cot* films follow the success of Okereke's *Girls Cot* (2006) series, which borrowed its name from Dickson Iroegbu's unrelated hit film *Women's Cot* (2003). The word "cot" has generated a considerable amount of confusion in online Nollywood bulletins with no clear consensus on what the word means, but it may be short for "coterie."

17. For a further discussion of *Living in Bondage* as a Mephistophelian tale and an analysis of the film's popularity with local audiences, see Onookome Okome's "Introducing the Special Issue on West African Cinema: Africa at the Movies."

18. See, for example, Peter Geschiere, *The Modernity of Witchcraft: Politics and the Occult in Postcolonial Africa* and Jean and John Comaroff, "Alien-Nation: Zombies, Immigrants and Millennial Capitalism."

19. See Karin Barber's highly influential essay "Popular Reactions to the Petro-Naira."

20. Brenda Chalfin, for instance, describes one Ghanaian church whose logo combines the insignia of the Mercedes-Benz and the Cadillac. On the fancy cars of many Pentecostal pastors, see Birgit Meyer's "Prayers, Guns and Ritual Murder" as well as Rijk Van Dijk's "The Moral Life of the Gift in Ghanaian Pentecostal Churches in the Diaspora."

21. While most celluloid filmmakers do make their films with an African audience in mind, the films are, to their chagrin, rarely shown in local cinemas. Since it is more profitable for theaters to show films from America, Hong Kong, or India that draw large crowds, many African feature films are only shown in African theaters during festivals like FESPACO (the Pan-African Film Festival of Ouagadougou), the biannual festival held in Burkina Faso. Furthermore, African television stations have been reluctant to show African celluloid films, preferring foreign soap operas or even locally made television shows (many of which are filmed plays) that are less critical of African states, cheaper to purchase, and popular enough to command advertising money. According to the prominent Senegalese producer Clarence Delgado, the stations believe that if filmmakers want their movies aired

on television they should provide them for free, but filmmakers, insulted by such suggestions, have been unwilling to simply give their movies away.

22. Nollywood filmmaker Emem Isong explains in a recent interview that she tends to release her films in phases. She'll release only twenty to thirty thousand copies at a time in case the film is pirated and sold for cheaper. It is too risky, she says, to release a hundred thousand copies (Ryan 2014, 177–78).

23. See Giovanni Arrighi's "The African Crisis." Arrighi attributes Africa's economic collapse to the crisis in world capitalism—and the United States' responses to it—that began in the 1970s when the United States became a major debtor rather than lender and began to compete for capital. This, in effect, reversed the global flow of capital, and led to higher interest rates, structural adjustment programs, and a contraction in money supply that had a drastic affect on sub-Saharan African countries. These conditions, according to Arrighi, led to an economic crisis when African countries, for the first time, experienced a surplus of workers instead of a deficit.

24. By contrast, the first Ghanaian video-makers, who had begun experimenting with videocassette technology slightly before the Nigerians, were those who had been involved in exhibiting or distributing celluloid films rather than theater or television (Garritano 2013, 67).

25. As John McCall points out, Nollywood is also a huge job creator. McCall argues that a 2002 study that estimated that the video industry has created some three to four thousand jobs is, in fact, on the low end. He writes, "I think this figure is quite conservative. It seems to account for production jobs only and it is unclear whether it includes the market vendors who distribute and sell millions of videos each year, or supporting sectors, such as Nigeria's printing industry that has been revitalized by demand for posters and video packaging" (2012, 20). This impressive employment impact is also a source of pride for Nollywood practitioners.

26. As Birgit Meyer suggests, the Lagos and Accra presented in video films look and feel like modern cosmopolitan cities, devoid of the gridlock traffic, pollution, and infrastructural deficiencies that its occupants find inevitable. She writes, "The city of Accra features in video films in at least three different manners. Firstly, much effort is put into visualizing Accra as part and parcel of a particular kind of urban modernity, with the car, good roads and high buildings as characteristic markers. Movies are usually replete with long scenes—in fact, too long for spectators from outside—in which cars take the audiences on a ride passing by key sites of modernity—and, interestingly, these scenes are usually accompanied by Western style music" (2008, 263).

27. Metz points out that capitalist cinema may be closer to a daydream than an actual dream, not simply because it is a waking activity but, more importantly, because the daydream is a conscious fantasy rather than an unconscious wish.

28. As Garritano argues, "Occult narratives should not be read as remnants of 'traditional' or 'primitive' beliefs, but as a dynamic, modern discourse that reflects

and attempts to make sense of contemporary capitalist forces" (2012a). I am using the term "modern" here in the way that Garritano does, to indicate that the films are part of the contemporary, neoliberal moment.

29. John McCall argues that the vulture is a common figure in Nigerian urban legend. He writes, "In the village, little exists in the way of garbage, but in urban areas, mountainous stacks of refuse collect at dump-points throughout the cities, and these are perpetually covered with large vultures picking through the malodorous monuments to capitalist surplus. The vulture has clearly taken a place in Nigerian popular cosmology as a symbol of predatory capitalism" (2002, 91).

30. For a discussion of this film and an important critique of male violence in Ghanaian video films, see Wisdom S. Agorde's "The Triad of Men's Violences in *Time*: A Ghanaian Occult Video Film."

31. All translations of the Yoruba lyrics to "Yahoozee" have been provided by Aderinsola Ajao.

32. One interesting exception to this is the film *Blackberry Babes,* which opens with a broken-down car and winds up being a satire of telecommunication technologies (Tsika 2015, 121).

33. According to Tsika, this accident inspired several films and was notably referenced in Afe Olumowe's film *Show Girls* (2011) that Okereke was supposed to star in before her crash (Tsika 63). After *Show Girls,* films like Ubong Bassey Nya's *Blackberry Babes Reloaded* (2012), Ejike Chinedu Obim's *Twist* (2013), and Ike Nnaebue's *Under Your Skin* (2014) have also featured crashes that complicate the lives of main characters and often kill or harm their loved ones.

34. Though concurrent with this trend of big-budget films is one that moves in the opposite direction: the surge in low-budget and inexpensive Akan-language films in Ghana and the production of films produced in less common native languages like Bini and Ibibio for hyperlocal markets in Nigeria (Haynes 2014, 57).

35. In a recent interview, Nigerian filmmaker Tunde Kelani was asked how he felt about the promised government funding for Nollywood offered by President Goodluck Jonathan in 2010. His response was that he would have much preferred investment in infrastructure and the construction of cinemas: "Put the money in electricity. Let the electricity come! Even if I go out and select ten [movies] to watch over a weekend, the point is, there is no electricity to watch the movies!" (Ryan 2014, 182).

5. Women in Traffic

1. See Agnes Apusigah for a discussion of the way that Ghana, in the beginning of the 1990s, was faced with a mixed economic reality. Apusigah writes that the Economic Recovery Program (ERP) succeeded in halting the rapid economic decline of the late 1970s and early 1980s and was able to improve road networks,

schools, and hospitals. However, she also argues that "the cost sharing, downsizing and cutbacks that marked the neo-liberal efficiency model of adjustment resulted in the devaluation, and to some extent, total neglect, of social concerns" and "that social cost of adjustment, especially for vulnerable groups such as the rural poor, women, and working class, was tremendous" (2015).

2. Just after *Faat Kiné's* release, the Senegalese people voted out the socialist party that had been ruling the country since independence. In an interview with Stuart Klawans of the *New York Times,* Sembene links women like Faat Kiné to the move away from the socialist government, arguing that their leadership was pivotal during the presidential runoffs of 2000.

3. For Nnaemeka, *nego-feminism* is the "feminism of negotiation," and it also "stands for 'no ego' feminism" (2004, 377). She writes, "In the foundation of shared values in many African cultures are the principles of negotiation, give and take, compromise, and balance. Here, negotiation has the double meaning of 'give and take/exchange' and 'cope with successfully/go around.' . . . African feminism (or feminism as I have seen it practiced in Africa) . . . knows when, where, and how to negotiate with or negotiate around patriarchy in different contexts" (377–78).

4. As Gibreel M. Kamara argues, Sembene, who has always had the liberation of African women as his top priority, should be considered part of the Senegalese feminist literary circle. See his article, "The Feminist Struggle in the Senegalese Novel: Mariama Ba and Sembene Ousmane." Likewise, David Murphy in *Sembene: Imagining Alternatives in Film and Fiction* has a wonderful discussion of Sembene's feminism and the representation of women in Sembene's films and novels.

5. As Apusigah writes, "Laudable as the PAMSCAD was, its stress on job creation, above all else, was indicative of its neo-liberal roots and emphasis on efficiency. Ignoring the deficiencies of the reforms in the ways that they contributed to the heightening of vulnerability and intensification of exclusion, the plan found an 'easy way out' through compensatory programs that provided a quick fix, not sustained relief" (2015).

6. Amadiume argues that African precolonial practices show that, contrary to what Levi- Strauss suggests in his famous theory of the incest taboo, the exchange of women was not necessarily the marker of the beginning of civilization because when a female husband would take on a wife for purposes of power consolidation, women were not being exchanged by men (2005, 88).

7. As Berlant writes, "The holding pattern implied in 'impasse' suggests a temporary housing" (2011, 5).

8. Andrade notes that although Bâ did not refer to herself as feminist, the novel, which is one of the most commonly taught African Francophone novels, is a key text in the African feminist literary canon and Bâ's work is a progenitor (2011, 72).

9. Tuzyline Jita Allan writes, "Lacking voice [Fusena] is unable to articulate even her anger. In fact, Fusena's entire range of self-expression is compromised of eight

brief statements, four of which are one-to-five-word interrogatives. But judging from her reaction—the dangerously reckless manner in which she drives out of the house to go to work on the day she gets the news—her rage is tremendous" (1991, 181).

10. See chapter 1 for a further discussion of the hum.

11. See Slaughter's *Human Rights, Inc.: The World Novel, Narrative Form, and International Law.*

12. As Aidoo notes in her talk "Ghana: To Be a Woman," "The solution does not lie with you, the individual woman, married or unmarried, no matter how keenly aware you are of the problems in your environment" (263).

13. The second film in the trilogy, *Moolaadé,* is about a woman who offers protection to four young girls who have refused to submit to the ritual of female circumcision. *Brotherhood of the Rats* was slated to be the third film, but Sembene passed away before the film went into production.

14. I thank Tsitsi Ella Jaji for bringing "the original Faat Kiné" to my attention.

15. In Lomé the Nana Benzes even have their own radio station, Nana FM.

16. The film's English subtitles translate Kiné's statement, "Je l'ai déja conduit," into "I have already laid him" rather than "I have already driven him," and they do not translate the Wolof modifier "bu baxx."

17. See John Mowitt's *Re-Takes* (127–29) for a discussion of the way in which Sembene repeats several of the same motifs in the two celebration scenes but rearranges the enunciative marks of the failed copulation in *Xala.*

18. Though this might also be Sembene's way of crafting a feminist politics that is inclusive of men.

Conclusion

1. In his article "'Africa Rising': TIME Magazine Agrees with the *Economist*" for the website "How We Made It in Africa," Jaco Maritz writes, "At the end of 2011, *The Economist* magazine caused quite a stir when it came out with a cover titled 'Africa Rising' together with an illustration of a boy flying a rainbow-coloured kite the shape of the continent. The reason for all the fuss was that 11 years earlier the publication called Africa 'the hopeless continent' on one of its covers. The accompanying article painted a picture of a continent ravaged by war, famine and disease."

2. Furthermore, Jacobs takes *TIME* magazine's Africa bureau chief Alex Perry to task for arguing that young Africans must now choose Africa Rising over African Uprising, a statement that glosses over the oppressive regimes that often hold back these very youth.

3. See "Driving to an Early Grave" for a discussion of the rising accident rates in the world's poorest regions.

4. For more on the economic ramifications of these developments, see Dele Fanimo's "Nigeria: New Automotive Policy's Mixed Grill."

Bibliography

Adas, Michael. 1990. *Machine as the Measure of Men: Science, Technology, and Ideologies of Western Dominance.* Ithaca: Cornell University Press.

Adejunmobi, Moradewun A. 2010. "Charting Nollywood's Appeal Locally and Globally." *Film in African Literature Today* 28:106–21.

———. 2015. "Neoliberal Rationalities in Old and New Nollywood." *African Studies Review* 58, no. 3: 31–53.

Adesokan, Akin. 2011. *Postcolonial Artists and Global Aesthetics.* Bloomington: Indiana University Press.

Adichie, Chimamanda. 2014. *Americanah.* New York: Anchor Books.

Agorde, Wisdom S. 2007. "The Triad of Men's Violences in *Time*: A Ghanaian Occult Video Film." *Postcolonial Text* 3, no. 2. http://postcolonial.org/index.php/pct/article/view/516.

Aguiar, Marian. 2003. "Smoke of the Savannah: Traveling Modernity in Sembène Ousmane's *God's Bits of Wood*." *Modern Fiction Studies* 49, no. 2 (Summer): 284–305.

———. 2011. *Tracking Modernity: India's Railway and the Culture of Mobility.* Minneapolis: University of Minnesota Press.

Aidoo, Ama Ata. 1968. Introduction to *The Beautyful Ones Are Not Yet Born,* by Ayi Kwei Armah, vii–xii. Toronto: Macmillan.

———. 1984. "Ghana: To Be a Woman." In *Sisterhood Is Global,* ed. Robin Morgan, 258–65. New York: Anchor Books.

———. 1991. *Changes: A Love Story.* New York: The Feminist Press at the City University of New York.

Alber, Erdmute. 2002. "Motorization and Colonial Rule: Two Scandals in Dahomey, 1916." *Journal of African Cultural Studies* 15, no. 1: 79–92.

Allan, Tuzyline Jita. 1991. Afterword to *Changes: A Love Story,* by Ama Ata Aidoo, 171–96.

Amadiume, Ifi. 2005. "Theorizing Matriarchy in Africa: Kinship Ideologies and Systems in Africa and Europe." In *African Gender Studies: A Reader,* ed. Oyèrónkẹ́ Oyěwùmí, 83–98. New York: Palgrave Macmillan.

Amenechi, Andy, dir. 2005. *The Master.* DVD.

Andrade, Susan Z. 2011. *The Nation Writ Small: African Fictions and Feminism, 1958–1988.* Durham: Duke University Press.

Andrade-Watkins, Claire. 1996. "France's Bureau of Cinema—Financial and Technical Assistance, 1961–1977: Operations and Implications for African Cinema." In *African Experiences of Cinema,* ed. Imruh Bakari and Mbye B. Cham, 112–27. London: British Film Institute.

Appadurai, Arjun. 1996. *Modernity at Large: Cultural Dimensions of Globalization.* Minneapolis: University of Minnesota Press.

———. 1999. "Things to Come: Emergent Regimes of Materiality." *CODESRIA Bulletin,* nos. 3–4: 36–40.

Apter, Andrew. 1999. "IBB = 419: Nigerian Democracy and the Politics of Illusion." In *Civil Society and the Political Imagination in Africa: Critical Perspectives,* ed. John Comaroff and Jean Comaroff, 267–308. Chicago: University of Chicago Press.

Apusigah, Agnes Atia. 2015. "Gender Mainstreaming the Ghana Poverty Reduction Strategy or is it?" *Isis International.* http://www.isiswomen.org/index.php?option=com_content&view=article&id=512:gender-mainstreaming-the-ghana-poverty-reduction-strategy-or-is-it&catid=116&Itemid=452.

Armstrong, Nancy. 2005. *How Novels Think: The Limits of British Individualism from 1719–1900.* New York: Columbia University Press.

Arrighi, Giovanni. 2002. "The African Crisis." *New Left Review* 15 (May–June): 5–36.

Audouin-Dubreuil, Ariane. 2005. *Crossing the Sands: The Sahara Desert Track to Timbuktu.* Deerfield, Ill.: Dalton Watson Fine Books.

Auslander, Mark. 1993. "'Open the Wombs!': The Symbolic Politics of Modern Ngoni Witchfinding." In *Modernity and Its Malcontents: Ritual and Power in Postcolonial Africa,* ed. Jean Comaroff and John Comaroff, 167–92. Chicago: University of Chicago Press.

Austen, Ralph. 1987. *African Economic History: Internal Development and External Dependency.* London: James Currey.

Bâ, Amadou Hampaté. 2000. *The Fortunes of Wangrin.* Bloomington: Indiana University Press.

Bâ, Mariama. 1981. *So Long a Letter.* Trans. Modupé Bodé-Thomas. Oxford: Heinemann.

Bakhtin, Mikhail. 1981. *The Dialogic Imagination.* Trans. Caryl Emerson and Michael Holquist. Austin: The University of Texas Press.

Barber, Karin. 1997a. "Popular Reactions to the Petro-Naira." In Barber, *Readings in African Popular Culture,* 91–98.

———, ed. 1997b. *Readings in African Popular Culture.* Bloomington: Indiana University Press.

———. 1997c. "Views of the Field." In Barber, *Readings in African Popular Culture,* 1–11.

Barthes, Roland. 1957. *Mythologies.* Trans. Annette Lavers. New York: Hill and Wang.

Bayart, Jean-François. 2007. *Global Subjects: A Political Critique of Globalization.* Trans. Andrew Brown. Malden, Mass.: Polity Press.

Bayo Lawuyi, Olatunde. 1997. "The World of the Yoruba Taxi Driver: An Interpretive Approach to Vehicle Slogans." In Barber, *Readings in African Popular Culture,* 146–50.

Beckman, Karen. 2010. *Crash: Cinema and the Politics of Speed and Stasis.* Durham: Duke University Press.

Bekolo, Jean-Pierre, dir. 1992. *Quartier Mozart.* VHS.

———. 2002. "Jean-Pierre Bekolo (Cameroon)." In Ukadike, *Questioning African Cinema,* 217–38.

———, dir. 2005. *Les Saignantes.* DVD.

Benjamin, Walter. 1968a. "On Some Motifs in Baudelaire." In *Illuminations: Essays and Reflections,* ed. Hannah Arendt, 155–94. Trans. Harry Zohn. New York: Schocken Books.

———. 1968b. "The Work of Art in the Age of Mechanical Reproduction." In *Illuminations: Essays and Reflections,* ed. Hannah Arendt, 217–52. Trans. Harry Zohn. New York: Schocken Books.

Berlant, Lauren. 2011. *Cruel Optimism.* Durham: Duke University Press.

Berliner, Brett. 2002. *Ambivalent Desire: The Exotic Other in Jazz-Age France.* Amherst: University of Massachusetts Press.

Berry, Sara. 1983. *From Peasant to Artisan: Motor Mechanics in a Nigerian Town.* Working Paper no. 76, African Studies Center, Boston University.

Beuving, Joost. 2009. "Striking Gold in Cotonou? Three Cases of Entrepreneurship in the Euro-West African Second-Hand Car Trade in Benin." In Gewald et al., *The Speed of Change,* 127–50.

Bloom, Peter. 2008. *French Colonial Documentary: Mythologies of Humanitarianism.* Minneapolis: University of Minnesota Press.

Böhm, Steffen, Campbell Jones, Chris Land, and Matthew Paterson, eds. 2006a. *Against Automobility.* Malden, Mass.: Blackwell.

———. 2006b. "Introduction: Impossibilities of automobility." In Böhm et al., *Against Automobility,* 3–16.

Brennan, Timothy. 2008. "Postcolonial Studies and Globalization Theory." In *The Postcolonial and the Global,* ed. Revathi Krishnaswamy and John C. Hawley, 37–53. Minneapolis: University of Minnesota Press.

Busch, Annett, and Max Annas, eds. 2008. *Ousmane Sembène Interviews.* Jackson: University of Mississippi Press.

Cabral, Amilcar. 1979. "The Role of Culture in Liberation Struggle." In *Communication and Class Struggle, Vol. 1: Capitalism and Imperialism, ed.* Armand Mattelart and Seth Siegelaub. New York: International General.

Cary, Joyce. 1962. *Mister Johnson.* New York: Time Reading Program.

Castells, Manuel. 1998. *The Information Age: Economy, Society and Culture,* Vol. 3: *End of Millennium*. Malden, Mass.: Blackwell.

Césaire, Aimé. 2000. *Discourse on Colonialism*. Trans. Joan Pinkham. New York: New York University Press.

Chalfin, Brenda. 2008. "Cars, the Customs Service, and Sumptuary Rule in Neoliberal Ghana." *Comparative Studies in Society and History* 50, no. 2: 424–53.

Chilson, Peter. 1999. *Riding the Demon: On the Road in West Africa*. Athens: University of Georgia Press.

Chinweizu, Onsucheka J., and Ihechukwu Madubuike. 1983. *Toward the Decolonization of African Literature*. Washington, D.C.: Howard University Press.

Comaroff, Jean, and John Comaroff. 1999. "Alien-Nation: Zombies, Immigrants and Millennial Capitalism." *CODESRIA Bulletin*, nos. 3–4: 17–28.

———. 2000. "Millennial Capitalism: First Thoughts on a Second Coming." *Public Culture* 12, no. 2: 291–43.

———. 2012. *Theory from the South; or, How Euro-America Is Evolving Toward Africa*. Boulder, Colo.: Paradigm.

Cooper, Frederick. 1996. *Decolonization and African Society: The Labor Question in French and British Africa*. Cambridge: Cambridge University Press.

———. 2005. *Colonialism in Question: Theory, Knowledge, History*. Berkeley: University of California Press.

Cooper, Frederick, and Ann Laura Stoler. 1997. "Between Metropole and Colony: Rethinking a Research Agenda." In *Tensions of Empire: Colonial Cultures in a Bourgeois World,* ed. Frederick Cooper and Ann Laura Stoler, 1–58. Berkeley: University of California Press.

Cresswell, Tim. 2006. *On the Move: Mobility in the Modern Western World*. New York: Routledge.

Curtain, Matthew. 2013. "EU Car Sales Slump." *Wall Street Journal*. http://online.wsj.com/news/articles/SB10001424127887323468604578244981638540410.

D'Almeida-Topor, Hélène, Chantal Chanson-Jabeur, Monique Lakroum, eds. 1992. *Les Transports en Afrique (XIXe-XXe siècle)*. Paris: L'Harmattan.

Debord, Guy. 1981. "Theses on Traffic." In *Situationist International Anthology,* ed. and trans. Ken Knabb, 69–70. Berkley: Bureau of Secrets.

de Certeau, Michel. 1984. *The Practice of Everyday Life*. Trans. Steven Rendall. Berkeley: University of California Press.

Deleuze, Gilles. 1986. *Cinema 1: Movement-Image*. Trans. Hugh Tomlinson and Barbara Habberjam. Minneapolis: University of Minnesota Press.

Deleuze, Gilles, and Felix Guattari. 1987. *A Thousand Plateaus: Capitalism and Schizophrenia*. Trans. Brian Massumi. Minneapolis: University of Minnesota Press.

Delgado, Clarence. 2007. Interview by author. March 29, Dakar, Senegal.

Diawara, Manthia. 1992. *African Cinema: Politics and Culture.* Bloomington: Indiana University Press.

———. "Toward a Regional Imaginary in Africa." 1998. In *The Cultures of Globalization,* ed. Fredric Jameson and Masao Miyoshi, 103–24. Durham: Duke University Press.

"Driving to an Early Grave." 2015. *Economist.* http://www.economist.com/news/international/21595031-rich-countries-have-cut-deaths-and-injuries-caused-crashes-toll-growing.

Drummond-Thompson, Philip. 1992. "The Development of Motor Transport in Nigeria: A Study in Indigenous Enterprise." In D'Almeida-Topor et al., *Les Transports en Afrique,* 223–47.

Dworkin, Gerald. 1988. *The Theory and Practice of Autonomy.* New York: Cambridge University Press.

Ehrenburg, Ilya. 1929. *The Life of the Automobile.* Trans. Joachim Neugroschel. London: Serpent's Tail.

Ekwuazi, Hyginus Ozo. 2000. "The Igbo Video Film." In Haynes, *Nigerian Video Films,* 131–47.

El-Erian, Mohamed A. 2013. "Into Africa." *Foreign Policy.* http://foreignpolicy.com/2013/04/29/into-africa/.

Ezeanyaeche, Ojiofor, dir. 1996. *Blood Money, I and II.* VHS.

Fanimo, Dele. 2014. "Nigeria: New Automotive Policy's Mixed Grill." *All Africa.* http://m.allafrica.com/stories/201408141304.html/.

Fanon, Frantz. 1963. *The Wretched of the Earth.* Trans. Constance Farrington. New York: Grove Press.

Featherstone, Mike. 2005. "Introduction." In Featherstone et al., *Automobilities,* 1–24.

Featherstone, Mike, Nigel Thrift, and John Urry, eds. 2005. *Automobilities.* London: Sage.

Ferguson, James. 2006. *Global Shadows: Africa in the Neoliberal World Order.* Durham: Duke University Press.

Field, Margaret J. 1962. *Search for Security: An Ethno-psychiatric Study of Rural Ghana.* Evanston: Northwestern University Press.

Flink, James. 1988. *The Automobile Age.* Cambridge, Mass.: MIT Press.

Ford, Henry. 2008. *My Life and Work.* Minooka, Ill.: The Richest Man in Babylon Press.

Foucault, Michel. 1978. *The History of Sexuality.* Vol. 1: *An Introduction.* Trans. Robert Hurley. New York: Random House.

———. 1994. "What Is Enlightenment?" In *Ethics: Subjectivity and Truth,* ed. Paul Rabinow, 303–20. Trans. Robert Hurley et al. New York: New Press.

Fraser, Robert. 1986. "The Road to Idanre." In *West African Poetry: A Critical History,* 231–50. Cambridge: Cambridge University Press.

Freud, Sigmund. 1959. *Inhibitions, Symptom, Anxiety.* Trans. James Strachey. The Standard Edition. New York: W. W. Norton.

Gandy, Matthew. 2006. "Planning, Anti-planning and the Infrastructure Crisis Facing Metropolitan Lagos." *Urban Studies* 43, no. 2: 371–96.

Garritano, Carmela. 2012a. "Blood Money, Big Men and Zombies: Understanding Africa's Occult Narratives in the Context of Neoliberal Capitalism." *manycinemas,* no. 3: 50–65. http://www.manycinemas.de/Carmela_Garritano/articles/Garritano_Nollywood.html.

———. 2012b. "The Extroverted African Novel and Its Local Engagements: Adaobi Tricia Nwaubani's *I Do Not Come to You by Chance.*" Paper presented at the African Literature Association Annual Meeting, Dallas, Texas, April 13.

———. 2013. *African Video Movies and Global Desires: A Ghanaian History.* Athens: Ohio University Press.

Gayet, M. G. 1957. "L'exemple des plans de development de l'Afrique Occidentale Française concernant les réseaux routiers." *Bulletin de la Selection de geographie du Comité des travaux historiques et scientifiques*: 21–34.

Geschiere, Peter. 1997. *The Modernity of Witchcraft: Politics and the Occult in Postcolonial Africa.* Charlottesville: University of Virginia Press.

Gewald, Jan-Bart. 2002. "Missionaries, Hereros, and Motorcars: Mobility and the Impact of Motor Vehicles in Namibia before 1940." *International Journal of African Historical Studies* 35, nos. 2–3: 257–86.

Gewald, Jan-Bart, Sabine Luning, and Klaas van Walraven. 2009a. "Motor Vehicles and People in Africa: An Introduction." In Gewald et al., *The Speed of Change,* 1–20.

———, eds. 2009b. *The Speed of Change: Motor Vehicles and People in Africa, 1890–2000.* Leiden: Brill.

Gibbs, James. 1995. "The Writer and the Road: Wole Soyinka and Those Who Cause Death by Dangerous Driving." *Journal of Modern African Studies* 33, no. 3: 469–98.

Gibson-Graham, J. K. 1996. *The End of Capitalism (As We Knew It): A Feminist Critique of Political Economy.* Minneapolis: University of Minnesota Press.

Giddens, Anthony. 1991. *Modernity and Self-Identity: Self and Society in the Late Modern Age.* Stanford: Stanford University Press.

Gikandi, Simon. 2001. "Globalization and the Claims of Postcoloniality." *South Atlantic Quarterly* 100, no. 3: 627–58.

Gilroy, Paul. 2010. *Darker Than Blue: On the Moral Economies of Black Atlantic Culture.* Cambridge, Mass.: Harvard University Press.

Godard, Xavier, and Pierre Teurnier. 1992. *Les transports urbains en Afrique à l'heure de l'ajustement.* Paris: Karthala.

Goerg, Odile. 1992. "Publicité et transports routiers en Guinée dans l'entre-deux-guerres." In D'Almeida-Topor et al., *Les Transports en Afrique,* 43–54.

Gomes, Flora. 2002. "Flora Gomes (Guinea-Bissau)." In Ukadike, *Questioning African Cinema,* 101–8.

Gould, Peter R. 1960. *The Development of the Transportation Pattern in Ghana.* Evanston: Department of Geography, Northwestern University.

Grace, Joshua. 2013. "Heroes of the Road: Race, Gender, and the Politics of Mobility in Twentieth Century Tanzania." *Africa* 83, no. 3: 403–25.

Graham, Julie. 1991. "Fordism/Post-Fordism, Marxism/Post-Marxism: The Second Cultural Divide?" *Rethinking Marxism* 4, no. 1: 39–58.

Graham, Sean, dir. 1952. *The Boy Kumasenu.* http://www.colonialfilm.org.uk/node/332.

Green-Simms, Lindsey. 2011. "'Just to See': Fanon, National Consciousness, and the Indiscreet Look." In *Indiscretions: At the Intersection of Queer and Postcolonial Theory,* ed. Murat Aydemir, 203–24. Amsterdam: Rodopi Press.

———. 2012a. "Hustlers, Homewreckers, and Homoeroticism: Nollywood's *Beautiful Faces.*" *Journal of African Cinemas* 4, no. 1: 59–79.

———. 2012b. "Occult Melodramas: Spectral Affect and West African Video-Film." *Camera Obscura: Feminism, Culture, and Media Studies* 27, no. 2: 25–59.

Green-Simms, Lindsey, and Unoma Azuah. 2012. "The Video Closet: Nollywood's Gay-Themed Movies." *Transition* 107:32–49.

Grewal, Inderpal. 2005. *Transnational America: Feminisms, Diasporas, Neoliberalisms.* Durham: Duke University Press.

Griswold, Wendy. 2000. *Bearing Witness: Readers, Writers, and the Novel in Nigeria.* Princeton: Princeton University Press.

Haardt, Georges Marie, and Alain Audouin-Dubreuil. 1924. *Across the Sahara by Motor Car.* Trans. E. E. Fournier D'Albe. New York: D. Appleton.

———. *The Black Journey.* 1927. New York: Negro Universities Press.

Hamid, Mohsin. 2013. *How to Get Filthy Rich in Rising Asia.* New York: Riverhead Books.

Haraway, Donna. 1991. *Simians, Cyborgs, and Women: The Reinvention of Nature.* New York: Routledge.

Harding, Frances. 2007. "Appearing Fabu-less: From Tender Romance to Horrifying Sex." *Film International* 5, no. 4: 10–19.

Hardt, Michael, and Antonio Negri. 2000. *Empire.* Cambridge, Mass.: Harvard University Press.

Harrow, Kenneth. 2007. *Postcolonial African Cinema: From Political Engagement to Postmodernism.* Bloomington: Indiana University Press.

Hart, Jennifer. 2016. *Ghana On the Go: African Mobility in the Age of Motor Transportation.* Bloomington: Indiana University Press.

Harvey, David. 1990. *The Condition of Postmodernity.* Cambridge, Mass.: Blackwell.

Hawkins, E. K. 1958. *Road Transport in Nigeria: A Study of an African Enterprise.* London: Oxford University Press.

Hay, A. M. 1971. "The Development of Road Transport in Nigeria, 1900–1940." *Journal of Transport History,* n.s., 1: 95–107.

Haynes, Jonathan. 1999. "African Filmmaking and the Postcolonial Predicament." In *African Cinema: Postcolonial and Feminist Readings,* ed. Kenneth Harrow, 21–43. Trenton, N.J.: Africa World Press.

———. 2000a. "Introduction." In Haynes, *Nigerian Video Films,* 1–36.

———, ed. 2000b. *Nigerian Video Films.* Rev. ed. Athens: Ohio University Center for International Studies.

———. 2014. "'New Nollywood': Kunle Afolayan." *Black Camera* 5, no. 2: 53–73.

Haynes, Jonathan, and Onookome Okome. 2000. "Evolving Popular Media: Nigerian Video Films." In Haynes, *Nigerian Video Films,* 51–88.

Hazemann, Yves. 1992. "Routes et routiers du Sénégal au XXe siècle: Les sources de l'histoire des transports." In D'Almeida-Topor et al., *Les Transports en Afrique,* 211–22.

Headrick, Daniel. 1988. *The Tentacles of Progress: Technology Transfer in the Age of Imperialism, 1850–1940.* New York: Oxford University Press.

Hebdige, Dick. 1988. *Hiding in the Light.* New York: Routledge.

Hinshaw, Drew. 2012. "Senegal's Taxi Sisters Break New Ground." *Global Post.* https://www.pri.org/stories/2010-05-04/senegals-taxi-sisters-break-new-ground.

hooks, bell. 1997. *Wounds of Passion: A Writing Life.* New York: Henry Holt.

Hopkins, A. G. 1973. *An Economic History of West Africa.* London: Longman Group.

Iliffe, John. 2007. *Africans: The History of a Continent.* 2nd ed. Cambridge: Cambridge University Press.

Jacobs, G., and A. Aeron-Thomas. N.d. "African Road Safety Review Final Report." U.S. Department of Transportation/Federal Highway Administration. http://safety.fhwa.dot.gov/about/international/africa/chap3.htm.

Jacobs, Sean. 2012. "TIME Magazine and the 'Africa Is Rising' Meme." *Africa Is a Country.* http://africasacountry.com/time-magazine-and-the-africa-is-rising-meme/.

Jain, Sarah S. 2005. "Violent Submission: Gendered Automobility." *Cultural Critique* 61:186–214.

Jameson, Fredric. 1986. "Third-World Literature in the Era of Multinational Capitalism." *Social Text* 15:65–88.

Jeyifo, Biodun. 2004. *Wole Soyinka: Politics, Poetics and Postcolonialism.* Cambridge: Cambridge University Press.

John, Elnathan. 2012. "How to Behave as a Car Owner in Nigeria." *Elnathan John's Dark Corner* (blog). http://elnathanjohn.blogspot.com/2012/07/how-to-behave-as-car-owner-in-nigeria.html.

Kaplan, Caren. 1996. *Questions of Travel: Postmodern Discourses of Displacement.* Durham: Duke University Press.

———. 2006. "Mobility and War: The Cosmic View of US 'Air Power.'" *Environment and Planning A* 38, no. 2: 395–407.

Kirby, Lynne. 1997. *Parallel Tracks: The Railroad and Silent Cinema.* Durham: Duke University Press.

Kiwanuka, M. Semakula. 1970. "Colonial Policies and Administrations in Africa: The Myths of the Contrasts." *African Historical Studies* 3, no. 2: 295–315.

Klawans, Stuart. 2001. "FILM; African Cinema's Main Man Celebrates Women." *New York Times.* http://www.nytimes.com/2001/03/11/movies/film-african-cinema-s-main-man-celebrates-women.html.

Kopytoff, Igor. 1986. "The Cultural Biography of Things: Commodization as Process." In *Social Life of Things: Commodities in Cultural Perspective,* ed. Arjun Appadurai, 64–91. Cambridge: Cambridge University Press.

Krings, Matthias, and Onookome Okome. 2013. "Nollywood and Its Diaspora: An Introduction." In *Global Nollywood: The Transnational Dimensions of an African Video Film Industry,* ed. Matthias Krings and Onookome Okome, 1–24. Bloomington: Indiana University Press.

Larkin, Brian. 2008. *Signal and Noise: Media, Infrastructure, and Urban Culture in Nigeria.* Durham: Duke University Press.

Lefebvre, Henri. 1971. *Everyday Life in the Modern World.* Trans. Sacha Rabinovitch. New Brunswick: Transaction.

Levine, Caroline. 2015. *Forms: Whole, Rhythm, Hierarchy, Network.* Princeton: Princeton University Press.

"L'évolution des marchés ouest-africains de l'automobile." 1966. *Le Moniteur Africain* 272:8–32.

Lyons, Harriet D. 1984. "The Uses of Ritual in Sembene's *Xala.*" *Canadian Journal of African Studies /Revue Canadienne des Études Africaines* 8, no. 2: 319–28.

Maintain, Olu. 2007. "Olu Maintain—Yahooze (Official Video—Naijapolis.net)." *YouTube.* https://www.youtube.com/watch?v=oJh8tCns-Bg.

———. 2013. "VIDEO: Olu Maintain Speaks On His Long Absence; Defends 'Yahoozee.'" *notjustok.* http://notjustok.com/2013/03/16/video-olu-maintain-speaks-on-his-long-absence-defends-yahoozee/.

Malaquais, Dominique. 2011. "Anti-teleology: Re-Mapping the Imag(in)ed City." In *African Cities Reader II: Mobilities and Fixtures,* ed. Ntone Edjabe and Edgar Pieterse, 7–23. Vlaeberg: Chimurenga and the African Centre for Cities.

Mamdani, Mahmood. 1996. *Citizen and Subject: Contemporary Africa and the Legacy of Late Colonialism.* Princeton: Princeton University Press, 1996.

Manovich, Lev. 2001. *The Language of New Media.* Cambridge, Mass.: MIT Press.

Maritz, Jaco. 2012. "'Africa Rising': TIME Magazine Agrees with the *Economist.*" *How We Made It in Africa.* http://www.howwemadeitinafrica.com/africa-rising-time-runs-with-same-title-as-now-famous-the-economist-cover/22337/.

Martin. 2012. "Import Limits on Used Cars." *Hotel Ivory.* http://hotelivory.wordpress.com/2012/01/15/import-limits-on-used-cars/.

Masquelier, Adeline. 2002. "Road Mythographies: Space, Mobility, and the Historical Imagination in Postcolonial Niger." *American Ethnologist* 29, no. 4: 829–56.

Mbembe, Achille. 2001. *On the Postcolony.* Berkeley: University of California Press.

———. 2007. "Afropolitanism." In *Africa Remix: Contemporary Art of a Continent,* ed. Njami Simon and Lucy Durán, 26–30. Johannesburg: Johannesburg Art Gallery.

Mbembe, Achille, and Sarah Nuttall. 2004. "Writing the World from an African Metropolis." *Public Culture* 16, no. 3: 347–72.

Mbembe, Achille, and Janet Roitman. 1996. "Figures of the Subject in Times of Crisis." In *The Geography of Identity,* ed. P. Yaeger, 153–86. Ann Arbor: University of Michigan Press.

McCall, John. 2002. "Madness, Money, and Movies: Watching a Nigerian Popular Video with the Guidance of a Native Doctor." *Africa Today* 49, no. 3: 79–94.

———. 2012. "The Capital Gap: Nollywood and the Limits of Informal Trade." *Journal of African Cinemas* 4, no. 1: 9–23.

McLuhan, Marshall. 2001. *Understanding Media: The Extension of Man.* Cambridge, Mass.: MIT Press.

McPhee, Allan. 1971. *The Economic Revolution in British West Africa.* London: Frank Cass.

McShane, Clay. 1994. *Down the Asphalt Path: The Automobile and the American City.* New York: Columbia University Press.

Melly, Caroline. 2013. "Ethnography on the Road: Infrastructural Vision and the Unruly Present in Contemporary Dakar." *Africa* 83, no. 3: 385–402.

Metz, Christian. 1977. *The Imaginary Signifier: Psychoanalysis and the Cinema.* Trans. Celia Britton, Annwyl Williams, Ben Brewster, and Alfred Guzzetti. Bloomington: Indiana University Press.

Meyer, Birgit. 2003. "Ghanaian Popular Cinema and the Magic in and of Film." In *Magic and Modernity: Interfaces of Revelation and Concealment,* ed. Birgit Meyer and Peter Pels, 200–22. Stanford: Stanford University Press.

———. 2006. "Prayers, Guns and Ritual Murder. Power and the Occult in Ghanaian Popular Cinema." In *The Power of the Occult in Africa,* ed. Jim Kiernan, 182–205. Münster: Lit Verlag.

———. 2008. "Sensuous Mediations: The City in 'Ghanaian' Films—and Beyond." In *Wildness and Sensation,* ed. Rob van Ginkel and Alex Strating, 254–74. Amsterdam: Het Spinhuis.

Miller, Daniel, ed. 2001a. *Car Cultures.* Oxford: Berg.

———. 2001b. "Driven Societies." In Miller, *Car Cultures,* 1–33.

———. 2010. *Stuff.* Malden, Mass.: Polity.

Moody, P. R. 1967. "Road and Bridge in Joyce Cary's African Novels." *Bulletin of the Rocky Mountain Modern Language Association* 21, no. 4: 145–49.

Morris, Rosalind. 2010. "Accidental Histories, Post-Historical Practice? Re-reading *Body of Power, Spirit of Resistance* in the Actuarial Age." *Anthropological Quarterly* 83, no. 3: 581–624.

Mottram, Eric. 1981. *Blood on the Nash Ambassador: Investigations in American Culture.* London: Hutchinson Radius.

Mowitt, John. 2005. *Re-takes: Postcoloniality and Foreign Film Languages.* Minneapolis: University of Minnesota Press.

Mrázek, Rudolf. 2002. *Engineers of Happy Land: Technology and Nationalism in a Colony.* Princeton: Princeton University Press.

Mulvey, Laura. 1994. "*Xala,* Ousmane Sembène 1976: The Carapace That Failed." In *Colonial Discourse and Post-colonial Theory: A Reader,* ed. Patrick Williams and Laura Chrisman, 517–34. New York: Columbia University Press.

Murphy, David. 2001. *Sembene: Imagining Alternatives in Film and Fiction.* Trenton, N.J.: Africa World Press.

Murray, Alison. 2000. "Le tourisme Citroën au Sahara (1924–1925)." *Vingtième Sciècle: Revue d'histoire* 68 (October–December): 95–107.

Newell, Sasha. 2012. *The Modernity Bluff: Crime, Consumption, and Citizenship in Côte d'Ivoire.* Chicago: University of Chicago Press.

Nfah-Abbenyi, Juliana Makuchi. 1997. *Gender in African Women's Writing: Identity, Sexuality, and Difference.* Bloomington: Indiana University Press.

Nganang, Alain Patrice. 2003. "Of Cameras, Trains, and Roads: French Colonial Conquest and Cinematographic Practice." *Black Renaissance/Renaissance Noire* 5, no. 1: 15–27.

Nnaemeka, Obioma. 2004. "Nego-feminism: Theorizing, Practicing, and Pruning Africa's Way." *Signs* 29, no. 2: 357–85.

Nnebue, Kenneth, dir. 1992. *Living in Bondage, I and II.* VCD.

Nossiter, Adam. 2013. "In Nigeria's Largest City, Homeless Are Paying the Price of Progress." *New York Times.* http://www.nytimes.com/2013/03/02/world/africa/homeless-pay-the-price-of-progress-in-lagos-nigeria.html?pagewanted=all&_r=1&.

Nwankwo, Nkem. 1975. *My Mercedes Is Bigger Than Yours.* London: Heinemann.

Nwaubani, Adaobi Tricia. 2009. *I Do Not Come to You by Chance.* Abuja: Cassava Republic Press.

Nyamnjoh, Francis B. 2005. "Fishing in Troubled Waters: *Disquettes* and *Thiofs* in Dakar." *Africa* 75, no. 3: 295–324.

Odoemene, Akachi. 2012. "Fighting Corruption without the State: Civil Society Agency and the Otokoto Saga." *Journal of Historical Sociology* 25, no. 3: 475–503.

Okereke, Afam, dir. 2007a. *Boys Cot, I and II.* DVD.

———, dir. 2007b. *The Return of Boys Cot, I and II.* DVD.

Okome, Onookome. 2007. "Introducing the Special Issue on West African Cinema: Africa at the Movies." *Postcolonial Text* 3, no. 2: 1–17.

Okpara, Enoch E. 1988. "The Role of Touts in Passenger Transport in Nigeria." *Journal of Modern African Studies* 26, no. 2: 327–35.

Okri, Ben. 1992. *The Famished Road*. New York: Random House.

Orekunrin, Ola. 2013. "Africa's Trauma Epidemic." *New York Times*. http://www.nytimes.com/2013/10/18/opinion/africas-trauma-epidemic.html?_r=0.

Oyěwùmí, Oyèrónké. 2005. "Visualizing the Body: Western Theories and African Subjects." In *African Gender Studies: A Reader*, ed. Oyèrónké Oyěwùmí, 3–22. New York: Palgrave Macmillan.

Packer, Jeremy. 2008. *Mobility with Mayhem: Safety, Cars, and Citizenship*. Durham: Duke University Press.

Pearson, George. 1948. "The Making of Films for Illiterates in Africa." In *The Film in Colonial Development: A Report of a Conference*, 22–27. London: British Film Institute.

Pfaff, Françoise. 1982. "Three Faces of Africa: Women in *Xala*." *Jump Cut*, no. 27: 27–31. http://www.ejumpcut.org/archive/onlinessays/JC27folder/XalaPfaff.html.

Piot, Charles. 2010. *Nostalgia for the Future: West Africa after the Cold War*. Chicago: University of Chicago Press.

Quayson, Ato. 2003. *Calibrations: Reading for the Social*. Minneapolis: University of Minnesota Press.

———. 2014. *Oxford Street, Accra: City Life and the Itineraries of Transnationalism*. Durham: Duke University Press.

Rajan, Sudhir Chella. 2006. "Automobility and the Liberal Disposition." In Böhm et al., *Against Automobility*, 113–29.

Reynolds, John. 1996. *André Citroën: The Henry Ford of France*. New York: St. Martin's Press.

Robbins, Bruce. 2007. "The Smell of Infrastructure: Notes toward an Archive." *boundary 2* 34, no. 1: 25–33.

Rodney, Walter. 1982. *How Europe Underdeveloped Africa*. Washington, D.C.: Howard University Press.

Ross, Kristin. 1995. *Fast Cars, Clean Bodies: Decolonization and the Reordering of French Culture*. Cambridge, Mass.: MIT Press.

Rostow, Walt W. 1960. *The Stages of Economic Growth: A Non-communist Manifesto*. Cambridge: Cambridge University Press.

Rubin, Gayle. 1997. "The Traffic in Women: Notes on the 'Political Economy' of Sex." In *The Second Wave: A Reader in Feminist Theory*, ed. Linda Nicholson, 27–62. New York: Routledge.

Ryan, Connor. 2014. "Nollywood and the Limits of Informality: A Conversation with Tunde Kelani, Bond Emeruwa, and Emem Isong." *Black Camera* 5, no. 2: 168–85.

Sacchi, Franco, dir. 2007. *This Is Nollywood*. DVD.

Sackey, Brigid M. 2006. "The Vanishing Sexual Organ Phenomenon." In *Sex and Gender in an Era of AIDS: Ghana at the Turn of the Millennium,* ed. Christine Oppong, Yaa P. A. Oppong, and Irene Odotei, 287–302. Accra: Sub-Saharan African Publishers.

Saint-Martin, Yves-J. 1973. "Les premières automobiles sur les bords du Niger: Félix Dubois et la Compagnie des transports par automobiles du Ṣoudan français, 1893–1913." *Revue francaise d'histoire d'outre-mer* 60, no. 221: 589–615.

Saro-Wiwa, Ken. 1994. *Sozaboy*. New York: Longman.

Schivelbusch, Wolfgang. 1977. *The Railway Journey: The Industrialization of Time and Space in the 19th Century*. Berkeley: University of California Press.

Schnapp, Jeffrey. 1999. "Crash (Speed as Engine of Individuation)." *Modernism/ Modernity* 6, no. 1: 1–49.

Schneider, William H. 1982. *An Empire for the Masses: The French Popular Image of Africa, 1870–1900*. Westport, Conn.: Greenwood Press.

Schwarz, Roberto. 1992. *Misplaced Ideas: Essays on Brazilian Culture*. Trans. and ed. John Gledson. New York: Verso.

Scott, David. 1999. *Refashioning Futures*. Princeton: Princeton University Press.

Seiler, Cotten. 2008. *Republic of Drivers: A Cultural History of Automobility in America*. Chicago: University of Chicago Press.

Sellers, William. 1954. "Mobile Cinema Shows in Africa." *Colonial Cinema* 12, no. 4: 75–81.

Sembene, Ousmane. 1960. *God's Bits of Wood*. Trans. Francis Price. Oxford: Heinemann.

———, dir. 1963. *Borom Sarret*. DVD.

———, dir. 1975. *Xala*. DVD.

———, dir. 2000. *Faat Kiné*. DVD.

———. 2008. Interview with Mamadou Niang. In Busch and Annas, *Ousmane Sembène Interviews,* 178–89.

Semi-Bi, Zan. 1976. "L'infrastructure routière et ferroviaire coloniale, source de mutations socials et psychologiques: Le cas de la Côte d'Ivoire, 1900–1940." *Cahiers d'Études africaines* 16, nos. 61–62: 147–58.

Sheller, Mimi. 2005. "Automotive Emotions: Feeling the Car." In Featherstone et al., *Automobilities,* 221–42.

Sheridan, Jim, dir. 2005. *Get Rich or Die Tryin*. DVD.

Simpson, Waleska Saltori. 2007. "'What Fashion of Loving Was She Ever Going to Consider Adequate?' Subverting the 'Love Story' in Ama Ata Aidoo's *Changes*." *English in Africa* 34, no. 1: 155–71.

Sissako, Abderrahmane, dir. 2002. *Heremakono*. DVD.

Slaughter, Joseph. 2009. *Human Rights, Inc: The World Novel, Narrative Form, and International Law*. New York: Fordham University Press.

Smith, Andrew. 2009. "Nigerian Scam E-mails and the Charms of Capital." *Cultural Studies* 23, no. 1: 27–47.

Smith, Daniel Jordan. 2001. "Ritual Killing, 419, and Fast Wealth: Inequality and the Popular Imagination in Southeastern Nigeria." *American Ethnologist* 28, no. 4: 803–26.

Sobchack, Vivian. 2004. *Carnal Thoughts: Embodiment and Moving Image Culture.* Berkeley: University of California Press.

Soyinka, Wole. 1965. *The Road.* Oxford: Oxford University Press.

———. 1967. "Death in the Dawn" and "Idanre." In *Selected Poems,* 6–7, 65–91. London: Methuen.

———. 1976. *Myth, Literature and the African World.* Cambridge: Cambridge University Press.

———. 1988. *Art, Dialogue, and Outrage: Essays on Literature and Culture.* New York: Pantheon Books.

Szeman, Imre. 2011. "Literature and Energy Futures." *PMLA* 126, no. 2: 323–25.

Tamo Tatiésté, Thomas, and Afané Bidja. 2002. "Impact of Automobile Lot and City Roads' Length on the Urban Mobility in Yaoundé (Cameroon)." In *La mobilité urbain pour tous,* ed. Xavier Godard and Innocent Fatonzoun. Lisse: A. A. Balkema.

Terranova, Charissa N. 2014. *Automotive Prosthetic: Technological Mediation and the Car in Conceptual Art.* Austin: University of Texas Press.

Thompson, Mike. 2008. "How the British Fixed the Independence Elections." *Africa Report* 9 (January–March): 53–55.

Touré, Moussa, dir. 1998. *TGV.* DVD.

"Transportation in Lagos (Part 4) Commercial Bus Services." 2013. *Naptu2's Blog.* https://naijachronicles.wordpress.com/2013/02/08/30/.

Tsika, Noah A. 2015. *Nollywood Stars: Media and Migration in West Africa and the Diaspora.* Bloomington: Indiana University Press.

Ukadike, Frank N. 1994. *Black African Cinema.* Berkeley: University of California Press.

———, ed. 2002. *Questioning African Cinema: Conversations with Filmmakers.* Minneapolis: University of Minnesota Press, 2002.

UNESCO. n.d. "Nollywood Rivals Bollywood in Film/Video Production." http://portal.unesco.org/en/ev.php-URL_ID=45317&URL_DO=DO_TOPIC&URL_SECTION=201.html.

Urry, John. 2000. *Sociology beyond Societies.* London: Routledge.

———. 2005. "The 'System' of Automobility." In Featherstone et al., *Automobilities,* 25–40.

Van der Geest, Sjaak. 2009. "'Anyway!': Lorry Inscriptions in Ghana." In Gewald et al., *The Speed of Change,* 253–93.

"Vans Carry Visual Education to Rural Areas in Nigeria." 1952. *Colonial Cinema* 10, no. 4: 92–94.

Verrips, Jojada, and Birgit Meyer. 2001. "Kwaku's Car: The Struggles and Stories of a Ghanaian Long-Distance Taxi-Driver." In Miller, *Car Cultures,* 153–84.

Vieyra, Paulin S. 1983. *Le cinema au Senegal.* Brussels: OCIC/L'Harmattan.

Virilio, Paul. 1984. *War and Cinema: The Logistics of Perception.* Trans. Patrick Camiller. London: Verso.

———. 2001. "From Modernism to Hypermodernism and Beyond." In *Virilio Live: Selected Interviews,* ed. John Armitage, 15–50. Interview by John Armitage. Thousand Oaks: Sage.

———. 2007. *The Original Accident.* Trans. Julie Rose. Malden, Mass.: Polity Press.

Weate, Jeremy. 2008. "Yahooze." *naijablog.* http://www.naijablog.co.uk/2008/02/yahoozee.html.

White, Luise. 2000. *Speaking with Vampires: Rumor and History in Colonial Africa.* Berkeley: University of California Press.

Willemen, Paul. 1993. "Negotiating the Transition to Capitalism: The Case of *Andaz.*" In *Melodrama and Asian Cinema,* ed. Wimal Dissanayake, 179–88. Cambridge: Cambridge University Press.

Williams, Raymond. 1978. *Marxism and Literature.* Oxford: Oxford University Press.

Wolf, James B. 1991. "Imperial Integration on Wheels: The Car, the British, and the Cape-to-Cairo Route." In *Literature and Imperialism,* ed. Robert Giddings, 112–27. London: Macmillan Press.

World Bank. N.d. "Motor Vehicles (per 1,000 People)." *World Bank.* http://data.worldbank.org/indicator/IS.VEH.NVEH.P3.

World Health Organization. 2013. "Road Safety in the WHO Africa Region: The Facts 2013." *World Health Organization.* http://www.who.int/violence_injury_prevention/road_safety_status/2013/report/factsheet_afro.pdf.

Yaeger, Patricia. 2007. "Introduction: Dreaming of Infrastructure." *PMLA* 122, no. 1: 9–26.

Yousef, Nancy. 2004. *Isolated Cases: The Anxieties of Autonomy in Enlightenment Philosophy and Romantic Literature.* Ithaca: Cornell University Press.

Index

Page numbers in italics refer to illustrations.

LINDSEY B. GREEN-SIMMS is assistant professor of literature at American University, Washington, D.C.